Ford 429/460 Engines

How to Build Max Performance

Jim Smart

CarTech®

CarTech®

CarTech®, Inc.
6118 Main St.
North Branch, MN 55056
Phone: 651-277-1200 or 800-551-4754
Fax: 651-277-1203
www.cartechbooks.com

Edit by Bob Wilson
Layout by Connie DeFlorin

ISBN 978-1-61325-604-6
Item No. SA507

Library of Congress Cataloging-in-Publication Data Available

Written, edited, and designed in the U.S.A.
Printed in China
10 9 8 7 6 5 4 3 2 1

DISTRIBUTION BY:

Europe
PGUK
63 Hatton Garden
London EC1N 8LE, England
Phone: 020 7061 1980 • Fax: 020 7242 3725
www.pguk.co.uk

Australia
Renniks Publications Ltd.
3/37-39 Green Street
Banksmeadow, NSW 2109, Australia
Phone: 2 9695 7055 • Fax: 2 9695 7355
www.renniks.com

Canada
Login Canada
300 Saulteaux Crescent
Winnipeg, MB, R3J 3T2 Canada
Phone: 800 665 1148 • Fax: 800 665 0103
www.lb.ca

CONTENTS

Acknowledgments

They say that it takes a village, and it most certainly does. I could never have accomplished what I have throughout my career were it not for the support and friendship from professional people, great friends who've stood by me. What I've learned from them cannot be measured.

Of all the people I've worked with through the years, four names stand out most: Jim Grubbs and Jeff Latimer of JGM Performance Engineering, John Da Luz of Luz Engineering, and the late Marvin McAfee of MCE Engines.

We lost Marvin in 2020 to the consequences of old age. He was 86. Marvin was sharp, confident, took pride in his work, and had six decades of experience. He was experienced and had wrenched on everything from race cars to Boeing 727 jets. He was an engine tuner and an extraordinary builder in his day. He was also an educator and mentor. He understood the heat energy process and the making of power. Admittedly, he was a cantankerous old curmudgeon who wasn't always easy and who knew of what he spoke. He never wavered from his routine and beliefs and never hesitated to let you know it. I loved Marvin the way I loved my father. I will miss him the rest of my life.

It has been Jim and Jeff's undying patience and commitment to my efforts for more than 20 years that has enabled us to produce great tech editorial for magazines, websites, and books. The same can be said for John Da Luz who has been a brother in arms for two decades and remains a great friend and mentor. Whenever I am stumped with a problem, I call John.

There's also Mark Jeffrey of Trans Am Racing in suburban Los Angeles who has worked with me on a wide variety of engine projects for more than 25 years. Mark is one of the nicest people I've ever known. I've gained a wealth of knowledge thanks to Mark's desire to educate and enlighten.

No acknowledgments section would be complete without Mark Houlahan, who has been technical editor for a variety of publications including *Mustang Monthly, Super Ford, Hot Rod's Mustang & Fords,* and *Muscle Car Review.* These days, Mark hangs his hat at Speedway Motors out of Lincoln, Nebraska, as a treasured website technical adviser and editor. If Mark cannot solve your technical challenges, they cannot be solved. Mark has always been my go-to guy anytime I am stumped. He has been an incredible friend.

Then comes the fabulous support system that I've had throughout my career. Alan Rebescher of Summit Racing Equipment/Trick Flow Specialties and Trent Goodwin of the Comp Performance Group have come to my rescue more times than I could ever count. Alan has become a close friend and cohort in crime over time. I'm grateful for his help and support time and time again.

Summit has supported untold car projects through the years. Summit's very heartbeat is the roar of internal combustion and extraordinary customer service. They never miss. If there's an issue, they solve it quickly.

Jeff Latimer

John Da Luz

Marvin McAfee

Comp, which was launched in 1976 as Competition Cams, was founded by John McWhirter, Ivars Smiltniks, Tom Woitesek, and Bob Woodard. Ron Coleman and Paul "Scooter" Brothers have been running the company in more recent years. They've never wavered in their passion for excellence.

Jim Grubbs of JGM Performance Engineering has great in-depth knowledge of Ford's 385-series 429/460 engines. He has built a lot of them in more than five decades in the business. Because he is passionate about these big-block Ford engines, he has studied them aggressively and applied what he has learned to his builds. He knows how to get power from them.

Finally, I want to thank Jon Kaase and Victor and Susan Moore for their support in the production of this book. They've provided quite a bit of content for this book. Anyone who knows Ford 429/460 and 351 Cleveland engines knows engine builder Jon Kaase of Kaase Racing Engines in the heart of Georgia.

As with most efforts like this, not everyone is going to agree with what is presented in the book. Put 50 engine builders in a room and ask them a question and you will get 50 different opinions. Most of what's in this book is a matter of opinion based on my own experiences and what I've learned from some of the best engine builders on the West Coast. What I am about to impart to you in this book is based on what I've been taught by professionals for four decades. It is my pleasure to present this book to you. It is my hope that you enjoy it as much as I have enjoyed writing it.

Jim Smart
Los Angeles, California

Introduction

Ford's legacy of powerful V-8 engines dates back to the flathead V-8 that was first introduced in 1932. Ford replaced the flathead with the company's first overhead valve V-8 for Lincolns and trucks in 1952, displacing 279, 302, 317, 332, 341, and 368 ci. The Ford and Mercury divisions got the more familiar Y-block overhead valve V-8 in 1954 in displacements of 239, 272, 292, and 312 ci.

FE/FT

Ford product planners and engineers saw the need for an even larger family of overhead valve V-8s displacing 332, 352, and 361 ci. The FE/FT engine was similar to the Y-block with skirted mains, but it had an unusual cylinder head/intake manifold combination beneath the valve covers along with shaft-mounted rocker arms like the Y-block. The FE/FT engine family evolved into larger displacements with greater levels of performance that made them terrific high-performance engines. The 332/352/361 grew to 390 ci in 1961, 406 in 1962, and the 427 in 1963. In 1966, Ford gave the FE more stroke to conceive the 410 Mercury and 428 Ford, both of which had 3.980 inches of stroke.

The large-bore 427 was little more than the 390 (3.780 inches of stroke) with large 4.230-inch bores. Ford learned that the 427 didn't deliver enough low-end torque to be a suitable luxury-car engine. This is why the longer-stroke 410 and 428 were born to power big Fords and Mercurys.

In 1968, Ford took the 428, fitted it with what were basically 427 medium-riser head castings and a hot hydraulic cam to conceive the 428 Cobra Jet, which had a very

Ford introduced the overhead valve Lincoln Y-block V-8 in 1952 for Lincolns and trucks displacing 217, 302, 317, 332, 341, and 368 ci, which ran from 1952 to 1957. Production ended with the advent of the MEL (Mercury, Edsel, Lincoln) big-block as well as the FE/FT series engines. The Lincoln Y-block was in response to the onslaught of overhead valve V-8 competition from Detroit.

The Ford/Mercury Y-block V-8 introduced in 1954 bears similarity to its Lincoln/Truck cousin; however, it is clearly different than its Lincoln counterpart. The Y-block is loved for the sound of its mechanical tappets and its throaty V-8 burble at the tailpipes. The flathead V-8 had run its course, especially against overhead valve competition. The Y-block V-8 was inevitable.

definite impact on NHRA drag race competition. Buyers saw this and wanted more. A legacy of powerful Cobra Jet intermediates and compacts was born.

The 428 Cobra Jet wasn't a mill developed inside of Ford but rather in Bob Tasca's race shop in Rhode Island. Bob Tasca Sr. was a Bristol, Rhode Island, Ford dealer who understood the value of "Race on Sunday, Sell on Monday." His message of performance was heard by Ford Motor Company and the consumer time and time again.

Tasca saw the 1967–1968 390 high-performance V-8 as lame by anyone's standards. This was when Tasca went to work getting the Mustang respect. He opted for off-the-shelf FE components, such as 427 medium-riser heads and intake, a hot cam, and the 428-ci short-block to conceive what would ultimately become the 428 Cobra Jet. He hopped into a 1967 Mustang equipped as such and drove it to Dearborn, Michigan, to present to Ford management. Although this story has been told several ways (depending upon who you ask), it was Bob Tasca Sr. who birthed the 428 Cobra Jet.

Because the FE 427 was the corporation's race-bred big-block, Ford had to further engineer this engine for not only power but also durability. In NASCAR competition, racers continued to scatter 427s all over racetracks everywhere, which was where the cross-bolted 406 and 427 blocks came from. Oil starvation led to a complete redesign of the 427 block to conceive the "Side-Oiler" in 1965. This development solidified the 427's place in racing history.

The FT (Ford Truck) was nothing more than an FE for trucks in displacements of 330, 359, 360, 389, and 391 ci. What made the FT different were components designed for heavy-duty truck use. FT engines had a forged steel crankshaft with a longer snout.

MEL

When the MEL (Mercury-Edsel-Lincoln) Ford big-block, also introduced in 1958, became long in the tooth in the late 1960s, Ford looked at a lightweight big-block replacement for the Lima, Ohio, engine plant. Ford needed a more efficient lightweight big-block (compared to the MEL). The new 385-series big-block in 370-, 429-, and 460-ci displacements was skirtless and resembled the small-block Ford architecturally.

The 385-series engine, named for its 3.850-inch stroke (460-ci engine), is a fiercely rugged and reliable big-block sporting less weight, yet it delivers abundant power. Though the 385 was an intended luxury-car mill, Ford went far with this engine,

In 1958, Ford introduced the MEL big-block in displacements of 383, 410, 430, and 462 ci. It was produced at the Lima, Ohio, engine plant through 1968. That same year, it was replaced by the 385 Series big-block.

Ford's FE/FT engine family displacing 332, 352, 360, 361, 390, 406, 410, 427, and 428 ci emerged in 1958 along with the MEL big-block, yet these two engines have very little in common. The FT (Ford Truck) engine family displaced 330, 359, 360, 389, and 391 ci. The FE/FT big-block is a skirted block like the Y-block and MEL, yet that's where the similarity ends. The FE/FT features a narrow cylinder head that shares valve covers with the intake manifold. This is the 1967 390 High Performance V-8.

as have drag racers. Drag racers took this mild-mannered big-block and made it a powerful engine to where it could rev to 7,000 rpm without consequence and make 400 hp and some 500 ft-lbs of torque. The darned thing was a beast. It has only grown more powerful with time.

The 460 with a 4.362-inch bore and 3.850-inch stroke was first in the 1968 Lincoln Continental and was followed by the lower-displacement 429 with the same 4.360-inch bore and 3.590 inches of stroke. Because these engines have the same bore size, it makes more sense to build a 460 than it does a 429 unless you happen to be building a bone stocker. At that, you can go 460 ci and no one will know it's in there but you. There are also more 460 cores available than 429s. Both employ the same block, so it doesn't matter.

The 429/460 has large 3.000-inch main journals with 2.500-inch rod journals. The 429/460 benefited from good Cleveland-style poly-angle valve wedge cylinder heads right out of the box. In 1970, Ford topped the 429 with large-port cylinder heads to birth the Cobra Jet and Super Cobra Jet engines.

The Cobra Jet yielded a whopping 11.0:1 compression ratio. The mechanical tappet Super Cobra Jet yielded even greater 11.5:1 compression. Compression was the key to power, much as it has always been. The 385's time as a factory high-performance V-8 (429-ci wedge) was short lived for just two model years (1970 and 1971) with a tremendous amount of horsepower and torque.

The 429 Cobra Jet was fitted with a Rochester Quadrajet carburetor with an iron spread-bore manifold. The more powerful Super Cobra Jet had the Holley 4150 with a Holley baseplate-compatible manifold. That makes it possible for you to go big atop the stock manifold.

I'm going to show you how to get real power from your 429/460. I've found it is easy to get brute power from these engines because they were designed this way. With standard iron heads, you can get 350 to 400 hp and comparable torque. If you opt for the big-port iron Cobra Jet heads or Ford's aftermarket aluminum heads, you can get more horsepower and torque than you ever imagined. The 385-series big-block is a big-block's big-block because it has so much power designed into it.

Boss 429

Ford Motor Company never gave up in its pursuit of a NASCAR-winning engine. When the 427 SOHC failed to endear NASCAR officials, Ford looked to its 385-series big-block for hemi-chamber inspiration. The objective was to conceive a hemi-head 429 and go after Chrysler's 426-ci Hemi and Chevrolet's big-block trackers. Ford called its hemi answer the "Blue Crescent." During development, the Blue

The 429 Cobra Jet and Super Cobra Jet were terrific powerhouses, especially for the larger Mustangs and Torinos. It made 360 hp at 5,800 rpm with nearly 500 ft-lbs of torque at 2,800 rpm. The Super Cobra Jet with a mechanical cam and Holley carburetion made upward of 375 hp. In truth, these engines made even greater power than advertised.

The 429 Cobra Jet with ram air and a Quadrajet carburetor.

The legendary Boss 429 impresses onlookers in size and mass with its awe-inspiring hemi heads. The street Boss 429 was detuned and not much of a match for the FE Series 428-ci Cobra Jet.

If you have deep enough pockets, you may opt for Ford's A460 block and just about any aftermarket head that you desire and build more than 1,000 hp.

Crescent actually had iron hemispherical chamber cylinder heads and surely weighed a ton. Aluminum heads weren't far behind.

The Blue Crescent was a purpose-built racing engine developed for NASCAR competition, in particular the 1969 Torino Talladega and Mercury Cyclone Spoiler II race cars. Somewhere in all of that, it became known as the Boss 429. To meet NASCAR homologation requirements, Ford had to produce a minimum of 500 street versions of the Boss 429 engine and a corresponding number of vehicles in which it would be raced.

Short-lived Ford President Semon E. "Bunkie" Knudsen came up with a way to get the most mileage out of the Boss 429 engine. He made the decision to produce at least 500 Torino Talladegas with 428 Cobra Jets and at least 500 Boss 429 Mustangs. Mercury Cyclone Spoiler II street cars (Mercury's Talladega) were fitted with the 351W.

Although the Boss 429 was good for marketing mileage, it was an incredibly bad idea from a logistics and manufacturing standpoint. Producing Boss 429 Mustangs involved bucking and building the cars at Dearborn and then shipping them to Kar-Kraft in Brighton, Michigan, to be fitted with their Boss 429 powertrains. The Atlanta and Lorain assembly plants had to be shut down for a time to build the NASCAR-bodied long-nose Torino and Spoiler II street cars. To add insult to injury, Ford and Mercury dealers couldn't give these cars away. No one wanted them.

The Boss 429 Mustang and 428 Cobra Jet Torino Talladegas did not sell because they were impractical for the average buyer. Some sat on Ford dealer lots for years before they were sold. The Mustang's Boss 429 engines were detuned for the street and loaded down with the Thermactor emissions system, which made them performance pigs compared to their NASCAR cousins.

The Boss 429 engine was another exotic offering from Ford like the 427 SOHC "Cammer," which made it decidedly temperamental and expensive for so many reasons. This made the Boss 429 a disappointing street engine, yet as legendary as Detroit iron gets on Woodward Avenue, Van Nuys Boulevard, and racetracks everywhere.

370 6.1-Liter Truck

You will rarely hear this 385-series engine mentioned; however, it is significant. The 385-series 370-ci medium-duty truck V-8 engine was introduced in 1977, replacing the 361-ci FT V-8. The 370 had the same stroke as the 429 (3.590 inches) with a smaller 4.050-inch bore. In 1979, Ford took the 370 metric with a displacement of 6.1L. The 370 was dropped in 1992, and the 429 took its place in truck applications.

Building Basics

Engine building technology has made huge strides over the past 40 years, and Ford's 385-series big-block 429/460-ci engine is no exception. I've learned over time that the details can make or break an engine regardless of the amount of technology you have. The two biggest details are double-checking clearances throughout and closely inspecting your work.

We get in a hurry to finish an engine and hear it self-destruct because we missed critical details in the process. We learn when an overlooked rod bolt fails halfway down the track and we run over our crankshaft. We also learn when a carelessly seated valve keeper escapes at high RPM.

Planning an engine build before you begin is the most effective approach to any project. A large part of building an engine is to know what you can afford and then not giving in to ego and temptation. Don't build an engine to impress others. Build it to impress yourself.

Think of an engine project this way: You wouldn't build a house or landscape your backyard without a blueprint and a corresponding plan, would you? What do you want your engine to do? Forget the notion that you can build a radical racing engine for the street and use it for the daily commute because, no matter what the buff magazines will tell you with claims of "800 streetable horsepower on pump gas," it is a long shot to mix street and race engines without conflict. There are strictly street engines, weekend bracket-racing engines, and all-out racing engines. Street and weekend bracket racing work well if you achieve a comfortable balance of the two.

Weekend horsepower should be realistic with peak horsepower somewhere around 6,000 rpm and peak torque at 4,500 rpm. In the real world, you want a broad powerband on the street, where torque begins to come on strong around 3,000 and peaks at 4,000 rpm. This enables you to achieve good quarter-mile elapsed times and still have something that you can live with for the daily commute.

Organization

I cannot stress enough the importance of keeping a clean, organized shop for your engine-building project. Do your engine teardown where

Block building begins with a thorough thermal cleaning and a battery of machine work including boring and honing cylinders to the next oversize. The maximum you want to go is 0.060-inch oversize. However, builders I work with suggest no more than 0.040-inch over. Sonic check the walls if you're considering 0.060-inch.

Boring takes cylinder bores to 0.005-inch shy of the overbore size. Wet honing takes the bore that additional 0.005 inch for a piston match.

The block should receive align-honing to ensure journal trueness and a good crosshatch pattern for bearing crush and security. Main saddles excessively out of true must be line-bored and then honed. If main caps are replaced or you're doing a four-bolt main conversion, the block must be checked and align-bored/honed.

All bolt holes should be chased and cleaned to ensure clean threads and smooth application of torque. Flush out the bolt holes with brake cleaner.

When you're computing compression ratio using a graduated cylinder, everything above the piston and within the chamber must be measured for volume. Valve reliefs and dishes add volume and reduce compression ratio. So does all volume above the piston rings.

you can catalog all parts and keep them properly stored. Keep engine parts and fasteners in jars or plastic containers labeled with a marker. Haul the block, heads, crankshaft, and connecting rods to a reputable machine shop immediately upon disassembly. This avoids any confusion and keeps you moving. Oftentimes, we tear down engines, catalog parts, and store everything, forgetting much of what you've seen in the teardown. Do not tear down an engine until you're ready to take it all to a machine shop.

If you cannot afford a machine shop at the time, leave the engine assembled until you are ready. I speak from experience on this one because too much is lost both mentally and physically once the engine is disassembled. Take plenty of pictures as you disassemble the engine. Keep disassembly, cleaning, machine

Hidden Power

Power is found anywhere you can reduce or eliminate internal friction. Anything you can do to make the going smoothly frees up power. Keep in mind that finding power costs money, but look at the dividends. When you set your clearances more liberally, the initial cost is free. What you tend to sacrifice is longevity if clearances are excessive. Some engine life is lost in the long term, especially when it comes to bearing and piston-to-cylinder wall clearances. Friction-reducing parts such as a dual-roller timing set and Torrington bearings cost more, but free up power.

work, and assembly as cohesive as possible. Know what you're going to do and when you're going to do it. Then, get busy and see your engine project through to completion. Nothing's more discouraging than a disassembled engine that's going nowhere because you didn't have a plan, or money.

When it is time to assemble the engine, keep a clean, organized shop. Even simple house dust will damage an engine's cylinder walls and journals. Whenever you're not working on the engine, keep it bagged. When you are assembling parts, clean them first with brake cleaner or compressed air to remove any debris. Avoid engine assembly on a windy day, which generates its share of dust. Automotive bodywork and sheet-metal repair create harmful dust that will damage engine parts. Keep this kind of work well away from your engine. Make sure engine assembly lube and oil are clean. Any kind of stray matter, no matter how small, can do engine damage.

When it is time for assembly, everything should be in the proper order. Pistons should be matched to each bore. This means each bore should have been checked with a micrometer and honed to the piston's specific size if you're working with a reputable builder. Each piston should be numbered to the bore that was honed for that match, not to mention dynamic balance. All piston rings should have been individually gapped for each bore. All of your engine's critical parts should be laid out on the workbench in proper order. Take organization to the extreme, which will mean never being sorry later. Number each cylinder with a felt-tip marker at the block deck. Lay out pistons and rods on the bench in cylinder number order. You would be amazed how many engine builds I've witnessed where the pistons were installed with the "front" reference notch to the rear. One of them actually made a magazine cover, which generated its share of laughter.

Keep cans of brake cleaner on your workbench to last-minute clean parts during assembly. This eliminates any chance of dust particles and stray matter where it doesn't belong. Use lint-free tack rags (static cloths) for your last-minute cleanup work. Do not use those cheap red linty shop towels, terry cloth, or paper towels for engine assembly. Keep plenty of engine oil and assembly lube close by. Keep these items covered to keep dust and debris out. I stress clean because I've seen the damage dust can do to an engine.

Begin your Ford big-block project with good healthy parts. Because the 385-series engines have a reputation for flawed castings depending upon when and where they were cast, you must be very cautious selecting yours. If you're buying a junkyard core, get a written money-back guarantee. First thing you want to do is inspect a potential core for obvious issues: leaks, cracks, overheating, voids in castings, and poor workmanship. What you don't want is a block that cannot be bored any farther. The most you want to go with a 429/460 is 0.040-inch oversize, though you can get away with 0.060-inch over. Cylinder walls should be sonic checked for thickness if you're pushing the limits.

Rarely is poor workmanship found in original factory-assembled engines. You will, however, find plenty of it in rebuilt or remanufactured engines. Incorrect parts, mismatched parts, defective pieces reused, poor machining and assembly technique, and the obvious absence of maintenance all play into why an engine failed. Disassembly is a forensics study where you get to learn all about the engine's past. Sometimes, you have a salvageable core. Other times, you have scrap iron. You never really know what you have until you measure cylinder bores, perform a sonic check, clean castings, and do magnetic particle inspection to check for cracks. Of course, you need to inspect the crank, measuring journals and checking for runout. You also need to check for irregular wear patterns. This is also important for connecting rods, checking them for abnormal wear, trueness, and journal dimensions.

Parts Selection

Once you understand what you want your engine to do, you can plan

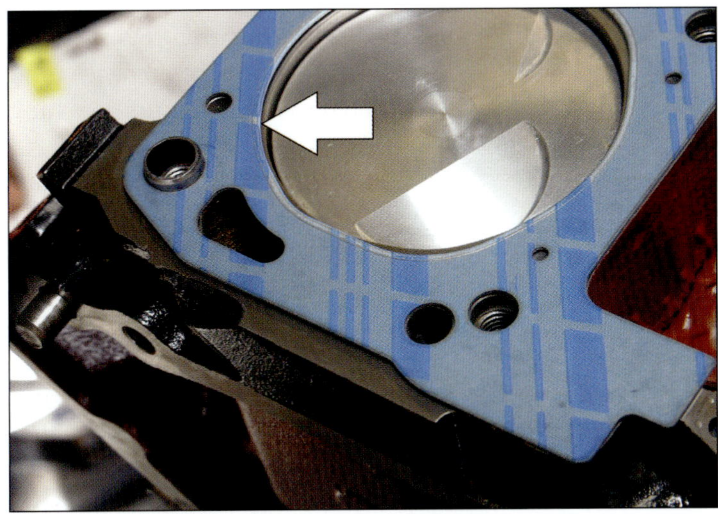

Cylinder head gasket thickness adds to volume above the piston, which affects compression ratio.

Combustion chamber volume is measured the same way you measure valve relief volume using a graduated cylinder.

This Mahle forged and dished piston increases volume, which reduces compression ratio. The volume of the dish is figured into compression ratio.

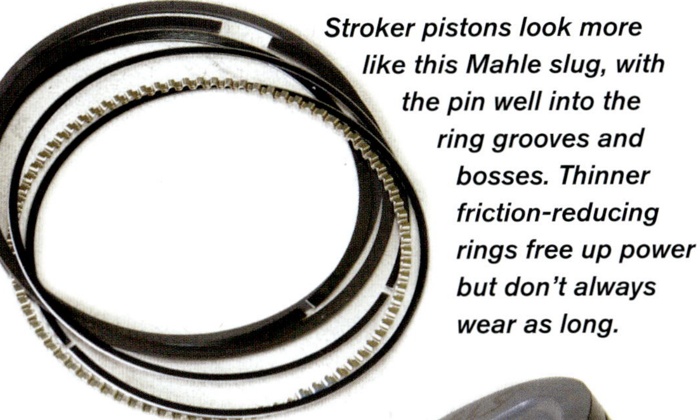

Stroker pistons look more like this Mahle slug, with the pin well into the ring grooves and bosses. Thinner friction-reducing rings free up power but don't always wear as long.

Here's a forged and coated Speed Pro stock piston for the 429 Super Cobra Jet build elsewhere in this book. The stock connecting rod has been reconditioned and fitted with new bolts.

the engine's basic architecture beginning with good bones. You've got to know what's going to work well together and what won't. The proper block and head combination. A solid bottom end (crank, rods, and pistons) and a cam that will work well with all of these components and work well within your driving agenda.

Even if you're building a warmed-up stock 429/460 with a factory cast crank and rods along with hypereutectic or forged pistons, you're going to need to know your engine's physics. Again, I am going to presume you've got no larger than a 4.422-inch bore. There are sticky issues such as compression height, swept volume, piston dimensions, and chamber size to think of. You can wind up with too much or too little compression. Knowing these issues going in, you can know almost exactly what your 429/460 is going to do when it is fired.

Compression Ratio

What is compression ratio and how is it calculated? One popular misconception is that pistons alone determine compression ratio; however, this has never been true. Compression ratio comes from not only piston dome or dish features but also stroke, bore, and combustion chamber size. Compression comes from piston travel from bottom dead center (BDC) to top dead center (TDC) with both valves closed. You are squeezing cylinder volume (displacement) into the area above the piston. Compression ratio is cylinder volume at BDC versus cylinder volume with the piston at TDC. If cylinder volume with the piston at BDC is 10 times more than it is with the piston at TDC, then you have a compression ratio of 10.0:1, or simply 10 to 1.

Five basic factors affect compression ratio: cylinder swept volume, piston dome or dish volume, head gasket thickness, clearance volume, and combustion chamber size.

Swept volume is the amount of air, or volume, the piston displaces during its journey to the top of the bore, hence the word "swept." If you enlarge swept volume by boring the cylinder oversize or increasing stroke, you increase compression ratio. You may also increase or decrease compression ratio by changing the piston dome. If you "dish" the piston, you lose compression. This is common with stock pistons, which are often dished to control compression. A good example are 429/460 engines with dished pistons. To raise compression ratio, you "dome" the piston with a surface shaped more or less like the combustion chamber. This reduces clearance volume at the top of the bore. When you reduce clearance volume, you increase compression ratio.

Whenever you go to an aftermarket head, keep combustion chamber size in mind. Combustion chamber size can wind up greater than your stock chambers. If you desire greater compression, you can make adjustments with proper piston selection. Cylinder volume is figured using a simple formula. Using a standard 460-ci bore and stroke (4.362 x 3.850 inches), let's work the following numbers.

4.362 x 4.362 x 3.850 x 0.7854 =
57.5337 x 8 =
460 ci (rounded off)

When you apply this formula, you come up with 57.5337 ci per cylinder. Multiply this number by eight and you have 460 ci. Truth is, you have 460.27, which is closer to 460 ci. If you bore the 460 to 4.392 inches (0.030-inch oversize), you have 58,328 ci per cylinder, which comes out to 466.62 ci.

See the following table for quick answers.

Bore size (inches)	Stroke (inches)	Displacement (cubic inches)
4.362	3.850	460.27 (460)
4.392	3.850	466.62 (467)
4.402	3.850	468.74 (469)
4.422	3.850	472.98 (473)
4.440	3.850	476.87 (477)
4.362	4.000	478.20 (478)
4.392	4.000	484.80 (485)
4.402	4.000	487.01 (487)
4.422	4.000	491.44 (491)
4.440	4.000	495.45 (495)
4.362	4.250	508.09 (508)
4.392	4.250	515.10 (515)
4.402	4.250	517.45 (517)
4.422	4.250	522.16 (522)
4.440	4.250	526.42 (526)
4.362	4.500	537.97 (538)
4.392	4.500	545.40 (545)
4.402	4.500	547.89 (548)
4.422	4.500	552.87 (553)
4.440	4.500	557.90 (557)

If you take a standard 4.362-inch bore and overbore it 0.030 inch to 4.392 inches, compression will increase by a fraction of a point. If you have a compression ratio of 10.0:1, compression will increase by less than a point with a 0.030-inch overbore. You compute compression increase (or decrease) by figuring the clearance volume, which is the area left above the piston when it reaches TDC. It is important to understand that the piston doesn't always reach TDC flush with the block deck. In most applications, the piston comes within 0.005 to 0.020 inch below the deck surface. It looks more flush with the block deck than it actually is. This is called piston deck height. Piston deck height affects compression because it determines clearance volume at the top. If you have a lot of clearance volume, you have less compression. The greater the piston deck height, the lower the compression ratio.

The following is a formula for figuring clearance volume.

Clearance volume =

0.7853982 x Bore² x Deck height

Again, let's look at our 460-ci engine with a 4.392-inch bore and 3.850-inch stroke. Our 460 has a piston deck height of 0.015 inch below the block deck. When you use the formula of 0.7853982 x 4.392 inches squared x 0.015 inches, you get 0.227 ci or just a fraction of the cylinder's 58.327 ci. If the deck height increased any amount, compression would drop. If deck height decreased any amount, compression would increase.

After figuring how to compute displacement in each cylinder and how to figure in the piston deck height effect on compression, it's time to figure in the piston's role in all of this. Remember that if you dish the piston, you lose compression. If you dome the piston, you increase compression. Most piston manufacturers give you the specifications on a piston. If it is dished, the manufacturer tells you how much. Likewise, for a domed piston where you also learn how much. This is performed in cubic centimeters (cc's). How many cc's are in the dish? How many cc's of volume make up the dome?

If you are baffled by cubic centimeters versus cubic inches, you're not alone. A lot of us are confused by metric versus SAE. Follow this formula and end your confusion.

Piston dome/dish in cubic inches =

cc's x 0.0610237

Let's get back to our 460 engine. Say that you have pistons with 4.000-cc dishes. Using the formula, you come up with 0.244 ci. This lowers compression ratio because you have more clearance volume above the piston. If you dome the piston by the same amount, you increase compression accordingly.

The next factor in compression ratio is cylinder head gasket volume, which contributes to clearance volume above the piston. The thickness of the head gasket affects compression ratio. The thicker the head gasket, the greater the clearance volume. This lowers compression. The thinner the head gasket, the lower the clearance volume, which increases compression. To figure the head gasket volume (displacement), use the following formula.

Cylinder head gasket

volume/thickness =

0.7853982 x Gasket bore² x

Compressed thickness

Again, let's look at our 460-ci engine with a 4.362-inch bore as an example. It has a cylinder head gasket that is 0.040 inch thick. You take 0.7853982 x 4.362 inches squared x 0.040 inch to arrive at the clearance volume.

With all of these issues out of the way, it's time to focus on combustion chamber volume. Combustion

Although time consuming, do a short-block mockup using pistons without rings to check internal clearances even if you're building a stocker. You want to make sure rods, rod bolts, piston skirts, counterweights, and the block stay clear of each other. You want a minimum of 0.100-inch clearance.

Piston ring installation must be performed gently. Oil rings get gently rolled into the groove. If you distort a ring, discard it immediately. Oil rings are carefully positioned around the expander, which ends should butt, never overlap. This is a piston ring expansion tool, which gently opens the rings for installation. The other accepted approach is rolling on these rings like the oil ring. Do not distort the ring.

When you're installing pistons, check ring end gap positioning, where the end gaps are 45 degrees apart. Generously lubricate rings, lands, and skirts with 30-weight engine oil or ring-specific assembly lube.

Before degreeing the camshaft, check true TDC on cylinder number-1. It is crucial to ascertain the piston's exact TDC in order to confirm valve timing events. Always degree the camshaft, even if it has been in the engine before. Very few production camshafts are ground per the cam card, which is why they should be degreed. Write down findings and compare them with the cam card.

This is the 429 Super Cobra Jet bottom end with four-bolt main caps. Use a windage tray for improved oil control. For street and road racing applications, opt for a road race pan to keep oil where it belongs around the pickup. Drag racing calls for a deep sump pan.

If your budget permits, use a one-piece Fel-Pro pan gasket. If you're going for a factory-original restoration, opt for the four-piece cork and rubber combination. Use sealer sparingly because you need so little. Just a thin film of Permatex The Right Stuff forms a perfect seal. If sealer is oozing out, you've used too much.

If you're using a conventional pan gasket, these end gaskets can be a pain because they don't always fit properly. Make sure these end gaskets seat properly in the rear main cap and timing cover.

chamber volume is the actual size of the chamber in cubic centimeters (cc's). Think of the combustion chamber as the ultimate clearance volume (volume above the piston). Early 429/460 chamber size runs 75 to 77 cc. Combustion chamber volume is figured with a graduated scale using fluid. You meter fluid into the chamber and figure how much fluid is used. You get this figure in cubic centimeters. The sample cylinder head has 77-cc chambers. Here's how you turn cubic centimeters into cubic inches.

Combustion chamber volume in cubic inches =
cc's x 0.0610237

Based on the formula above at 77 cc, you have 4.70 ci of volume in the chamber alone. Now, we have all of the information needed to compute compression ratio in our 460-ci engine. Use the following formula.

Cylinder volume + Clearance volume + Piston volume + Chamber volume + Gasket volume ÷ Clearance volume + Piston volume + Head gasket volume + Chamber volume

Our 460ci engine, with its 4.392-inch bores and 3.850-inch stroke, 0.020-inch deck height, 0.040-inch head gasket thickness, 77-cc chamber heads, and 4.000-cc dished pistons winds up like this.

58,328 ci + 0.188 cc + 0.244 cc + 4.70 ci + 0.502 ci ÷ 1.504 ci + 0.244 ci + 0.502 ci + 4.70 ci =
10.10:i

When you work this formula, you are taking cylinder volume, clearance volume, piston volume, chamber volume, and gasket volume, and adding them together to arrive at 58,328 ci. Then, you add up clearance volume, piston volume, head gasket volume, and chamber volume to get 4.834 ci. Then, you take 48.816 ci and divide it by 4.834 ci to arrive at 10.098, which, rounded off to the nearest tenth, is 10.10:1.

The Physics of Power

You've long been led to believe horsepower is what "power" is all about. But horsepower is rooted more in Madison Avenue advertising rhetoric than fact. In the power picture, horsepower doesn't count for much, especially on the street. What counts is torque and when you have the most of it. Truth is, engines make torque (grunt!) when you feed fuel and air into combustion chambers and squeeze the mix. Torque is the grunt that gets you going, and horsepower is the force that keeps you moving at speed.

Engines are doing their best work when they reach peak torque where they are making low- and middle-range twist. That's what you want from an engine. When an engine is below the torque peak, it has more than enough time to completely fill the cylinder with air and fuel. When engine RPM rises above the torque peak, there isn't enough time to completely fill the cylinders with air and fuel, which is where real power comes from.

The power you feel from an engine is torque multiplied by engine speed (RPM) to produce a number that tells you something about the engine's output. This theory dates back to steam engines and inventor James Watt. Watt invented the steam engine in the 1800s. Watt's theory was a simple one. It compared the work his steam engine could do with the same work an equal number of horses could do. Watt determined that a single horse could pull a 180-pound load 181 feet in 1 minute's time. This formula figured out to 32,580 ft-lbs per minute. Watt rounded it off to 33,000 ft-lbs per minute. He divided this figure by 60 seconds, which worked out to 550 ft/lbs per second, and this became the standard for one horsepower. As a result of Watt's calculations, horsepower has become a measure of force in pounds against a distance in feet for the brief period of one minute. Then, you take this formula and apply it to an engine's crankshaft at each journal throw to arrive at horsepower. This is based on the number 5,252.

Torque and RPM are divided by 5,252. In addition, torque and horsepower always equal out at 5,252. If you are able to solve this equation at 5,252 rpm, RPM cancels out, ultimately leaving horsepower equal to the torque figure. In fact, if you work this out on a graph, the torque, horsepower, and RPM lines should always intersect.

When you look at torque alone, it is the measure of an engine's work. Horsepower is a measure of how quickly the engine does the work. Torque comes mostly from displacement and stroke. This means the real power you derive from an engine comes in the torque curve. The broader the torque curve, the better the power package. A broader torque curve comes from making the most of the air/fuel mixture across a broader RPM range. This is best accomplished with a longer stroke and a larger bore, and this is what strokers are all about: making the most torque across the broadest range. Truth is, you're never going to get the best of everything, even with fuel-injected engines. Engines need to be planned and built based on the way you're going to use them. What you choose in terms of a camshaft, cylinder heads, and induction system determines how the engine will perform.

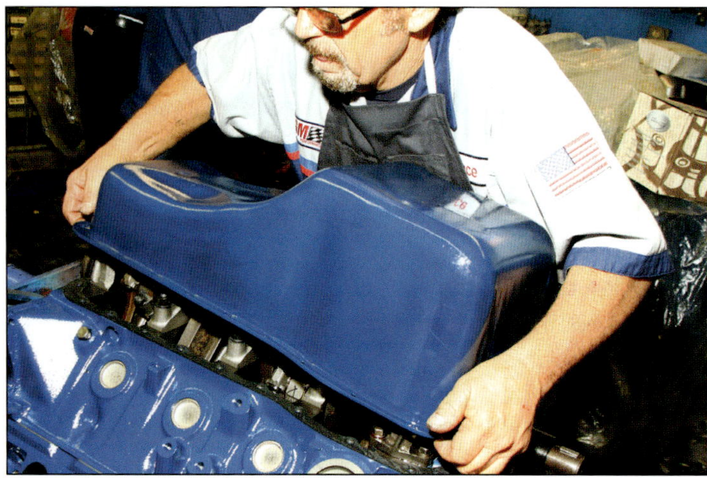

Once the pan gasket is properly seated, take extra care placing the pan and getting it seated. Make sure there's no gasket distortion. Crisscross tighten the pan bolts, gradually increasing torque in one-third values.

Cylinder head installation should begin with hospital-clean surfaces. Use Permatex The Right Stuff conservatively at coolant passages and where the cylinder head and intake manifold gaskets meet.

The 1970-1971 429 Super Cobra Jet cylinder heads with their drive-through intake ports are true factory horsepower castings. They're factory rated at 375 hp with roughly 500 ft-lbs of torque. These heads have had mild port work and JGM Performance Engineering managed to get 467 hp with a hotter cam with nearly 500 ft-lbs of torque.

Ryan Peart of JGM Performance Engineering stresses the importance of tightening fasteners and getting it right. You must apply smooth pressure on the torque wrench and slowly get to the desired torque in one-third values. Always be sure bolt and hole threads are clean and lubricated.

All oil gallery plugs should be threaded (including ones that were press-in plugs from the factory) with sealer applied to the threads.

I suggest the use of intake manifold and valve cover studs from ARP for ease of installation and security. Apply a thin bead of Permatex The Right Stuff around cooling passages and along the bottom of intake ports. Don't overdo it.

Follow the crisscross pattern in your Ford Shop Manual for intake manifold bolt tightening and do not overtighten. Then, go back and check your torque.

Wasted Power

When you're planning for power, you rarely stop to consider how power gets wasted in an engine's design and construction. Friction is the power pickpocket, hiding in all sorts of places inside engines. Most of the friction occurs at the pistons and rings. Some of it gets lost at the bearings and journals. Even more of it gets consumed at piston wrist pins, lifters and bores, cam lobes and lifters, rocker arm fulcrums, and valve stems.

Your objective needs to be compromised between having tolerances that are too loose and too tight. Piston-to-cylinder wall clearances are critical in order to have good cylinder sealing, yet not too much friction where you consume unnecessary power. The same is true for rod and main bearing clearances. You want liberal clearances for good oil flow and heat transfer yet less friction.

Another power-robbing issue is engine breathing. You want an induction system that helps your engine breathe well at the RPM range it is designed and built for. This means choosing the appropriate intake manifold and carburetor. Go small on carburetor sizing and you limit breathing. If ports don't match in terms of uniform size, you restrict breathing. Opt for cylinder heads

TECH TIP

Use a Torque Plate

Does your machine shop use a torque plate during cylinder honing? If not, find another machine shop. The torque plate simulates cylinder head installation by getting the block where it would be with the heads installed and bolts torqued. The reason for this is simulation, simulating the installation of cylinder heads on the block when the machinist is honing the bores. You want cylinder walls dimensionally where they would be if heads were installed. If you hone a block without a torque plate, you then bolt on the cylinder heads; cylinder wall dimensions change as the bolts are torqued. ■

It makes perfect sense to go with good aftermarket roller rocker arms such as these Crane Classics to reduce internal friction and improve valve lift.

where port sizing is too limited for your displacement and you restrict breathing.

On the exhaust side, you want a scavenging system that makes sense. You don't have to have long-tube headers for great breathing. Shorty headers will do the job and without the shortcomings of long-tube headers. Go too large on header tube size and you limit torque. Go too small and you hurt power on the high end. This is where your exhaust system has to work hand-in-hand with the heads, camshaft, and induction system.

Building a 429/460 Stroker Engine

A stroker is an engine with increased or decreased stroke. By increasing an engine's stroke, the distance the piston travels in the cylinder bore, you gain displacement. By the same token, when you decrease an engine's stroke, you reduce the distance the piston travels in the bore, which changes when and how the engine makes power. Short-stroke engines like high RPM, where they make the most torque. The focus here is more about increasing stroke in order to achieve greater amounts of torque and horsepower.

Stroking an engine does more than just increase displacement. It increases torque by giving the engine more of a mechanical advantage. When you increase stroke, you increase the engine's crankshaft arm or lever, which makes the most of a combustion cycle. The longer the stroke, the greater the torque or twist. Increase rod ratio via a longer rod and you improve piston dwell time at each end of the cylinder. This yields greater levels of power.

Stroke comes from the length of the crankshaft's rod journal arm. Then, you double that length to come up with the engine's stroke. You double the length of the crankshaft's arm because you get that arm in two directions: TDC then BDC. This is a simple 2:1 ratio. Take the crankshaft arm, measured from the crankshaft centerline, and double the measurement. If the arm is 1½ inches, you have a 3-inch stroke.

How do you get more power from a stroker? You get power from the greater mechanical advantage of a longer crankshaft arm, but there's more. You are also filling the cylinder with a greater volume of air and fuel, which gives you more power all by itself. From stroke and cylinder swept volume, you get torque. Torque is the truest measure of an engine's power output.

When you consider the crankshaft's arm, the distance from the crankshaft centerline to the center of the rod journal, this is where torque is born. Torque is an engine's "grunt" factor. "Grunt" is that physical pressure at your backside when the accelerator is pressed. So, what is torque, exactly? Think of the crankshaft's arm as a simple lever, like you were taught in high school physics class. Torque equals the downward force of the stroke times the length of the lever or arm. If you look a 460 engine's 500 ft-lbs of peak torque, this means each cylinder bore is producing 740 pounds of pressure on each power stroke. You increase torque when you increase the length of the arm. When you increase the length of the arm, you increase stroke.

A stock 460's engine's arm is 1.925 inches. This means the 460 engine has a 3.850-inch stroke. If you add 1/4 inch to the arm, this increases the arm to 2.175 inches. Double the 1¼ inches and you have 3.850 inches to achieve 460 ci with the standard 4.360-inch bore. This gives you 40 additional foot-pounds of torque.

Along with the advantages of a stroker, there are disadvantages as well, especially if you're bent on pumping the most displacement possible into a 429/460. When you stroke the 429/460 to its limits, you lose piston skirt, which hurts stability. You also push the piston pin into the piston ring land area, which weakens piston design. It also puts the pin close to the piston dome, which exerts too much heat on the pin and boss. These are disadvantages that shorten engine life.

Another factor with stroking is rod length. When you haul that piston deep into the cylinder bore, you are also bringing it closer to the crankshaft counterweights, which creates conflict. This means you need a longer connecting rod to get the piston down there without interference with the counterweights. Sometimes,

TECH TIP

Valve Clearancing

A mock-up should always include valve-to-piston clearances, which can actually be performed when you are degreeing the cam. This step gives you sold mechanical confirmation. You want at least 0.0100-inch clearance between valve and piston. Check piston-to-valve clearances by using modeling clay on top of the pistons (and, yes, check all eight bores) and running the crank through with the heads and valvetrain in place. Valves open, touching the clay and yielding actual clearances.

you can find off-the-shelf connecting rods to complete your stroker, and sometimes, you are forced to custom fabricate connecting rods that will work. More expensive stroker kits have custom parts, such as rods and pistons. More affordable kits have off-the-shelf parts that have made the kit possible without expensive tooling costs.

Whenever you have to custom make connecting rods, this drives up the cost of a stroker kit. The same is true for custom pistons. Stroker kits often mandate custom pistons to keep things friendly at the top of the bore. A 535-ci stroker, for example, has custom pistons with pin bosses pushed way up into the ring lands. This drives up cost. It also shortens engine life for reasons just explained.

Stroker Power Pointers

There are plenty of myths about making power, especially in the Ford camp. Folklore tells us it's easier to make power with a Chevrolet than a Ford, but this is nonsense. You can make just as much power with a Ford for the same amount of money you can a Chevy. What gives the Chevrolet an advantage is numbers, sheer volume. Chevys are simply more commonplace than Fords. But even this is changing because Ford's popularity has grown dramatically. When it comes to seat-of-the-pants performance, there's no black magic here, just the simple physics of taking thermal expansion and turning it into rotary motion that makes you feel good about your engine.

To learn how to make power, you have to understand how power is made to begin with inside an engine. How much power an engine makes depends on how much air and fuel you can pump through the engine, plus what you do with that fuel and air mixture during that split-second it lives and dies in the combustion chambers.

You should think of an internal combustion engine as an air pump. The more air and fuel you can "pump" through the cylinders, the more power you're going to make. This is why racers use big carburetors, manifolds, heads, superchargers, turbochargers, and nitrous oxide. Racers understand this air pump theory and practice it with reckless abandon, sometimes with catastrophic results. But good racers also understand the "too much of a good thing" theory. Sometimes it can cost you a race. Sometimes it can cost you an engine.

Getting power from your "air pump" takes getting liberal amounts of air and fuel into the chambers, then squeezing the mixture as hard as you can without damaging the engine. When you raise compression, you increase the power your mixture yields. It is the intense heat of compression coupled with the ignition system that sparks the yield of energy from the mixture. The more compression you have, the greater the heat you have to ignite the mixture.

The problem is that when there's too much compression and resulting heat, the air/fuel mixture can ignite prematurely resulting in preignition and detonation. So, you have to achieve the right compression ratio to get the most from the fuel you have. Today's street fuels won't tolerate much more than 10.5:1 compression. This means you have to look elsewhere for answers in the power equation, like more aggressive camshaft profiles, better heads, port work, hotter ignition systems, exhaust headers that breathe better, state-of-the-art intake manifolds and carburetors, even electronic fuel injection where you never thought of using it before.

The thing to remember about gasoline engines is this. The air/fuel mixture does not explode in the combustion chambers, it "lights off" just as your gas furnace or water heater does. Because the mixture is compressed and ignited, it lights off more rapidly. Combustion in a piston engine is just that, a "quick fire" that sends a flame front across the top of the piston. Under ideal circumstances, the flame front travels smoothly across the piston dome, yielding heat and pressure that act on the piston and rod uniformly to create rotary motion at the crankshaft.

A bad "light off" that originates at two opposing points in the chamber is that preignition or detonation factor I was talking about earlier. The opposing flame fronts collide creating a shock that hammers the piston and the valves, which is the pinging or spark knock you hear under acceleration. The objective is to get a smooth light-off, with the flame front traveling in one smooth direction for maximum power. An abnormal light-off can also happen prematurely from advanced ignition timing or red-hot carbon in the chamber.

Power management is having the right balance of ignition timing, fuel mixture, compression ratio, valve timing events, and even external forces such as blower boost or nitrous input. All of these elements have to work together if you're to make productive power. Let's talk about some of the elements you need to make power.

The science of making power must tie in with how you intend to use your engine, and that's where most of us get it wrong all too often. In our quest for stroker torque, we sometimes forget how the vehicle is going to be driven and used. If you are building a stroker to go drag racing, the way you build your engine is going to be different than the person who builds one for trailer towing. By the same token, road racing engines should be executed differently than drag racing engines.

How do you approach each engine building game plan? Street engines for the daily commute need to be planned for good low- and mid-range torque. Drag racing engines need to make power at high-RPM ranges. Road racing engines need to be able to do it all: down low, in the middle, and at high RPM because they're going to live in all of these ranges during racing. Engines scheduled for trailer towing need plenty of low-end torque. They also need to be able to live comfortably at mid-range when you're going to be pulling a grade.

Assembly Techniques

With proper selection of parts out of the way, you can assemble an engine using tried and proven techniques employed by professionals. When it comes to assembly practices, engine building professionals stress two main areas: cleanliness and double-checking your work. Never assemble an engine in the same area where it was torn down. Even minute amounts of dirt, dust, or grit can stop an engine cold by scoring bearing surfaces and cylinder walls. I stress double-checking your work because this approach actually saves time. If you think it's inconvenient to check your work two and three times, consider the inconvenience involved in a teardown because there's high oil consumption or having to collect the pieces of a blown engine because something critical was missed during the assembly process. Check it thrice and sleep better.

Engine building is an exacting exercise in physics where every detail must be covered to ensure success. Power comes from taking all of that thermal energy and harnessing it above the piston during light-off. The light-off should be a smooth quick-fire with a nice flame front across the tops of the piston converted to rotary motion with an attitude.

The easiest way to make power is to raise compression. However, you don't want too much compression. Compression ratio depends upon your plan and the fuel available. The other quickest way to unleash power is less internal friction. You reduce internal friction with obvious means such as with roller tappets, double roller timing set, and lightweight full roller rocker arms. However, there are other ways, such as more liberal clearances and lightweight components, which is a balancing act in itself because you also want durability, good oil pressure, and low oil consumption.

Even with all details covered, it is no guarantee an engine will stay together or make the power expected. It is those troublesome areas you cannot see, material weaknesses and defects, that can fail when least expected. This means you must be attentive to everything you have control over in the build process. When in doubt, check it out.

Stop Leaks

Gasket technology and engine sealing have come a long way since the 429/460 was introduced in 1968. Fel-Pro is the only gasket I use. Although, there are those who prefer to use other brands–and there are excellent gaskets out there. I've had tremendous luck with Fel-Pro and stick with what I know.

Help your gaskets work better by using The Right Stuff from Permatex in areas that could become compromised, such as between rear main seal halves at the block and the main cap. A respected engine builder I work with, Jeff Latimer, discourages staggering the rear main seal tips away from the main cap and block mating surfaces.

He is of the belief the seal tips can be compromised (bunched) in the number-5 main cap and leak. ■

Mock-Up Phase

Savvy engine builders begin assembly with a mock-up phase where the bottom end is assembled and lubed up without piston rings and checked for proper clearancing throughout. A mock-up allows you to check critical clearances all around. This means rods and journals have to be checked to make sure they're going to clear the bottoms of the bores and piston skirts. You must have a minimum clearance of 0.0100 inch between every rod and the block. Be careful how much iron is ground away because you risk going all the way through into a water jacket or the world outside. The most you're going to be able to get into a 460 is 550 ci with a 4.440-inch bore. A 4.440-inch bore is discouraged unless you are very confident of a sonic check.

Run Cooler

Run a high-flow water pump along with a 180-degree F thermostat. It is suggested you stay away from a 160-degree F thermostat, which makes the engine run too cool. Never run your Ford big-block without a thermostat. If you are running an engine-driven fan, go with a Flex-A-Lite flex fan or a factory thermostatic fan clutch for efficient cooling. The fan must be halfway into a shroud for best results, and yes, always use a fan shroud for improved air velocity through the radiator. ■

JGM Performance Engineering has been building powerful 385-series engines for nearly 40 years. JGM is building an affordable and certainly powerful (500 hp) street/strip 460 for this chapter with ported iron heads. Torque is comparable to horsepower.

The 429/460 block is one and the same, with both the 429 and 460 sharing the same block on two-bolt mains. This is a hardy block that can take a tremendous amount of punishment. If you stud the mains and install a stud girdle, this block can stand 500 to 600 hp. Some builders insist it will withstand more. You may also convert this block to four-bolt main caps with a Milodon kit.

Ford Part/Casting Numbers

Ford part numbers and casting numbers can be confusing, especially if you've never dealt with them before. There are actually two part-numbering systems. The most common one that applies to engines addressed in this book is for 1950–1998. Things changed in 1999 with a new numbering system I will get into shortly. Here's how the 1950–1998 system works:

Ford part/casting number example: C5ZZ-9510-K

Prefix	C5ZZ
Basic part number	9510
Suffix	K

The prefix tells you when the part was originally released for production, what car line it was released for, and what engineering group it came from. The prefix breaks down like this.

A closer look at the 460 main cap reveals why you should opt for a stud girdle or four-bolt main caps if you are planning big horsepower.

The 429/460 block is a brute casting, meaning it can withstand horsepower numbers courting 600. This is the 1970-1971 429 Cobra Jet block with four-bolt main caps, identifiable by the "CJ" in the lifter valley. Most 429/460 Police Interceptor blocks are four-bolt mains.

Use brass core and water jacket drain plugs, which are corrosion resistant and last virtually forever. You want wide-lip core plugs, which are more secure and less likely to blow out. Raw steel core plugs can corrode and cause leaks, or worse yet, seize to the block and become impossible to remove. Stainless core and drain plugs offer the same look without corrosion issues.

First Position	
Letter	**Decade**
B	1950–1959
C	1960–1969
D	1970–1979
E	1980–1989
F	1990–1999

Second Position
The second position (the year of the decade) indicates the year that the part was released by Engineering for production.

Third Position	
Letter	**Car Line**
A	Ford
D	Falcon
G	Comet, Montego, and Cyclone
J	Marine and industrial
K	Edsel
M	Mercury
O	Fairlane and Torino
S	Thunderbird
T	Ford truck
V	Lincoln
W	Cougar
Z	Mustang

Fourth Position	
Letter	**Engineering Group**
A	Chassis
B	Body
E	Engine

However, if you are talking about a service replacement part, the fourth position indicates division as follows:

Fourth Position (for Service Replacement Parts)	
Letter	**Division**
Z	Ford Division
Y	Lincoln-Mercury
X	Original Ford Muscle Parts Program
M	Ford Motorsport SVO or Ford Racing Performance Parts

Basic Part Numbers

The basic part or casting number is the same whether it is an engineering number or a service number. For example, "9510" is the basic number for all carburetors. A finished engine block would be "6015" as another example. Each engine part receives another basic part number.

The suffix tells you the change level. "A" means original status of released part. "B" indicates at least one engineering change. The entire alphabet is used except the letters "I" and "L," which could be mistaken for the number "1." When Ford goes through the entire alphabet, it starts over again at "AA," "AB," "AC," "AD," and so on.

It is important to understand that part, casting, engineering, and service numbers rarely match each other. The casting number is derived from the actual casting or part and typically does not match the part, engineering, or service numbers. Unless the casting has been revised, the basic casting number does not change. It means the number you see in the casting will not match the part number in the Ford Master Parts Catalog, and if the catalog you are using is dated, as most are, expect even more changes in your Ford dealer's microfiche or computer when it comes to suffixes. When demand for a part falls below a predetermined level, Ford will discontinue or "N/R" the part. "N/R" means "Not Replaced."

Ford Basic Part Numbers (Engine Only)	
Basic Part Number	**Component/Group**
6000-6898	Engine
8000-8499	Radiator
8500-8699	Water pump and cooling fan
9002-9256	Fuel tank
9301-9420	Fuel pump
9421-9499	Intake manifold and related parts
9500-9599	Carburetor and related parts
9600-9699	Air cleaner
9700-9999	Accelerator linkage
10000-10499	Alternator and generator
10500-10653	Voltage regulator
10654-10756	Battery
11000-11388	Starter
12000-12390	Ignition system
12402-12425	Spark plugs
14197-14689	Electrical wiring
18250-18699	Heater
18800	Radio and related accessories
19000	Fuel

Date and Foundry Codes

Ford makes it easy to identify engine castings because there are three foolproof systems in place. First is the casting number, which tells you the engineering level. Second is the casting date code, an alphanumeric code that tells you the exact date the item was cast at the foundry. There is also a foundry logo cast into the piece that tells you where it was cast. Finally, unless any machine work has been performed, a manufacturing date code is normally stamped into a machined surface that confirms when the component was manufactured. Casting and manufacture date codes look like this example: 9A26.

9	Year (1969)
A	Month (January)
26	Day

If this code is cast into the piece, it indicates the date the piece was cast at the foundry. If the date code is stamped or inked, it indicates the date of manufacture. When a cylinder block or deck is milled, the stamped manufacture date code is normally lost in the machining process.

Also expect to see foundry codes such as "DIF" (Dearborn Iron Foundry) and "M" with a circle around it indicating Michigan Casting. Michigan Casting, which is now the Ford/Mazda joint-venture Mustang assembly plant in Flat Rock, Michigan, was a Ford iron foundry in the 1970s and 1980s. Also, some iron and aluminum castings were produced by unknown outside suppliers.

Ford Muscle Parts

In the early 1970s, Ford released two supplements to its original *Muscle Parts Story* catalog. Because the 429/460 didn't become a high-performance engine until 1970, there was no reference to the 385-series engines prior to 1970. Supplement No. 1 listed parts interchange and description. One chapter is dedicated to the 385-series engines, which included the 429, Boss 429, and the 460. This chapter included technical data for each engine including detail on the design and engineering elements of major components such as the block, heads, induction, crankshaft, connecting rods, and pistons. The intent was to get enthusiasts connected to the 385-series engine family.

Supplement No. 2 soon followed, addressing the performance enhancements for the Boss 302, 351 Cleveland, and 429. The 429 wedge modifications were detailed in three kit levels: Impressor, Controller, and Dominator. Each of these kits included a laundry list of parts and Ford part numbers used to project predicted horsepower ratings.

Good, Better, Best

The Impressor kit predicted 434 hp, which was an increase over the 429 Cobra Jet's 370 hp.

Stage 1

Stage 1 was the addition of the 429 Super Cobra Jet induction system, which was good for 12 hp at 6,200 rpm and 45 ft-lbs of torque at 2,800 rpm. Big deal, right? However, there's more.

- D0ZZ-9510-Z: Holley 780-cfm Carburetor (Boss 302 with manual choke)
- D0ZZ-9510-N Holley 780-cfm Carburetor (429 SCJ with manual transmission)
- D0ZZ-9510-R: Holley 780-cfm Carburetor (429 SCJ with automatic transmission)

Stage 2

Stage 2 included the following:

C9AZ-6250-A: 429 Cobra Jet Hydraulic Cam with 428 Cobra Jet valve springs (yes, 428 FE Cobra Jet)

Using the C9AZ-6250-A 429 Cobra Jet hydraulic camshaft got you 37 more hp at 419 at 5,200 rpm. Torque remained the same, but at a higher rpm (3,200 rpm).

Stage 3

Stage 3 of the Impressor kit included long-tube headers, getting you 15 additional horsepower at 5,200 rpm for a total of 434 hp. Ford suggested 34-inch-long primary header tubes, $2^1/_8$ inches in size with a 10- to 12-inch-long collector (secondary) tube. The Impressor kit delivered 419 hp. These numbers may leave you scratching your head. These engines made more than the advertised 370/375 hp.

Controller Kit

The next performance level from Ford was the Controller kit, which was good for greater power, some 99 hp over the advertised 370/375 at 469 hp. Stage 1 of the Controller kit is the same as Stage 1 of the Impressor kit, which was where I began. Stage 2 adds the 429 Cobra Jet/Super Cobra Jet valvetrain, ported 429 CJ/SCJ heads and ignition. Here's what you need valvetrain-wise.

Part Number	Item
C9ZZ-6A527-A	Non-positive stop rocker-arm studs
C9ZZ-6A528-A	Sled fulcrums
C9ZZ-6564-A	Stamped steel rocker arms
C8AZ-6A529-A	Rocker arm stud nuts
C9ZZ-6A529-B	Lock nuts
D0AZ-6A564-A	Pushrod guide plates
D0OZ-6565-B	Hardened pushrods
7HA-6518-A	Valve keepers
D0OZ-6514-A	Valve spring retainers
D9OZ-6A536-A	Valve spring seats/ cups
D0OZ-6313-A	429 CJ/SCJ valve spring/damper assembly
Note: Stage 3 employs the 429 CJ/SCJ valve springs instead of the 428 CJ valve springs in Stage 2.	

Stage 3 of the Controller kit is the same as Stage 1's long-tube headers.

Stage 4 includes the following modifications:

Part Number	Item
D0OZ-6049-A	429 CJ/SCJ cylinder heads (bare castings)
D0OZ-6507-A	Intake valves, 2.250 inches
D0OZ-6505-A	Exhaust valves, 1.730 inches

When you add these modifications, you should get 99 more hp over the base 429-4V engine.

Dominator Kit

The Dominator kit is the final step to the maximum of *Ford's Muscle Parts Story* of the 385-series engines. It is here you add a larger carburetor, a hotter mechanical camshaft, ported CJ/SCJ cylinder heads, a stroker kit, and forged pistons. Horsepower will go skyward to 487 to 542, depending on how far you go.

The 780-cfm Ford Holley gets replaced with an 850-cfm Holley, which is good for 17 hp more at 6,200 rpm, which is 17 over the 600-cfm Quadrajet and 5 over the Holley 780. Here's what you should get.

Part Number	Item
R-4223-AAS	Holley 850-cfm carburetor
R-4781-AAA	Holley 850-cfm carburetor

Stage 3 is the same as the Impressor kit with the addition of long-tube headers.

Stage 4 goes with the 429 heads with a full-on port job with the 429 CJ/SCJ's larger intake and exhaust valves.

Part Number	Item
D0VZ-6049-A	429-4V heads
D0OZ-6507-A	Intake valves, 2.250 inches
D0OZ-6505-A	Exhaust valves, 1.730 inches

Stage 5 employs more stroke via a 460 cast crank (3.850 versus the 429's 3.590-inch stroke) tied to a good forged piston (11.1:1 compression). For durability, opt for the 429 CJ/SCJ connecting rod. Here's how the Ford part numbers add up.

Part Number	Item
C8VY-6303-A	460 cast crankshaft
D0OZ-6200-A	429 CJ/SCJ connecting rods
D1OZ-6108-A	429 CJ/SCJ forged pistons for 11.1:1 compression

It is important to note most of the suggested Ford part numbers listed here are no longer available. However, the aftermarket offers plenty of options. Back in the day, the aftermarket offered virtually nothing for the 429/460 because it was considered a luxury car engine. What you have available today far surpasses anything that the *Ford Muscle Parts Story* catalog had at the time.

Ford 385-Series Big-Block General Engine Specifications			
Displacement (ci)	**429**	**460**	**Boss 429**
Horsepower	320 at 4,400 rpm (2V); 360 at 4,600 rpm (4V); 360 at 5,800 rpm (CJ); 375 at 5,600 rpm (SCJ); 208 at 4,400 rpm (4V) (1972 SAE net); 202 at 4,400 rpm (4V) (1973 SAE net)	365 at 4,600 rpm; 224 at 4,000 rpm (SAE net)	375 at 5,200 rpm
Torque	476 at 2,800 rpm; 480 at 2,800 rpm; 298 at 2,800 rpm (SAE net); 327 at 2,800 rpm (SAE net); 327 at 2,600 rpm (SAE net)	500 at 2,800 rpm; 342 at 2,800 rpm (SAE net); 357 at 2,800 rpm (SAE net); 338 at 2,800 rpm (SAE net); 360 at 2,800 rpm (SAE net); 350 at 2,800 rpm (SAE net); 355 at 2,800 rpm (SAE net); 386 at 2,800 rpm (SAE net)	450 at 4,500 rpm
Carburetion	Rochester Quadrajet; Holley 4150 (SCJ)	Autolite/Motorcraft; 4300/4350	Holley 4150
Compression	10.5:1 (2V); 11.01:1 (4V); 11.5:1 (CJ/SCJ); 8.0:1 (1972–up)	10.5:1 (1968–1971); 8.5:1 (1972–up)	10.5:1
Bore size (inches)	4.362	4.362	4.362
Stroke (inches)	3.590	3.850	3.590
Crank type	nodular iron	nodular iron	steel
Piston type	cast aluminum	cast aluminum	forged
Connecting rod length (inches)	6.600	6.600	6.600
Valve size (inches)	intake: 2.090; exhaust: 1.660	intake: 2.090; exhaust: 1.660	intake: 2.250; exhaust: 1.720
Lifter type	hydraulic; mechanical (SCJ)	hydraulic	hydraulic (1969); mechanical (1970); mechanical (race); mechanical (820-A and 820-T engines after June 1, 1969)
Rocker arm ratio	1.75:1	1.75:1	1.73:1
Rocker arm type	bolt/fulcrum; stud mounted (SCJ)	bolt/fulcrum	shaft mounted (adjustable)
Engine balance	internal	internal (1968–1978 2Y crank); external (1979–up 3Y crank)	internal

Note: Some engine specifications are unavailable.

The Block

When Ford conceived the 385-series engine prior to 1968, the goal was to introduce a lightweight, skirtless big-block that could grow to greater displacements, primarily for luxury cars and trucks. Ford was also thinking about strength with a rugged, well-thought-out casting that could take a lot of punishment and still have room for growth. Known as the "Lima" engine for its manufacturing plant in Lima, Ohio, the 385-series engine was long on potential both as a luxury car engine and as a racing mill. In the years since 1968, the 429/460 has become legendary as a racing engine.

The 429/460 block is hardy in its most basic form as a grocery-getter luxury-car powerplant. It is strong and can withstand incredible amounts of power. Thick main webs and robust cylinder walls make the 429/460 block virtually indestructible if you build and tune it properly. This means that you can build on any 429/460 and have little concern when infusing a lot of power into this block.

The 429- and 460-ci displacements are completely interchangeable blocks because both have a 4.360-inch cylinder bore. In fact, there's only one block for both displacements. The sole difference in these engines is stroke: 3.590 inches for the 429 and 3.850 inches for the 460. Drop a 460 crank into a 429 block and you have a 460, and vice versa. Aftermarket stroker kits allow you to huff as much as 500-plus ci into this block. It is true there are more 460 cranks than there are 429s because the 429 was dropped early in production during the early 1970s.

The 429/460 block is identifiable by its casting numbers: C8VE, DOVE, and D1VE-A. You can also expect to see truck blocks with D5TE, D6TE, D7TE, D8TE, D9TE, and the like. All 1970–1971 Super Cobra Jet blocks had four-bolt mains (three center mains only). There are also Police Interceptor 429 blocks with four-bolt mains, although this can get very confusing. Not all Police Interceptor blocks had a four-bolt main. In the end, it doesn't really matter unless you're doing a concours restoration and are obsessed with casting numbers and date codes. Even with

The 429/460 block is basically the same from 1968 to 1996 with the exception of extended cylinder skirts and thicker webbing in the 1979–1996 D9TE truck block. This is the DOVE block with two-bolt main caps. Based on discussions I've had with seasoned engine builders and racers, the D9TE truck block appears to be the strongest due to thicker main webs and overall a thicker casting.

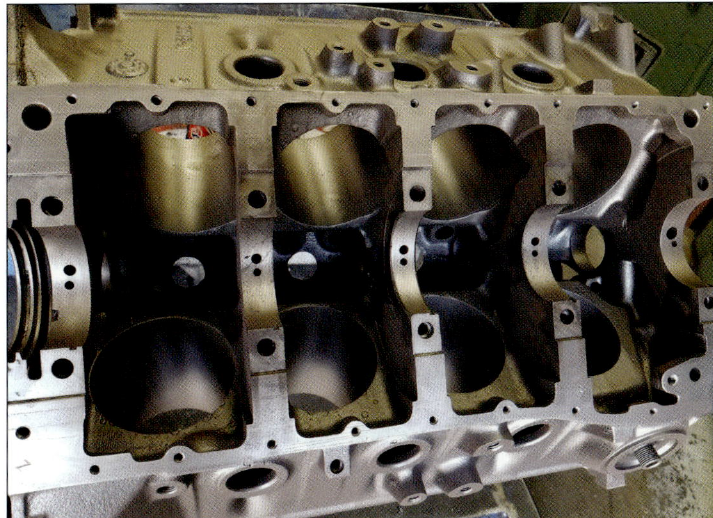

Although the 429/460 block was originally developed to be a passenger car and heavy-duty truck engine, it ultimately became a high-performance racing engine for Ford and Mercury muscle cars and marine applications with its five thick main webs and wide main caps. Although four-bolt main blocks are in high demand, the two bolt blocks can withstand 500 to 600 hp. With four-bolt main caps, it can withstand another 100 to 200 hp.

Virtually all 429/460 blocks have this "460" in the casting because they're all the same block regardless of displacement and stroke. The "14" is a casting cavity number. Even if you have a 429, expect to see "460" on these castings.

two-bolt main journals, a 385-series block is engineered to stay together under grueling conditions. The later D5TE, D6TE, D7TE, D8TE, and D9TE truck blocks with thicker main webs are among the strongest.

All 1968–1978 385-series block castings are basically the same with the exception being four-bolt main blocks, which have thicker mains and are drilled and tapped for four-bolt main caps. The D9TE truck block employs extended cylinder skirts, which calls for the correct corresponding crankshaft with smaller counterweights. This generation of 460 is an externally balanced rotating assembly with a slide-on counterweight.

This "460" can be found inside some 460 blocks just ahead of the number-5 rear main bearing saddle, but not all. You can also expect to see a reversed "460" in some blocks.

The block casting date code can be found in the lifter valley. This is an alphanumeric code consisting of the year, month, and day. This is 9M17 meaning December 17, 1969. When the date code is stamped into the block, this indicates the date the engine was manufactured.

The D0VE-A casting number (1970) is a very common casting number. Expect to see C8VE, C8VY, C9VE, C9VY, D0OE, D0VE, D1VE, D1ZE, D5TE, D6TE, D7TE, D8TE, and D9TE. Optimum choice is the truck block with a "T" code.

These blocks were cast in two foundries: Dearborn and Michigan Casting. "DIF" indicates the Dearborn Iron Foundry. It was cast at Dearborn and shipped to the Lima, Ohio, engine plant for machining and assembly.

The D9TE block with its extended skirts (roughly 0.1875 inch deeper into the block) was conceived for a reason. The extended skirts improved piston stability at BDC. It also needed to be a more robust block to handle the demands of even heavier trucks that it was asked to power when the larger Super Duty truck engine was discontinued.

If you want strength without the challenges of a D9TE truck block, opt for the D0VE-A early block with its thicker main webs. Finding a good serviceable D0VE-A block is an enormous challenge. If you can find one and the seller knows its worth, get out your wallet because rarity and condition dictate price. If casting numbers and authenticity are of little importance to you, opt for a late-model 460 truck block and get the corresponding crank.

When you see this "M" logo, it indicates the block was cast at Ford's Michigan Iron Foundry, also known as Michigan Casting, which also cast 351M and 400 blocks. Michigan Casting was at Flat Rock, Michigan, and is now the joint-venture Ford/Mazda assembly plant where Ford builds the Mustang.

This bellhousing bolt pattern is common to both the 429/460 and the 400 and 351M blocks as well. Note the reversed "460" in the back of this block on the right-hand side.

A broad look at the front of the 429/460 block. Because bore size is the same on all 429/460 blocks, you can build them as either a 429 or 460. The best advice is to grow displacement, go 460+. You can shoehorn a lot of displacement into these blocks, upward of 500 ci.

Because a lot of 429/460 blocks were installed in Ford vehicles, the vehicle identification number (VIN) was stamped in the back of the block like this. Lincoln consecutive unit numbers began at 600001. This one is 608277. Mercury began at 500001. Ford units began at 100001. F-Series trucks and E-Series vans were numbered differently.

This is a D9TE-AB 460 truck block, which was designed for its own unique crankshaft with smaller counterweights designed to clear extended cylinder skirts. You cannot use a pre-1979 429/460 crank in this block.

Ford 385-series engine blocks never had a one-piece rear main seal. All were two-piece.

The Boss 429 block is a completely different casting from the standard 429/460 variety. Most obvious are these four-bolt main caps, but there's more. This is high-nickel cast iron for strength, screw-in freeze plugs for cooling system security, more aggressive oil galleries, and thicker decks and main webbing. Look for "HP429" in Boss 429 block castings.

Aftermarket Blocks

A number of aftermarket 385-series blocks are available for your Ford big-block project. There are plenty of cores out there to build on, but not as many as there used to be. Jon Kaase Racing Engines offers a variety of aftermarket block options. The Eliminator Premier cast-iron block is Kaase's top-of-the-line iron block with steel four-bolt main caps on all five journals. It employs a 10.3-inch deck height, sports siamesed cylinder bores, and is therefore capable of a whopping 4.700-inch bore diameter.

The affordably priced Eliminator Premier ships to your door complete with five machined billet 8620 steel four-bolt main caps, A1 fasteners, a really stout valley tray, a cam tunnel machined to 2.500 inches, and all the trimmings you expect from a Kaase product. It is currently priced at $3,195.00 (price subject to change), which is not bad for a brute aftermarket block.

Kaase also carries the older Ford Racing SVO 385-series iron block, which is a more affordable alternative to the A-460 block I'm about to get into. Here's what you get with the SVO 385, which reads virtually the same as the newer A-460 block.

- High-strength block for professional competition
- 10.322-inch deck height (plus or minus 0.005 inch)
- Cast-iron block with four-bolt main caps on journals 2, 3, and 4
- Nodular-iron main caps
- 3.000-inch main journal diameter
- Siamesed cylinder bore design
- Can be bored/stroked to 598 ci
- Bore range from 4.360 to 4.600 inches (also available in a "big bore" version, part number M-6010-A460BB)
- Wet-sump oiling system design
- Priority main journal oiling system
- Weighs approximately 275 pounds

Siamesed blocks are solid between cylinder bores. There are no water passages between cylinder bores. This is done to increase block strength.

Ford's A-460 race block from Jon Kaase Racing Engines has long been the gold standard for affordable race blocks and here's why.

- 10.322-inch deck height (plus or minus 0.005 inch)
- Rugged cast-iron race block with four-bolt main caps on journals 2, 3, and 4
- Nodular iron main caps
- Can be bored/stroked to produce 598 ci
- Siamesed cylinder bores
- Rough bored to 4.490-inch (plus or minus 0.003 inch)
- Maximum recommended bore size is 4.600 inches
- Wet-sump oil system design
- 3.000-inch main journal diameter
- Weighs approximately 275 pounds
- High-strength cast-iron block for professional competition
- Siamesed blocks are a solid casting between the cylinder bores for extraordinary strength. This means there are no water jackets between them. This is a matter of design to increase block strength.
- The A-460 is also available in standard bore version, Ford part number M-6010-A460.

The Kaase cast aluminum race block is the high-priced spread and there's a reason why. This is a super lightweight cast aluminum race block developed solely for racing with full water jackets. It is priced from $5,900.00 to $6,730.00. It is available in four versions.

- 4.900-inch bore spacing x 10.320-inch deck height
- 4.900-inch bore spacing x 11.200-inch deck height
- 4.900-inch bore spacing x 11.700-inch deck height
- 5.000-inch bore spacing x 12.000-inch deck height

For those of you with really deep pockets and a serious passion for professional drag racing, there's the Kaase/Bear billet aluminum block with 5.000-inch bore centers. This is an all-out race block engineered for professional racers. It is priced at $15,000.00. Yeah, that's what I said. Takes a lot of time and resources to CNC cut a block of billet aluminum into a solid race block. Chances are you're probably not in the market for a solid billet aluminum race block because it is way beyond most budgets.

Budget Blocks

The aftermarket is loaded with reconditioned 429/460 blocks that are ready for final detailing and assembly. For less than $1,000, you can get into a reconditioned and fully machined block from Competition Products, as one example of what's available though there are more. The Competition Products block is fully machined and prepped; it's ready for assembly. You only have to check all dimensions and make sure your pistons are matched to the bores.

Competition Products begins with select Ford cores and puts them through an extensive cleaning and machining process. All are chemically cleaned and Magnafluxed for cracks and then bored and honed on Sunnen Equipment. Decks are milled and checked. Then, blocks get final prep including freeze plugs and Dura-Bond cam bearings.

These reconditioned blocks are sold as race blocks and, therefore, no warranty is expressed or implied. This means you must thoroughly examine your block when it arrives. This goes for any used or reconditioned block you may purchase. You will want to confirm the block's condition the minute it arrives. You don't want to find out months or years later you have a flawed block. Do not wait. Have a trusted machine shop inspect and confirm condition before you begin assembly. The Competition Products block, as one example of what's available from the aftermarket, looks like this:

Part type	Engine Block
Application	Ford 460
Engine block style	Stock/OEM
Engine block material	Cast iron
Main journal type	460 main
Deck height	10.300 inch
Cylinder bore (as shipped)	4.440 inch
Cylinder bore diameter	4.440 inch
Finished cylinder bores	Yes
Main caps included	Yes
Main cap material	Cast iron
Main bolt style	Two-bolt (all 5 caps)
Main cap fasteners included	Yes, OEM
Lifter bore diameter	0.874 inch
Camshaft bore	Standard
Provisions for OEM roller lifters	No
Main bearings included	No
Rear-main seal style	Two-Piece
Oil pan rail type	Stock/OEM
Raised cam location	No
Cam bearings included	Yes, Dura-Bond
Freeze plugs included	Yes
Manufacturer	Tri Star
Manufacturer's part number	PMB460-080
Warranty	Race application (no warranty expressed or implied)

Boss 429 Block

It may interest you to know the 385-series 429/460-ci engine was under development for six years before being introduced in 1968. Ford product planners and engineers envisioned an engine family to replace the FE-series big-block and the rather unusual MEL-series fat-block developed for Mercury, Edsel, and Lincoln in the 1950s. Ford even put the MEL in Thunderbirds. More interesting yet with the 385 is the bore spacing. The MEL and the 385 have the same bore spacing, but that's about it in terms of shared engineering. Nothing from either engine family fits the other.

Ford's legendary and powerful Boss 429 has its own distinctive four-bolt main block (the first four mains are four-bolt) specific to the Boss 429. Look for the "HP429" on the front of the Boss 429 block. Not all Boss 429 blocks will have the "HP429" in the casting. Service replacements did not have the "HP429" in the casting.

The Boss 429 block is a high-nickel block developed exclusively for NASCAR with a unique Boss 429-specific oiling system similar to the FE 427 Side Oiler with quad oil galleries mid-block. There's no other 385-series block like it. It is a standalone block casting exclusively for the Boss 429. Aside from the obvious differences, the Boss 429 employed O-ring cylinder head sealing instead of conventional cylinder head gaskets.

The Boss 429 block includes more beef all around, and especially in the lifter valley, which is the block's most central strength point. This is an "S" code block, which is said to be primarily 1969, the early cars.

The only casting number I've ever seen on Boss 429 blocks is C9AE-E. It is unknown how many Boss blocks were produced.

The quickest way to identify the Boss 429 block, aside from the obvious screw-in freeze plugs, four-bolt mains, and the "HP429," is this quartet of oil galleries around the camshaft, which ensures the rotating assembly down under gets plenty of oil. No other 429/460 block has this oil gallery configuration. If you see a pair of oil galleries, it isn't a Boss 429 block.

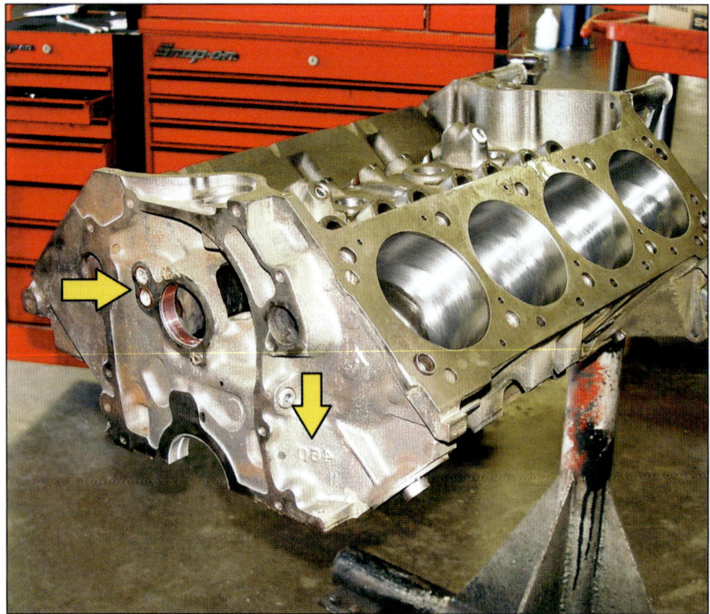

Here's another look at the Boss 429 block with its dual oil gallery plugs in front. Note the reversed "460."

This is the right-hand side of the Boss 429 block with the C9AE-E casting number and screw-in freeze plugs. Installed in a vehicle with the starter installed, the block casting number is not visible. The starter must be removed.

Head on, the differences in the Boss block are significant. Note the thicker main webs and a more generous oiling system.

Main saddles from the factory typically didn't have a crosshatch pattern. Most builders I work with suggest having your block line-honed for improved main bearing security and crush.

One way to identify a Boss 429 block, aside from four-bolt mains (mains 1-4), is the "S" code in the lifter valley on early Boss 429 block castings and the four oil galleries surrounding the cam journals. The Boss 429 service replacement block will have a "460" and an "A" cast in the front of the block instead of the "HP429" just mentioned. Expect to see variations out there with both "429" and "460." No other 429/460 block has the four oil galleries and four-bolt main journals on number-1 through number-4. I've often wondered how many Boss 429 blocks have wound up in engine builds where the builder had no idea what they had. Swap meets have been known to come up with the most unusual finds.

Block Identification

There has always been some confusion when it has come to 385-series block identification. The 429/460 block castings, despite different casting numbers, are all basically the same and can all be converted to four-bolt main caps with help from a qualified machine shop. All have the same thick main webs and pan rails. If you take away the casting numbers and date codes, these blocks tend to defy detection from each other except for minor casting changes.

429/460 Block Identification			
Displacement and Years Available	Ford Part/Casting Number (6010)	Bore Size (inches)	Additional Information
429/460 ci (1968–1970)	C8VE-F	4.360	—
429/460 ci (1969–1970)	C9VE-B	4.360	—
429-ci (1970–1971) Cobra Jet, Super Cobra Jet, and Police Interceptor	D0OE-B	4.360	Four-bolt mains
429/460 ci (1971–up)	D1VE	4.360	—
429/460 ci (1971–up)	D1ZE-AZ	4.360	—
429/460 ci (1975–up)	D5TE	4.360	Truck block
460 ci (1976–up)	D6TE	4.360	Truck block
460 ci (1977–up)	D7TE	4.360	Truck block
460 ci (1978–up)	D8TE	4.360	Truck block
460 ci (1979–up)	D9TE	4.360	Truck block; Extended cylinder skirts with smaller crankshaft counterweights; Slide-on crankshaft counterweight; Externally Balanced.
429-ci Boss 429	C9AE-E	4.360	Boss 429 Block HP429
429-ci Boss 429	C9AE-E	4.360	Boss 429 Service Block 460A
NOTE: Not all block castings are shown here. These are all known castings.			

Block Preparation

You want a block with perfectly machined surfaces that will mate well and seal tight without conflict. This calls for extreme measures in machining and painstaking attention to detail. This is why you must enlist an experienced and trusted machine shop. Before you spend a lot of money on a block, it must first be cleaned and inspected, then confirmed fit for service. This is a good investment, especially if you discover you have a bad block.

You're not going to find a machine shop that will clean and machine a block and then refund your money because it is cracked, bored oversize beyond salvage, was windowed by a stray connecting rod and repaired, or suffers from some other type of defect.

You must know going in if you have a usable block. Begin with a pressure test to confirm integrity. Then, perform a complete thermal cleaning, including removing all welch and oil gallery plugs followed by a visual and magnetic particle inspection. This is an investment you will have to make in a block casting before you spend real money on machine work.

Go into water jackets with a high-power magnet to catch slag and other metal debris that can cause cooling system troubles. You would be amazed at how much you will find in there from the foundry, which can cause hot spots and overheating. I've seen freeze plugs (also known as Welch plugs) inside water jackets, knocked inside by careless rebuilders and factory autoworkers. Do this even if it's a new block, and especially if it's a new block. Measure cylinder bore size from top to bottom, and sonic check cylinder walls and block decks. While you're at it, perform a pressure test. The line bore should also be checked. Check the cam bore-to-line bore centerlines. Check the cam journals for any irregularities. Examine lifter bores.

Block cleaning should be an ongoing process throughout the machining phases. It is suggested you have your machinist clean the block after each machining phase to ensure debris doesn't accumulate in oil galleries, water jackets, and other cavities. Not all will agree with this because it's labor intensive and adds to cost; however, it is just good housekeeping.

The logic in repeat cleaning is that even the smallest metal particle and grit can and will damage moving parts. Even a hair-thin score in a block journal can cost you oil pressure. Oil galleries and other passages must have a thorough cleaning with long and aggressive rifle cleaning brushes again and again until you are confident all debris is gone. Another aspect of cleaning is slag and stress riser removal. Slag can impede oil and cooling system passages. Stress risers can lead to cracking.

Machine work includes cylinder boring and honing if bores are tapered beyond 0.0010 inch. Maximum wear limit is 0.010-inch over before you must go to the next oversize. Where possible, bore and hone to 0.020-inch oversize instead of 0.030-inch, which buys you more block life. If wear is minimal and boring unnecessary, you must at least do a fine-finish hone and ridge removal. The purpose of boring is not only to take cylinders to the next oversize but also to match each piston to a hone-matched bore. In other words, you measure each piston and hone a cylinder to match, but do so only once dynamic balancing is complete and you have eight slugs and rods balanced to a specific location on the crankshaft.

Piston rings should be end gapped and installed. One more thing: make sure your machine shop uses a torque plate for honing, which simulates cylinder head installation and gets the bores as they will be once heads are installed and torqued down. Hone without a torque plate and you have cylinder bores that will be irregular when heads are installed and torqued. Always use a head gasket with the torque plate. It's that important. Three different stones are typically used in the honing process, becoming progressively finer as the process goes until the machinist achieves a fine crosshatch pattern.

Main saddles need to be align honed until they are true. Align honing puts a nice crosshatch pattern in the bearing saddles, which provides good bearing crush and security. Main saddles require boring when they are worn beyond limits, which involves milling main cap mating surfaces, then boring and honing the installed caps. This is on par with reconditioning connecting rods. One thing that machine shops rarely do is cam bore align honing. However, for good cam bearing security, ask them to check and hone yours if necessary. It's worth the expense to get a good crosshatch pattern.

Decks should be measured across and corner to corner, then milled the minimal amount necessary. Block

Before you have a block machined in the first place, mike all of the dimensions before you spend money on machine work. Cylinder wall thickness should be sonic checked as shown along with miking bore size going in. I suggest never going beyond 0.040-inch oversize, though some blocks will go 0.060-inch over.

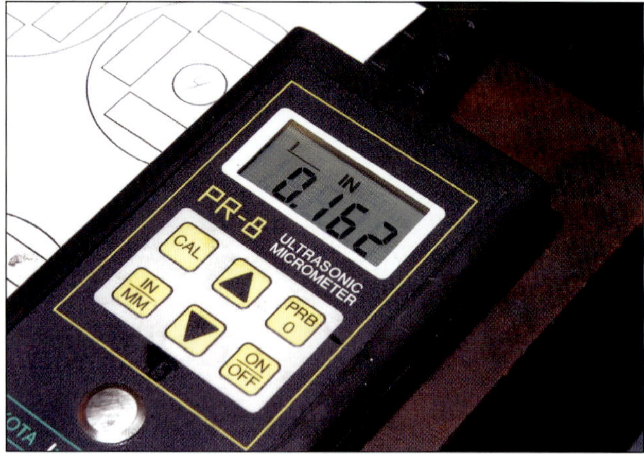

This sonic check shows 0.162-inch wall thickness. Check wall thickness on all eight bores from top to bottom and in four different locations around each bore. Wall thickness should never be less than 0.140 inch.

The 429/460 block in all its forms can be converted to four-bolt main caps. Milodon aftermarket main bearing caps add strength to factory two-bolt Ford big-blocks. They also add strength to 429/460 four-bolt main blocks by replacing the iron four-bolt main caps. These Milodon main cap kits are available in your choice of angle- or straight-side bolts depending upon your block type.

While you're ordering the Milodon four-bolt main caps, opt for ARP hardware consisting of studs and bolts for unequalled strength. You will want to chase bolt-hole threads and use a thread lubricant on the threads for positive torque readings.

deck warpage any greater than 0.003 inch across a distance of 6 inches or greater calls for deck milling. How much you remove from the deck depends on what you want the deck height to be.

Deck height is the distance from the crankshaft centerline to the top of each deck. Of course, you have to dial-in crank, rod, and piston dimensions to determine compression and quench, which involves a lot of math. Once the decks are milled, your machine shop should put a nice taper at the top of each bore for ease of piston/ring installation.

Once all machine work is complete, you've performed a thorough cleaning, and all oil gallery and freeze plugs are installed, perform a pressure test to confirm you still have a solid block.

Once the pressure test is complete, begin painting by properly masking off what should not be painted. This includes GE Glyptal inside where necessary. GE Glyptal on rough inside surfaces streamlines oil drainback and seals the casting.

Once your block is in paint, spray cylinder walls and interior surfaces with WD-40 for corrosion prevention. You don't want rusty cylinder walls and bearing saddles. In a damp climate, it doesn't take long for them to get that way.

Some block cracking can be repaired via welding or using J-B Weld. This product is a two-part catalyzed product that works well with cracked cast iron. Properly mixed and allowed time to cure, it will last the life of any engine block. For J-B Weld to work effectively you need a clean surface and a crack that has been carefully stop drilled at each end. Just a small 1/16-inch stop drill hole at each end slows and stops cracking. Then, weld or J-B Weld the crack. I suggest against the use of J-B Weld at the cylinder walls and decks where stresses can be extreme. Your machine shop will know best on what call to make on repair. Some blocks are cracked beyond repair.

The first order of business is to chase every bolt hole in the block, and especially the main cap bolt holes, then blast them out with brake cleaner and a drop of SAE 30-weight engine oil. Clean threads are important to proper fastener torque readings when it's time to put your block together.

Before any machine work is performed, ARP main studs are screwed into the main journal bolt holes. Never bottom out the main studs. Always run them down just short of the bottom of the bolt hole using a thread lubricant.

The block is machined by a JGM Performance Engineering for pinpoint accuracy. Main webs on each side of the main caps have to be machined down (arrow) to make way for the Milodon steel caps.

Prussian Blue is applied to the main webs where we're going to cut the block to accommodate the four-bolt main caps.

With Prussian Blue applied beneath the four-bolt main caps, lines will be scribed in the main web contact surfaces to outline where the block will be milled.

We're doing a test fit of the Milodon main cap to have some idea how the angle-side bolt holes will have to be drilled and tapped.

Main cap depth is checked with a dial indicator to determine how much metal will need to be milled off the main web.

Using a Bridgeport, with all dimensions having been checked, the main web is milled as shown to make way for the main cap.

Because we've altered the line bore with aftermarket steel main caps, the line bore will have to be bored and align-honed to proper dimensions. This is not a process you can conduct in your home shop. It must be handled by a professional machinist.

Ford 429/460 Block Specifications						
Engine	Cylinder Bore Diameter (inches)	Crank to Rear Face Runout (inch)	Main Bearing Bore (inches)	Lifter Bore Diameter (inch)	Distributor Shaft Bore Diameter (inch)	Head Gasket Surface (inch)
429/460	4.3600–4.3636; Maximum out of round 0.015	0.005	3.1922–3.1930	0.8752–0.8767	0.1560–0.5175	0.0003 in any 6-inch direction; no more than 0.0007 overall

Fasteners, Clean Threads, and Torque

Your block preparation should include thread chasing, which not enough of us do. Every bolt hole should be lubricated with WD-40 and chased with a thread chaser until fasteners roll smoothly. Damaged threads should be tapped or repaired with a Helicoil insert. Once threads are clear, blast them with a soapy solution and compressed air. Then, spray WD-40 in the hole for corrosion prevention. Fastener threads should also be chased while you're at it.

When it comes to fastener use, I suggest ARP fasteners throughout because there is no better fastener out there. You will find some ARP kits don't have all of the correct fasteners, which means you will need to do it piecemeal and order specific fasteners for your 429/460. There is also AMK Products for those who wish a factory look using OEM fasteners. Not all OEM-style fasteners are available. You may have to resort to new-old-stock fasteners where you can find them. AMK Products is meticulous about the quality of its fasteners, which makes them an excellent source for engine fasteners.

I suggest going with main studs even if you're building a stocker for greater bottom-end security. This is a nice, stealthy modification no one can see. Main studs offer greater structural integrity, which prevents main cap movement. Head studs make cylinder head removal difficult if you have to remove them in a car. However, if you're going to push the limits of a 429/460 block, such as nitrous, supercharging, or high RPM/high compression for extended periods, studs are the better choice. Give all fasteners a trial run through bolt holes to check for resistance.

Never torque fasteners without lubrication and always torque them in one-third torque values, then recheck torque. This means if you have a full torque value of 80 ft-lbs, the first phase should be 26.6 ft-lbs; the second 53.3 ft-lbs; and the final 80 ft-lbs. Then, check total torque.

Why is bolt torque so important? Tightening a fastener is about clamping force between two or more components and them staying together. As you tighten a fastener, you are working against threads in the process of pulling two or more components together. You're also contributing to bolt stretch and tension.

What is bolt torque and what is bolt stretch? Torque really is a measure of twist, how hard you twist something in inch- or foot-pounds. It is also about bolt tension and stretch. In truth, fasteners are designed to stretch just so much. This stretch and tension is what keeps components together. With each bolt tightening, the fastener loses strength. There are fasteners you should never use twice for this reason, while others stretch and tension are less of a consequence. We tend to reuse cylinder head and main cap bolts when we probably shouldn't. This is less of a consequence on street engines than those built for competition.

Torque is an immediate indication of fastener tension. You must be mindful of the many factors that affect bolt torque and contribute to tension, such as surface texture (rough or smooth), rust, grit, thread type, and material just to name a few. Torque wrenches offer this tension and indicate the amount of torque by the rotational force applied to the bolt.

As torque is applied, bolt threads draw the threaded face and bolt head closer together, which stretches the fastener and applies tension. Bolt tension works by loading the bolt head, which provides stretch before the nut is secure and tight. The tensioner is clamped to the bolt's threads and pushes against the flange in the surface being bolted. This provides a very consistent amount of bolt stretch, which ensures uniform bolt stretch and clamping force on components. This is why you must invest in a torque wrench and other appropriate tools. You should not tighten fasteners based on feel.

You must know, via a torque wrench, what your fastener torque is. What's more, know how to properly use a torque wrench. Always apply torque smoothly. Never jerk a torque wrench, and never use one to remove fasteners. Using a torque wrench to loosen fasteners will adversely affect calibration. At least once a year, have your torque wrench's calibration checked by a professional. This information can be found on the web.

Although "torque-to-yield" fasteners have never really been used on 385-series engines, it is good to know why they exist. Torque-to-yield is about more accurately determining bolt stretch and tension. Tightening a fastener to its "yield point" proves out high preloading of the bolt, which can significantly increase fatigue life. This means the fastener will last longer. When the applied torque load doesn't surpass the clamping force, the stress of the fastener will be lower than when the preload is less than the applied load. Torque-to-yield is beneficial in high-frequency high-load applications with a greater risk of fastener fatigue-involved failure, such as cylinder heads or main bearing caps. As a rule, torque-to-yield fasteners are generally one-time use only.

When you're assembling a 429/460, decisions are made about torque versus tension based on performance requirements and your budget. You cannot build an engine based strictly on budget. Do it on the cheap and it becomes expensive in the long term. You have to look at your engine's mission and how it will be used most of the time. Always use Grade-8 fasteners—no exceptions. Never use peanut-butter bolts (no head markings) or Grade-5s.

Another important issue concerning fasteners is thread type and spacing. Although thread types are often unnoticed unless you can't get a bolt to thread, threaded fasteners are a given when you're assem-

The 1970–1971 Cobra Jet blocks are marked in the lifter valley with a "CJ" (white arrow) and a casting date code (black arrow).

bling an engine. As a rule, you're going to have coarse thread fasteners throughout your 429/460. In some instances, you're going to see fine threads. Fine and coarse thread fasteners don't speak the same language. They are about thread spacing in threads per inch. However, let's keep the narrative simple.

When you're assembling a 429/460, the most common fastener you will see is Unified National Coarse (UNC) thread, often known as "National Coarse." UNC is most commonly used because they fit deeper and are certainly more common than fine thread. UNC also employs a higher tolerance during plating and manufacturing.

Unified National Fine (UNF) thread, also known as "National Fine," involves a more specific fit and has a finer tension adjustment with tighter tolerances. UNF threads have better torque-locking ability and can carry heavier loads because there are more threads per inch. You will see UNF with items such as carburetor studs and the like.

United National Extra Fine (UNEF) thread is used in very specialized applications, such as tapped bolt holes in thin material, tapped holes in hard material, or thin threaded walls.

With engines, coarse thread is better than fine thread unless you have a very specific purpose. Coarse offers better resistance than fine when it comes to cross threading and stripping. Coarse thread isn't as vulnerable to being damaged or nicked, so it doesn't have to be handled with special care as fine thread does. Coarse thread screws down more quickly, is not as adversely affected by plating buildup, and suffers from gagging and galling issues because there is more material (thread thickness) between each thread.

Although coarse thread types are ideal for many applications, fine threads also have their benefits. They sport more threads per inch, which means they're stronger in tension and shear strength than coarse threads due to their larger tensile stress area.

Another important issue is fastener material. Steel is certainly the most common type of bolt material. What you get from steel is a high degree of formability coupled with tensile strength and durability. Steel bolts are often processed with zinc or chrome plating for corrosion resistance but may also be produced without any plating or coating.

High-carbon steel is easily the most common type of steel used in engine fastener production. For your 429/460 project, you have a choice of Grades-2, -5, and -8, with Grade-8 being the standard for carbon-steel-based screws and bolts for engines and drivelines, with alloy carbon steel being optimum. High-carbon steel bolts deliver remarkable mechanical strength.

Here's how bolt grades stack up and what they're best used for.

The 429 Cobra Jet block sports four-bolt main caps. Note, this block has been studded for improved strength. If you find a 429 Cobra Jet block or a truck block with four-bolt mains that's damaged or bored to its limits, you can use these main caps for a two-bolt main block. Again, let a qualified machinist do this conversion.

If you're reaching for the stars, the Ford Performance A460 block will take you well beyond 1,000 hp with siamesed cylinder bores, thick main webs, four-bolt mains, thick decks, and more. The A460 can be used on the street, but it is a race block and really for competition only.

Ford's A460 block is unequalled in terms of brute strength, with a 10.322-inch deck, four-bolt main caps on journals number-2, -3, and -4, and nodular iron main caps. It can be bored/stroked to 598 ci, sports siamesed cylinder bores, and is rough bored to 4.490 inches (plus or minus 0.003 inch). The A460 is also available with a standard bore (part number M-6010-A460).

If you like the high-price spread ($15,000), JKRE and Bears Performance have teamed up to produce Billet cylinder blocks for 5.000 bore center applications. (Photo Courtesy Jon Kaase Racing Engines)

Grade-2

Grade-2 is a low-carbon steel material that's the least expensive and certainly the least durable. It should never be used in an engine. Grade-2 is the softest material and also the most common. Grade-2 bolts rarely have any identification on the bolt head.

Grade-5

Grade-5 bolts are made from non-alloy medium-carbon groups and are normally work-hardened to improve strength. Grade-5 is the most common grade of fasteners used in automobiles.

Grade-8

Grade-8 fasteners are medium-carbon alloys. They are work-hardened to a higher degree than Grade-5, which makes them stronger and well suited for engine, driveline, and suspension/brake systems. Never use anything less than Grade-8 in your 385-series build.

For the rest of us, fully machined and prepped Ford 460 blocks are ready for your engine builder or home garage. Competition Products begins with select Ford 460 cores, which are then fully machined. Each core is hot tanked and Magnafluxed for cracks and flaws, then bored and honed on precision Sunnen Equipment. These blocks are parallel decked. Each is fitted with new freeze and oil gallery plugs. Dura-Bond cam bearings are installed as a finishing touch. Ask for PN PMB460-080 when you call or order from their website. (Photo Courtesy Competition Products)

Alloy

Alloy is a metal formed with high-strength carbon steel that can be heat-treated for added strength. Alloy steel, due to its metal composition, has low corrosion resistance and typically benefits from additional treatment. There's high strength going on here, but also brittleness.

Stainless Steel

Stainless steel is a unique alloy combining the properties of low-carbon grade steel with chromium and nickel. The chromium

Sometimes, cylinder bores are so badly damaged or bored too far to where they must be sleeved. Summit Racing stocks the full complement of Melling cylinder sleeves for a wide variety of applications including the Ford 429/460. Cylinder sleeves get measured, and the block is bored for an interference fit.

Cylinder sleeves are always longer than the blocks they're designed to fit. Once they're inserted into the block, the excess is milled flush.

The block is bored slightly undersize compared to the sleeve's outside diameter. Every engine builder has their own approach. Sleeves are normally kept in a deep freeze where they shrink in size. The block is heated to where the bore expands, making room for the sleeve.

An industrial adhesive is applied to the cylinder wall, which will secure the sleeve.

The sleeve is carefully driven into the bore (shown) until it bottoms out. Then, the sleeve is bored and honed to piston size.

component lends stainless steel a high degree of corrosion resistance. A low carbon content prevents it from being hardened. However, this makes stainless stronger than most Grade-2 fasteners, yet weaker than many of the hardened Grade-5 and Grade-8 types.

Stainless is a material you need to do your homework with before making a decision. Stainless steel fasteners are not magnetic compared to steel fasteners. Stainless looks better than its steel counterparts; however, it is not always wise to use it in an engine. For securing valve covers, timing covers, oil pans, and the like, stainless works exceedingly well.

Rotating Assembly

The 385-series engine was engineered with an extraordinarily stout bottom end, which, even with a two-bolt main bottom end, makes it a terrific performance engine. You can make a lot of power with the 385 without concern of engine failure if you package and assemble it properly. Because the 385-series big-blocks are a simple, straightforward engine family with three basic displacements, crankshaft choice is quite simple to understand. You have two basic choices depending upon the stroke desired.

All 429/460 engines were fitted with 4U, 2Y or 3Y nodular iron crankshafts with the exception being the Boss 429, which is a close cousin to a steel crank. The Boss 429 was fitted with a forged steel crankshaft marked with Ford forging numbers for NASCAR competition, including street versions. You can expect to see C9AE-A, C9AE-B, or C9AE-C on a Boss crank.

The 385-series engines included three displacements but two strokes: 3.590 and 3.850 inches. Crankshafts are easily identified because they are marked accordingly. The 429 cranks are marked "4U" and "4UA." The 460 cranks are 2Y, 2YA, 2YAB, 2YABC prior to 1979. After 1978, they are marked "3Y." Also note not all 3Y crankshafts are marked. Some have no markings whatsoever. What makes the 3Y different than the 2Y or even the 4U is balancing. The 2Y and 4U are internally balanced. The 3Y is externally balanced. This means 460 engines from 1979 to 1996 are externally balanced and must be treated accordingly.

You've probably been led to believe that you must have a steel crank to do high-performance engine work. However, the 385-series nodular iron crankshaft, regardless of displacement, is a durable crankshaft thanks to main journal sizing and the good consistency of better nodular iron. Based on four decades of experience with this engine and the many people I've seen build 429/460 big-blocks, this is a crankshaft with a great reputation for durability, especially if you inspect and prepare it properly.

All 429/460 engines were fitted with cast-iron crankshafts from the factory, with the exception of the Boss 429 (1969–1970 only), which was fitted with a steel crank. Crankshaft identification is easy. The 429 engines were fitted with a 4U or 4UA crank with a 3.580-inch stroke. The 460 engine was fitted with a 2Y cast crank until 1979. From 1979 to 1996, the 460 was fitted with the 3Y crank with smaller counterweights to clear extended cylinder skirts.

Because there's plenty of room for displacement in the 429/460 block, you can bore and stroke this block enough to get more than 500 ci. You get displacement, power, and durability this way. If you want to keep your 429/460 stock internally, you have a great foundation on which to build because the 429/460 is extremely rugged in factory form. The 429/460 crank is a durable piece that can take up to 7,000 rpm. You must be very methodical in your approach if you want it to live. The main thing here is a detailed inspection and good prep work.

A crankshaft's primary job is to convert heat energy into rotary motion and power. There's often the question on what type of crankshaft to choose for a 429/460 project. Because the 429/460 is so simple in terms of parts, you have very few options when it comes to the crank and rods. There's either the 2Y (1968–1978, large counterweights) or the 3Y (1979–1996, smaller counterweights) externally balanced nodular iron crankshaft. Your choices are but two. The Boss 429 was the only 385-series engine with a steel crank. The 429 CJ and SCJ were never factory fitted with a steel crank.

Because there are many torsional stresses on a crankshaft, a lot of thought needs to be given to crankshaft selection. Although the hot ticket always seems to be steel crankshafts, they're truly unnecessary for a street build. Cast is good for anything up to 500 to 600 hp. If you're going to push it beyond 600 hp, you're going to want steel. If you're going to treat your 460 to nitrous or a blower, you're going to want steel to get durability.

A cast crank performs well with steady, consistent applications of power. It is the shock nature of nitrous and boosted induction that can break an iron crank. I believe that you can road race with an iron crank, depending on how fast you want to go. You can even drag race with a cast crank depending upon the type of drag racing you want to do. It is important to remember that crankshafts twist and flex as combustion pulses hammer on each journal, which oscillates the iron or steel back and forth like rubber. You load the crank with a wide-open throttle, then come off the throttle abruptly, causing even more twist. Aside from the obvious stresses, there are other loads, such as the oil pump and distributor, which also contribute to twist.

Twist and oscillation affect timing and power output. As pistons and rods rise to compression/ignition stroke, oscillation becomes more intense, acting on not only the crankshaft but also connecting rods and pistons. It all moves violently with changes in power application. The crank's torsional behavior rebounds against the piston and rod as they ascend on the compression stroke. There's also the harmonic damper, which acts as a shock absorber for crank twist. As the crank rebounds, it works on the balancer, which softens rebound shock and reduces the risk of crankshaft breakage. Regardless of how you look at this dynamic, cyclic fatigue issues affect crankshaft life.

How do you recondition a crankshaft to make the most of its durability? You might get nervous about turning a crankshaft beyond 0.010-inch undersize; however, crankshafts are stronger than you may think. Automakers engineer tremendous strength into even the most modest cast-iron crankshafts. Crankshafts do break from time to time, but it is rarely due to material failure. This means that you can machine your 385's crank beyond 0.010-inch undersize without consequence, especially if you're building a street engine.

You can comfortably turn the journals to 0.020-inch undersize and still have durability. Over the years, I've studied crankshaft failure and talked with those who have also studied it and concluded most failures occur in the journal's fillet radius where heat and stress occur most. If you study most crankshaft failures, look at where they fail. The fillet radius is the most common failure spot between journals and the rest of the crank. Rarely will you ever see a mid-journal failure or a break at a counterweight. This is exactly why you must pay close attention to the fillet area with proper machining and finishing technique, plus the bearing's relationship with the fillet. Radiuses must be identical.

When you grind and finish a crankshaft, it is so easy to overlook the fillet radius. It is remarkable how many miss this. As engine builders, we spend so much time focused on journal surfaces, oil hole chamfering, and balance that we forget to examine each fillet radius and the bearing's important relationship with that radius. To add insult to injury, builders sometimes install bearings backward, which is failure before you even get started. I've seen countless assembly errors that result in engine failure and by people who should know better. Some of this stuff is easy to miss, which is why methodical inspection as you go is so critical.

A good rule is to machine the crank journals to your bearings and swap bearings around to get

The 385-series cast-iron crank is a fiercely durable piece capable of handling most street/strip applications. It can safely handle 500 hp.

optimum clearances throughout. Micropolish the journals and fillet radiuses to get the best oil flow and wedge for the best results. Main and rod journals get extremely hot, especially under a load at high RPM, where oil temperatures can briefly court 350 to 400°F.

Conventional engine oil begins to break down at 260°F. Synthetic begins to break down at 300°F. Oil can tolerate extremely high temperatures for a short amount of time, which is why a steady volume across the bearings and journals is important. You want enough of an oil wedge at the journals to keep moving parts apart, yet enough flow to carry destructive heat away from the journals.

If the machining process and mock-up show excessive crankshaft endplay, King Engine Bearing has two affordable options: MaxFlange and ProFlange thrust bearings. MaxFlange is a process used on all King engine bearings. It reduces crankshaft endplay by supplying a flange on the high side of the tolerance to compensate for excessive crankshaft thrust wear.

Excessive thrust clearance is more common with manual transmission applications due to clutch release activity, which leans on the main thrust heavily each time the clutch is disengaged. ProFlange is a King line of bearing sets with oversize flanges, which allows the crank's thrust to be ground to 0.010-, 0.020-, or 0.030-inch undersize. Both approaches are designed to save crankshafts from rework or replacement.

Crankshaft Selection

Crankshaft materials vary considerably and require a lot of thought. The options are steel billet on the high end, forged steel, malleable steel, and nodular iron (cast iron). On stroker kit websites, you will see the words, "cast steel," which is marketing jargon for cast iron or nodular iron. It sounds more upscale than the words "cast iron," but it is nothing more than nodular iron.

What are the differences between nodular and cast iron? There are different grades of what is essentially cast iron. Grade depends on alloy and quenching (heat-treating). The different types of iron alloy are too involved to get into here; however, I will go over the basics. Engine blocks and heads, as two examples, are made from gray wall iron (ASTM A48), which has a hardness of 260 on the Brinell hardness scale. Crankshafts and camshafts, to name two examples, are ductile or nodular iron (ASTM A339) at 310 on the Brinell hardness scale. Iron with low carbon content is known as steel.

385-Series Crankshaft Identification

Engine Displacement	Casting/ Forging Number	Stroke (Inches)	Main Journal (Inches)	Rod Journal (Inches)	Additional Information
429; 429 Cobra Jet; 429 SCJ	4U, 4UA	3.590	2.9994–3.002	2.4992–2.5000	Cast iron
Boss 429	C9AE-A; C9AE-B; C9AE-C	3.590	2.9994–3.002	2.4992–2.5000	Forged steel
460 (1968–1978 only)	2Y; 2YA; 2YABC	3.850	2.9994–3.002	2.4992–2.5000	Cast iron
460 (1979–1996 only)	3Y	3.850	2.9994–3.002	2.4992–2.5000	Cast iron; smaller counterweights; externally balanced

Nodular iron is also known as ductile iron. The separation of graphite in nodular form is similar to separation of graphite in gray cast iron except that the additives included in the mix facilitate the graphite to take nodular shape, hence the term "nodular."

Ductile iron continues to find wide use in the automotive industry. The graphite structure in the iron is a primary reason for its higher strength and ductility. Ductile irons are used in the production of crankshafts, gears, rocker arms, and even disc brake calipers.

Although it is widely believed you shouldn't race with a cast (nodular) iron crankshaft, you can weekend race with a cast crank without consequence if you prepare accordingly. Preparation should include Magnafluxing, which is an electromagnetic process of checking for cracks, grinding, and polishing; radiusing the journals; and removing all of the stress risers. Removing stress risers is crack prevention. You also want to cross drill where necessary and chamfer oil holes to improve oil flow at the journals. Chamfering improves oil flow to bearings and journals by reducing resistance to flow. In other words, you have broader oil hole surface area at the journal, which increases volume.

Forged Steel Crankshafts

Cast, nodular iron, and cast steel crankshafts are the cheapest and most common because they're easy to manufacture. Molten liquid iron is poured into a sand-cast mold, cooled, heat-treated, and machined to what looks like a crankshaft. Forged steel crankshafts are a more involved process because there are more steps. A nearly molten steel alloy ingot is heated to approximately 2,200 to 2,600°F and rammed into the shape of a crankshaft in a die at more than 240,000 psi.

The aftermarket offers a wealth of cast and steel stroker kits and cranks. This is a steel stroker crank from Eagle, which adds plenty of stroke to a Ford A-460 block.

The forging is then heat-treated via a quenching process and allowed to cool before being machined into its final configuration. Once all machining is complete, the forged crank is heated to 400 to 600°F to relieve stress and carefully allowed to cool. Once cool, final polishing and finish work are performed.

Forged steel crankshafts are typically made of 4340 hardened steel. Others are made of 1038 steel, which isn't as pure as 4340, but still quite effective. Tom Lieb, founder of Scat Enterprises, has told me that specialized formulas for forged steel cranks vary from manufacturer to manufacturer. Scat's forging process differs from a lot of manufacturers in that it uses a pressure technique instead of a traditional "slam-bam" hammer approach to make its forged steel cranks. Instead of hammering molten 2,600-degree F metal into shape, it applies tremendous pressure to the nearly liquid metal. Once the forging is trimmed and machined, it gets nitrided for good surface hardening.

Scat has the edge because it manufactures some of the lightest cranks in the industry, which are what racers want. The lighter the crank as well as rods and pistons, the faster your big-block will rev.

Eagle Specialty Products has its own unique approach to forged steel crankshafts: a no-twist formula that comes from a special heat-treating and shot-peening process that ensures pinpoint accuracy at high RPM. Journals are cross drilled and chamfered for a good oil wedge between journal and bearing. A target bob weight of plus or minus 2 percent means less balancing time with the Eagle crank.

If you're rebuilding a 429/460 that already has a steel crank from a prior rebuild, your crank should be nitrided once all machine work and balancing is completed. This keeps journal surfaces hard and less inclined to wear.

Crankshaft Differences

I am asked from time to time how you tell the different between a cast and a forged crankshaft. A cast crank has fewer flaws as a rule and generally has a rough surface with narrow parting lines. A forged steel crank has smoother surfaces and wide parting lines due to the violent forging process.

If you take a small hammer and tap the forged crank, it will ring like a bell with a long resonance afterward. A cast-iron crank will ring, but it's not with the clarity and crispness of a forged crank. If you have a cracked crank, it won't ring at all or there will be a buzzy resonance. A cracked crank is like a bad bowling pin. Tap on it and you will hear the difference immediately. The sound goes flat.

The high-end billet crank begins life as a cylindrical steel ingot, which enters a labor-intensive process of many machining steps before it looks like a crankshaft. The reason you would want a steel billet crank is raw strength. It is the strongest crank you can buy for a 429/460, especially if you intend to spin it above 8,000 rpm, use nitrous, or supercharge it. The strength of a steel billet crank comes from its one-piece nature and alloy makeup, which has been machined into a crankshaft. Street 429/460 engines do not need a steel billet crank, which is purely a race piece for extreme duty use.

Magnum durable competition crankshafts from Callies are manufactured from AISI 4340 steel alloy, then are heat-treated several times, which gives them great wear and strength characteristics. I personally like their gun-drilled (cross-drilled) mains and fully profiled counterweights.

Aftermarket Crankshafts						
Brand	**Part Number**	**Type**	**Stroke (inches)**	**Main Journal (inches)**	**Rod Journal (inches)**	**Specifics**
Callies	994H29-MG	4340 Steel	4.300	3.000	2.200	Magnum; 2-piece rear main
Callies	99QH29-MG	4340 Steel	4.500	3.000	2.200	Magnum; 2-piece rear main
Callies	992H-29-MG	4340 Steel	4.150	3.000	2.200	Magnum; 2-piece rear main
Callies	99SH-29-MG	4340 Steel	4.750	3.000	2.200	Magnum; 2-piece rear main
Crower	95187C	4340 Steel	Custom	Custom	Custom	Custom
Eagle	104603850	Cast Steel	3.850	N/A	N/A	2-piece rear main; internal balance
Eagle	Z104603850	Cast Steel	3.850	N/A	N/A	2-piece rear main; internal balance
Eagle	104604140	Cast Steel	4.140	N/A	N/A	2-piece rear main; internal balance
Eagle	104604300	Cast Steel	4.300	N/A	N/A	2-piece rear main; internal balance
Eagle	446041402200	4340 Steel	4.140	N/A	N/A	2-piece rear main; internal balance
Eagle	446043002200	4340 Steel	4.300	N/A	N/A	2-piece rear main; internal balance
Eagle	446045002200	4340 Steel	4.500	N/A	N/A	2-piece rear main; internal balance
Lunati	70745002	4340 Steel	4.500	3.000	2.200	VooDoo series; 2-piece rear main; internal balance
Lunati	70743002	4340 Steel	4.300	3.000	2.200	VooDoo series; 2-piece rear main; internal balance
Scat	946010	Cast Steel	3.850	3.000	2.200	Pro Stock; 2-piece rear main; internal balance
Scat	946041	Cast Steel	4.150	3.000	2.200	Series 9000; 2-piece rear main; internal balance
Scat	946043	Cast Steel	4.300	3.000	2.200	Series 9000; 2-piece rear main; internal balance
Scat	946045	Cast Steel	4.500	3.000	2.500	Series 9000; 2-piece rear main; internal balance
Scat	44604750-3	4340 Steel	4.750	3.000	2.200	Super Light; 2-piece rear main; internal balance
Scat	44604750-2	4340 Steel	4.750	3.000	2.200	Pro Series; lightweight; 2-piece rear main; internal balance
Scat	44604500	4340 Steel	4.500	3.000	2.200	Standard weight; 2-piece rear main; internal balance
Scat	446-4500-3	4340 Steel	4.500	3.000	2.200	Super Light; 2-piece rear main; internal balance
Scat	44604500-2	4340 Steel	4.750	3.000	2.200	Pro Series; lightweight; 2-piece rear main internal balance
Scat	44604300	4340 Steel	4.300	3.000	2.200	Standard weight; 2-piece rear main; internal balance
Scat	44604300-3	4340 Steel	4.300	3.000	2.200	Super Light; 2-piece rear main; internal balance
Scat	44604300-2	4340 Steel	4.300	3.000	2.200	Pro Series; lightweight; 2-piece rear main; internal balance
Scat	44604150	4340 Steel	4.150	3.000	2.200	Standard weight; 2-piece rear main; internal balance
Scat	44604150-3	X	4.150	3.000	2.200	Superlight; 2-piece rear main; internal balance
Scat	44604150-2	X	4.150	3.000	2.200	PRO Series; lightweight; 2-piece rear main; internal balance
Speedmaster	PCE276-1106	Cast Steel	4.150	3.000	2.500	Procomp; 2-piece rear main; internal balance
Speedmaster	1-276-015	4340 Steel	4.150	3.000	2.200	2-piece rear main; internal balance
Speedmaster	PCE276-1099	Cast Steel	3.850	3.000	2.500	2-piece rear main; internal balance (stock replacement)
Speedmaster	PCE276-1127	4340 Steel	4.140	3.000	2.200	2-piece rear main; internal balance
Speedmaster	PCE276-1066	4340 Steel	4.500	3.000	2.200	2-piece rear main; internal balance
Speedmaster	PCE276-1064	4340 Steel	3.850	3.000	2.200	2-piece rear main; internal balance
Speedmaster	PCE276-1065	4340 Steel	4.130	3.000	2.200	2-piece rear main; internal balance
Speedmaster	PCE224.1002	Cast Iron	N/A	N/A	N/A	Slide-on counterweight

Connecting Rods

Seven factory connecting rods were used in the 385-series engine family. The original C8VE-A 429/460 rod was conceived for luxury cars and heavy-duty applications in 1968. The D0OE-A Cobra Jet/Super Cobra Jet rod has more beef at the big end. If you can't find these rods, opt for the D6VE-AA truck rod, which is basically the same rod forging. Have these rods shot peened and fitted with ARP bolts and you're ready to build real durability into your street/strip 429/460-ci big-block.

If you're going with a stock crank and rods, connecting rods have to be inspected, reconditioned, shot peened, and fitted with new ARP bolts. This process makes your stock rods the best they can be. Reconditioning should include removal of stress risers prior to shot peening to reduce the risk of rod failure. The large end is resized and centered to get it true. The small end should be checked for irregularities. The press-fit 429/460 rod has a 1.0400- to 1.403-inch diameter by 3.290- to 3.310-inch-wide wrist pin, with center-to-center being 6.6035 to 6.6065 inches.

Stock connecting rod (top) versus a stronger aftermarket H-beam connecting rod. H-beam rods are stronger. However, the aftermarket offers a variety of high-strength I-beam rods. You don't need an H-beam rod for anything under 500 to 600 hp.

A 460 rod is being check here on a jig to confirm trueness (twisted or bent).

You can recondition 429/460 rods, shot peen them for added strength, and fit them with ARP bolts and get the equivalent of a Cobra Jet/truck rod. All 429/460 connecting rods are the same forgings. Both the standard 429/460 rods and Cobra Jet rods were manufactured from the same D0AE forgings. The D6VE truck rods were machined like the Cobra Jet connecting rods.

You can recondition 429/460 rods, shot peen them for added strength, and fit them with ARP bolts and get the equivalent of a Cobra Jet/truck rod. All 429/460 connecting rods are the same forgings. Both the standard 429/460 rods and Cobra Jet rods were manufactured from the same D0AE forgings. The D6VE truck rods were machined like the Cobra Jet connecting rods.

An important part of connecting rod reconditioning is eliminating stress areas, such as this parting line in the forging. It must be carefully ground smooth and worked gently to eliminate the ragged edges.

Aftermarket Connecting Rods

The automotive aftermarket offers a wealth of connecting rod types for the 429/460. Scat, in particular, offers several different types of high-performance connecting rods ranging from Pro-Stock to Pro Sport. Scat rods are made from a two-piece chrome-moly steel forging for maximum strength and durability, which is what you want from a connecting rod.

What's more, Scat connecting rods are precision machined and finished by master machinists on state-of-the-art equipment right here in the United States. The Scat Pro-Stock I-beam rod is available in press-fit pin or bushed. This is a lightweight I-beam rod designed to yield increased strength and quicker revs thanks to its lightweight design. Scat fits these guys with ARP Wave-Loc bolts for added security. The Pro Sport H-beam rod sports a special doweled cap for very specific cap-to-rod alignment.

Eagle H-beam connecting rods are forged from certified 4340 chrome-moly steel. Not all 4340 steel is the same according to Eagle. To be classified as "4340 steel" certain alloy elements must be present in certain percentages. AISI/SAE specifications call for 1.65- to 2.00-percent nickel content in 4340 steel. While this may appear to be a small difference, please understand that this is almost an 18-percent variation. Eagle says 4340 steel with 1.65-percent nickel will act differently than 4340 steel with 2.00-percent nickel content. This is just one of many alloying elements involved in creating just the right 4340 steel for Eagle rods.

Procomp Electronics H-beam connecting rods are a nice rod for the money. They're good for supercharged and nitrous applications. They have a special dowel-pinned cap for specific cap-to-rod alignment and are profiled with additional clearance for stroker applications. They are manufactured from 4340 chrome-moly steel with all surfaces shot peened and stress relieved.

Ever wonder what a connecting rod forging looks like right out of the forge? Scat then machines it into the H-beam piece on the right.

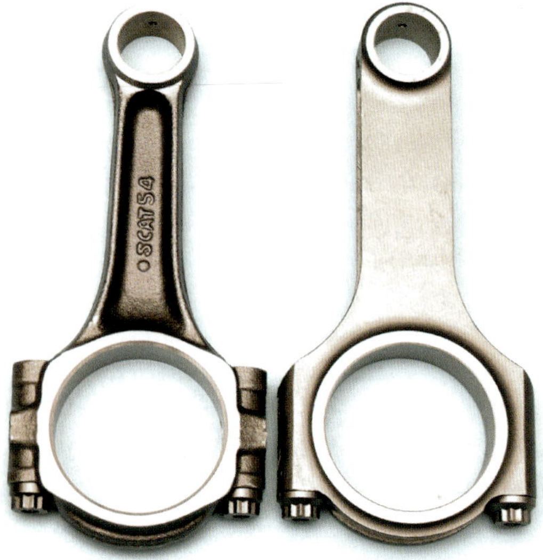

A comparison of two Scat connecting rods. On the left is an affordable high-performance I-beam rod. On the right is a stronger H-beam rod. The choice depends on RPM and horsepower. Below 500 hp you can get by with the I-beam rod. Beyond 500 hp calls for the H-beam rod.

Aftermarket Connecting Rods				
Brand	Part Number	Type	Length (inches)	Other Specifics (inches)
Eagle	SIR6700B	I-beam	6.700	2.200 journal; 0.900 pin; 860 g
Eagle	SIR6800B	I-beam	6.800	2.200 journal; 0.900 pin; 870 g
Eagle	CRS6605F3D	H-beam	6.605	2.4990 journal; 1.040 pin; 835 g
Eagle	CRS6605F3D2000	H-beam	6.605	2.4990 journal; 1.040 pin; 835 g
Eagle	CRS6605F990	H-beam	6.605	2.4990 journal; 0.990 pin; 830 g
Eagle	CRS67003D	H-beam	6.700	2.2000 journal; 0.990 pin; 800 g
Eagle	CRS67003D2000	H-beam	6.700	2.2000 journal; 0.990 pin; 805 g
Eagle	CRS67003DL19	H-beam	6.700	2.2000 journal; 0.990 pin; 810 g
Eagle	CRS68003D	H-beam	6.800	2.2000 journal; 0.990 pin; 800 g
Eagle	CRS68003D2000	H-beam	6.800	2.2000 journal; 0.990 pin; 810 g
Eagle	CRS68003DL19	H-beam	6.800	2.2000 journal; 0.990 pin; 815 g
Oliver	F6700BB8	I-beam	6.700	2.235 journal; 0.990 pin; 818 g
Oliver	F6800BB8	I-beam	6.800	2.235 journal; 0.990 pin; 835 g
Oliver	F6700BBMX8 358 Max	I-beam	6.700	2.235 journal; 0.990 pin; 844 g
Oliver	F6800BBMX8 358 Max	I-beam	6.800	2.235 journal; 0.990 pin; 855 g
Oliver	F6700BBMXP8 Max Plus	I-beam	6.700	2.235 journal; 0.990 pin; N/A
Oliver	F6800BBMXP8 Max Plus	I-beam	6.800	2.235 journal; 0.990 pin; N/A
Scat	2-460-6605-2500	H-beam	6.605	2.500 journal; 1.040 pin; N/A
Scat	2-460-6605-2500A	H-beam	6.605	2.500 journal; 1.040 pin; N/A
Speed-master	PCE274-1055	H-beam	6.605	2.500 journal; 1.040 pin; N/A

Rod Ratio

When you're looking for a stroker package, rod ratio should be a chief consideration, but not necessarily the only one. Rod ratio is connecting rod length divided by stroke. The distance a piston travels is cast in stone by crankshaft stroke. How quickly it travels in each direction and how long it sits at each end of the bore is determined by connecting rod length or rod ratio. The longer a piston dwells, depending upon cam profile, the more productive the air/fuel charge. You want as much connecting rod as you can fit into the block without consequence, meaning excessive cylinder wall and bottom-end loading.

With a longer connecting rod comes mechanical advantage. To determine the maximum amount of rod you can get into a block, subtract the known compression height and half the stroke length (actual crank throw length) from the block's deck height.

429/460 Stock Rod Ratio Index			
Displacement	Stroke (inches)	Rod length (inches)	Rod ratio
429	3.590	6.6035 to 6.6065	1.84:1
460	3.850	6.6035 to 6.6065	1.72:1

Piston Selection

Selecting a piston boils down to what you want your engine to do. When you're planning an engine build, it is easy to go overboard and build more engine than you actually need. It is best to watch your money and build an engine as conservatively as possible based on what you know the engine will do. If you're building a daily driver, weekend cruiser, or tow vehicle, you don't need a steel crank, H-beam rods, and forged pistons.

Even if you intend to spin your 429/460 to 6,500 rpm on occasion, you can get away with a cast crank, stock shot-peened rods with ARP bolts, and cast or hypereutectic pistons. Hypereutectic pistons are a nice compromise between cast and forged. Though "hypereutectic" sounds high tech, the process has been around since 1902. Hypereutectic means a high-silicon cast piston, which is made of a harder cast material, yet without the expansion issues you see with forged pistons. Hypereutectic pistons are more durable than cast versions without the high price tag and those expansion issues just mentioned.

Cast pistons are the most basic type of slug you can stuff into an engine. Because I've used Mahle pistons extensively through the years, I suggest considering them across the board for your mild street or all-out race build. The Mahle ECOFORM cast piston is designed for modern engine building today. It is a lighter piston thanks to fresh casting technology, and it is more durable than your average cast piece.

When I spoke with Trey McFarland of Mahle Pistons about the ECOFORM, he said, "Our cast ECOFORM pistons are 20 to 25 percent lighter than cast pistons we were making 16 years ago."

This feature enables you to get good throttle response from your engine because there's less reciprocating weight to sling around.

All cast pistons have a certain amount of silicon (sand) in them for strength and hardness. The thing is, cast pistons are also brittle and can't take the kind of extreme shock loads and heat that forged race pistons can. This is where you need to know up front how you're going to use your big-block. What you get from a cast piston is stability, predictable expansion properties, and quiet operation in the cold.

Though cast pistons have their place, I am more inclined to suggest hypereutectic pistons as a base piston selection for any 429/460 build because they are more durable than cast yet don't have the issues you see with forged. Hypereutectic means a mixture of alloys melted together at just above the point where they become liquid. This is an oversimplification, of course, but suffice it to say it defines how alloys are melted together temperature-wise. In other words, hypereutectic is a process of how alloys are blended together. As I understand it from those who design pistons, cast pistons have roughly 10-percent silicon in the aluminum alloy. The hypereutectic piston has higher amounts of silicon, which calls for heat-treating to where the silicon blends into the aluminum creating a harder surface. Make no mistake, a hypereutectic piston is not a forged piston nor does it have the same strength.

Forged pistons cost considerably more because they call for many more manufacturing steps to get a finished product. Once piston forgings are slammed (forged) into shape under very high pressure molten aluminum, they have to be machined through a series of complex steps.

What makes forged pistons more challenging is what the machinist has to think about during the block machining process. Because forged pistons possess greater expansion properties, the machinist has to allow for this in how the cylinders are bored and honed to size. There has to be sufficient piston-to-cylinder wall clearances.

The first company to develop forged pistons was Federal-Mogul's Sealed Power division in the 1960s.

You dish a piston to increase volume on top to reduce compression. This happens when you increase stroke, which creates greater compression. Pistons are also dished when you run boost via a supercharger, turbocharger, or nitrous.

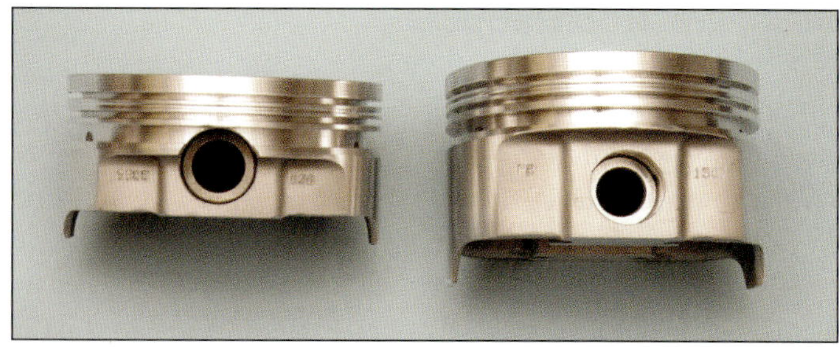

Piston design has changed considerably to remove the weight and mass. A conventional piston is on the right, with a stroker piston on the left. Note how much less skirt there is with the stroker piston. The stroker piston yields more room for stroke while employing less skirt for crank counterweight clearance.

There were learning curves as we saw with the Boss 302 engine in 1969–1970 with cracked piston skirts and other failure issues, causing a lot of warranty claims and engine replacements. Sealed Power developed forged pistons using the VMS75 aluminum alloy, which has been a factory piston alloy for ages.

Strokers yield great mechanical advantage because there's more arm (leverage) involved. The engine doesn't have to work as hard. Stroke yields torque at low RPM and horsepower at high RPM.

The aftermarket industry utilizes the 2618 alloy for race pistons with great success because it can withstand up to 575°F. One shortcoming of 2618 is hardness. It isn't as hard as another widely used alloy known as 4032, which has higher amounts of silicon, which makes aluminum alloys very hard. The 4032 piston makes more sense for street and racing use. As always, chat with your favorite piston manufacturer for best results before making a decision. Make sure you speak with an engineer or sales person qualified to help you make a decision, not a sales person who may not be as knowledgeable.

Whenever you're preparing to dial-in a camshaft, the first order of business is to check true TDC. If it is off, cam timing will also be off.

Choosing a piston evolves from material to dimensions, which can get tricky if you don't know what you're doing. This is why you want to be positive about crank throw, block deck height, compression height, and more. It is so easy to get this wrong and wind up with pistons that don't fit. This is why you must first select a crank and rod before settling on a piston. Manufacturers make this easier because engine kits typically include pistons.

Not only does piston design and shape affect compression ratio, so does how deep or out of the bore the piston is. Head gasket thickness adds volume, which reduces compression ratio. Even the area above the top ring is considered into volume.

It is important to make sure the rod and cap are installed to where the bearing fillet faces the fillet radius. It is so easy to get this backward. The bearing tang is not there to keep the bearing from turning. It is there as a reference point. Bearing crush is what keeps the bearing from turning.

Your machine shop should chamfer the oil holes in the crank journals for improved oil flow across the bearings and journals. Journals should also be micropolished for the same reason

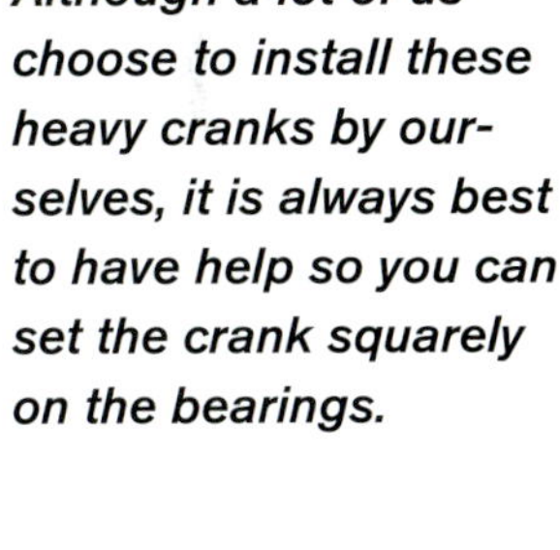

Although a lot of us choose to install these heavy cranks by ourselves, it is always best to have help so you can set the crank squarely on the bearings.

From 1968 to 1978, 429/460 engines employed this spacer between the harmonic damper and the crank.

From 1979 to 1996, when the 460 became externally balanced, the "hatchet" counterweight spacer was employed for offset balance.

When you're upgrading to a stroker kit, all clearances must be checked between the crank and block, and the rods and block. This is an A-460 block, which should pose few, if any, clearance issues. However, minimum clearance between the counterweights, rod bolts, block, and pistons is 0.100 inch.

The late Marvin McAfee of MCE Engines explained the importance of checking all crankshafts for runout at the main journals whether you've opted for a stock crank or an aftermarket forging.

Crankshaft endplay should be 0.004 to 0.010 inch. If it comes in tighter than 0.004 inch, sand the thrust bearing using a piece of plate glass or a proven flat metal surface using 400-grit paper. The two bearing halves should be clamped together using a radiator hose clamp and worked evenly across the paper using automatic transmission fluid or Marvel Mystery Oil. Then, wash thoroughly with solvent and a tack rag.

Jon Kaase of Jon Kaase Racing Engines grew tired of leaking rear main seals. This new seal is a one-piece rear main seal (left) that replaces the conventional two-piece seal in 429/460 engines.

Stroker Kits

Without question, the greatest power investment you can make is displacement. With displacement comes compression you can dial into your build. Displacement and compression remain the quickest paths to power. You want to keep compression conservative around 10.0:1 if you're running pump gas. You can stroke a 429/460 to approximately 500 ci with some room to spare because this is a block with plenty of room.

Forty years ago, you needed a lot of imagination and talent to increase a 460's stroke. You needed a seasoned crankshaft grinder who knew how to offset grind the crank, or a good source like Scat Enterprises to come up with a suitable stroker package. These days, you have quite a choice when it comes to 429/460 stroker kits. Choose your 385-series stroker package wisely and don't waste valuable cash on parts you do not need. A steel crank and H-beam rods are good for bench racing and tough talk when you're building a street engine; however, you really don't need them. A cast steel crank, heavy-duty I-beam rods, and hypereutectic pistons work very well in a street 429/460. With additional stroke and displacement, you get torque mostly, which is what you want on the street.

It is when you get down to serious weekend and full-time racing that you want the steel crank, heavy-duty I-beam or H-beam rods, and forged pistons. You want parts that can take the extremes of nitrous, supercharging, or turbocharging. But wait, there's more. Any time you're pushing power numbers beyond 500 without aided induction (nitrous or blower), you need to seriously consider a steel crank, heavy-duty I- or H-beam rods, and forged pistons.

You want a bottom end that will stay together under the most grueling circumstances. You also want to plan ahead if you intend to pump up the power later on. If you're planning a hotter cam, bigger heads, and any form of serious racing down the road, build for these upgrades now.

Today, there are a variety of stroker kits available for the 429 and 460 big-block engines. Good time-proven sources for bottom end kits are Coast High Performance, StrokerKits.com, Scat Enterprises, and Eagle depending on what you're building and what you intend to do with it.

On its outer surface there is a dot, a small indentation, that represents the exact place to cut the Jon Kaase seal with a razor blade for installation. Once cut, the seal can be wrapped around the crank and a daub of silicone sealer placed at the end joint.

Before lowering the crank into the crankcase, a light film of silicone is applied to the outer perimeter surface of the seal, and the joint is rotated to position it in the main cap.

Once the Kaase one-piece rear main seal is installed and the crank seated, there should be no more leak issues. Jon Kaase tells me there are numerous causes for rear main seals that leak: insufficient lubrication at the sealing lip edge, shaft roughness, lip hardening, lip softening, and installing the seal with the lip pointed outward. The lip must always be pointed toward the crank.

JGM Performance Engineering uses billet ring compressors because they do a lot of engines with different bore sizes. Adjustable ring compressors work fine in the home shop.

Ryan Peart of JGM Performance Engineering carefully guides the connecting rod to the crank journal. I advise the use of rod bolt protectors and a lot of patience doing this. It's too easy to be careless and damage a rod journal.

When you're torquing rod bolts, check the crank for freedom of rotation as you go. Check rod fitment at the crank before tightening fasteners. Torque bolts in one-third values, then check bolt torque and crankshaft freedom of rotation.

I will always stress the use of high-tech one-piece Fel-Pro gaskets where possible. Because this 429 Cobra Jet is for a concours restoration, JGM is installing an OEM-style cork gasket. I stress a light film of Permatex The Right Stuff on these gaskets and seals. If you have excess sealer coming out, you've used too much.

Building a Stroker

When I contacted Ronnie Besselman of Bessel Motorsports, better known as www.strokerkits.com, he offered excellent advice on how to shop for a stroker kit for your 429/460.

- Go for the longest connecting rod possible to minimize frictional losses and reduce side loading. This also makes for a quieter engine.
- Use the lightest bottom-end components possible, which frees up power and improves efficiency.
- Use a windage tray and pan that keep oil away from the crank and rods (windage). You want effective lubrication. You just don't want it hindering power and efficiency.
- Remember, when you add stroke (displacement), you no longer have a 429 or a 460. You have a higher displacement engine. Go with cylinder heads, cam profile, and headers that are up to the increased displacement.
- Be sure to tighten up cam lobe centerline to optimum by 1 degree of every 16 ci of displacement increased.
- Increase valve lift proportionately with displacement because you're moving more air.
- Increase induction capacity to keep up with displacement.
- Keep the induction system cool, which is important with a stroker.
- Step up header capacity (pipe size) at the primaries, secondaries, and collectors.

Bottom line with a stroker kit is to treat it like a big-displacement big-block because you now have 500 to 600 ci and all the power that goes with it. Cooling system capacity must also increase along with induction; cylinder head port/valve size, cam selection, and exhaust scavenging. You have to think of it all while you're increasing displacement.

Because of the ever-changing nature of stroker kits in an involved marketplace, I'm not going to list all of the stroker kits available. However, when you're shopping for a stroker package, look to companies with an abundance of stroker kit development and experience. Scat Crankshafts, Eagle Specialty Products, Oliver Racing, Callies, Speedmaster, and Stroker Kits.com are among the better choices for stroker kits.

While you are shopping for a stroker kit, pay close attention to each of these kits and what their limitations are. What are your block's limitations? Will the crank counterweights and connecting rods clear the cylinder skirts, block webs, and pan rails? Much of this cannot be determined without doing a block mock-up to ascertain clearances. Cylinder skirts can be conservatively notched to clear rod bolts. Pan rails and webs can be carefully shaved to clear crank counterweights. Crank counterweights can also be machined to clear the block by a seasoned machinist.

Strength in Stud Girdles

What makes the 385-series engine different than its predecessors is its skirtless block design. This makes it different than the FE/FT series and MEL big-blocks, which enjoyed the strength of a skirt surrounding the bottom-end internals. In fact, if you study the 429/460 closely, it is an enlarged version of the small-block Ford V-8, with similar characteristics. The block skirt was eliminated for weight reduction and ease of manufacture. Ford learned that eliminating the block skirt was an error in judgment in terms of block strength. It has returned to skirted blocks in its modern Modular and Coyote V-8s.

Although the 385-series big-block yields abundant strength in both two- and four-bolt blocks, there's always room for an equalizer, the main girdle. Canton Racing offers the bolt-on main cap girdle for the 429/460 to reinforce the main cap alignment and to counter the limited main journal webbing in these skirtless blocks. Canton's main cap supports are laser-cut from 1/2- to 5/8-inch steel and offer CNC-machined mounting holes and rod notches for stroker kit clearance. These main cap girdles bolt directly to the caps, eliminating the need for bushings, spacers, or unnecessary machining of the main caps for installation.

D.S.S. also offers a nice main cap girdle for the big-block Ford. The D.S.S. Support System features steel plates machined from 3/4-inch 6061 T6 billet aluminum, which beefs up the bottom end, virtually eliminating main cap shift and annoying and destructive harmonics. When you add the main cap/stud girdle to a four-bolt main cap conversion, it makes your 460 block indestructible without the weight penalty.

Harmonic Dampers and Flywheels

Harmonic dampers are generally elastomeric with an outer ring separated from the inner hub by a rubber shock band. Because there are two types of 460 engines, internally and externally balanced, you need to know what you have before ordering a flywheel/flexplate and harmonic damper. The internally balanced 429/460 engines with 4U and 2Y cranks call for a different damper and flywheel/flexplate than those with the 3Y crank that are externally balanced.

I've always called this component the harmonic "balancer"; however, it really is a "damper" (some call it a "dampener"). It takes the destructive vibration of a spinning crank and absorbs torsional stresses from combustion pulses. Torsional stress and vibration come from torque placed on the crank as each piston rises on the compression/ignition stroke and the light-off exerts force on each journal. Piston and rod not only smack compression but bounce off compression with combustion and linear force. Because this happens in rapid succession even at idle, it sets up a harmonic known as resonance. Resonance is that weird "wow and flutter" you hear when two race cars roar down the track at the same time to create a musical harmony. Same thing happens to a crankshaft as well as other parts in the engine, especially at full throttle. The harmonic balancer absorbs destructive resonance by allowing a soft rebound with each combustion pulse.

Harmonic dampers normally have two components designed to both absorb vibration and help momentum. The outer ring and rubber elastomeric band absorb shock. In other words, as cylinders fire, the crank can twist as much as 1- to 2-degrees at wide-open throttle, which is a lot of twist. If it did this without something to absorb the twist, the crank could eventually break. The ring and rubber allow the crank to softly rebound from twist with less shock. Because harmonic dampers have to cope with vibration, centrifugal force, and the elements of heat, ozone, and road film, they deteriorate and should be replaced from time to time. Harmonic dampers ordinarily last the life of an engine build, which means you need a new one when you build.

With skirtless blocks, such as the 385-series, a stud girdle is suggested to give the main saddles added strength.

Jim "JC" Beattie of ATI Performance out of Baltimore, Maryland, tells me harmonic damper choice depends on how you intend to use your 429/460. He first asks what application you are going to build for. Cast cranks normally absorb more low-range torsionals (twist) on a low-RPM engine that makes a lot of torque. A forged steel or a steel billet crank will live longer and take more horsepower and high RPM; a cast crank is less tolerant.

JC adds that crank weight is very important to torsional issues too. If you go too light, expect to have bearing failure and busted cranks regardless of damper selection. He says that when a crank is heavy, the

I visited ATI Performance Products and talked with Jim Beattie, president of the company. He told me the patented ATI Super Damper is the only harmonic damper designed exclusively for Ford high-performance engines from across the generations. The ATI Super Damper eliminates torsional crankshaft vibrations, exceeds SFI 18.1 specs, is tunable, is rebuildable, and is extremely efficient at all RPM ranges.

damper should be heavier too with a softer rubber compound within for best results. It is true some sanctioning racing organizations such as NASCAR and NHRA do not allow aluminum dampers or related parts for reasons of safety. Steel dampers are the only choice for road and circle track racing. It is important to confirm before ordering a damper.

Steel main caps are vital for torsional dynamics, as are fasteners. If you experience damaged main and rod bearings, take a closer look at the crank and harmonic damper. If bearings are worn from the middle out, and worn to the edges of each journal, that's normal wear. If there is wear only in the middle of the journal and bearing or at the edges, you have torsional twist in the crank. Look to ATI for answers.

Street engines need little more than a stock steel over rubber over iron damper. If you're going to drive high RPM, you're going to want a damper engineered to dampen the vibration and smooth out the spin. You're also going to want an SFI-approved balancer engineered to stay together at high RPM. ATI pioneered the race-ready harmonic damper. Each type of ATI damper is engineered for a specific engine family based on a lot of research and development time for each type. Jim Beattie, who founded ATI Performance, comments that harmonic balancers dampen the "spring" effect of an engine's crankshaft.

What makes the ATI damper unique is its design using rubber O-rings, which are there to take up the inertia, the back-and-forth twisting of the crank. Beattie further comments that ATI dampers go the

Inner and outer shells are available in aluminum or steel. They contain a steel inertia weight. This inertia weight has six (two-ring design) or eight (three-ring design) computer-machined grooves to retain the proper durometer O-rings. Each application is dyno tested.

Each type of Super Damper is designed for a specific application. This example is counterweighted for an externally balanced application.

Here's an ATI Super Damper on a 1,000-horse A-460 stroked to 598 ci. Note the 1979–1996 slide-on counterweight.

Summit Racing tells me you don't have to sacrifice safety or quality to save money. Their affordable Summit Bracket Racer SFI-legal SUM-C4272 dampers have been spin-tested to 12,500 rpm and carry an SFI-18.1 rating. This is an affordable alternative to more expensive options. (Photo Courtesy Summit Racing Equipment)

For a few bucks more than the SUM-C4272, you may opt for the TFS-19008 damper from Trick Flow. Put the engineering expertise of Trick Flow to work with a Track Max harmonic damper. It is SFI-18.1 rated and easy to read with a timing light. (Photo Courtesy Summit Racing Equipment)

Procomp Electronics Speedmaster harmonic dampers are yet another choice if you're on a budget because they're a great value for the money and priced competitively. They are SFI 18.1 rated for racing. This one is 7.250 inches in diameter. (Photo Courtesy Summit Racing Equipment)

distance when they're chosen based on a particular application. Choose a high-performance aftermarket damper based on the kind of driving you intend to do. JC adds that it takes a seasoned professional to see what has happened to a damper over the course of time and use. He suggests rebuilding or replacing your damper at every engine rebuild.

The patented ATI Super Damper is the only harmonic damper designed specifically for high-performance Ford engines, yet it is forgiving enough for everyday driving. ATI's proven elastomer is actually two dampers in one consisting of a 4.000-inch inner diameter ring and a 5½-, 6³/₈-, 7-, or 8-inch-diameter outer damper in two shells that bolt to the crank hub. All ATI dampers are SFI certified, and they exceed SFI specification 18.1. Extensive dyno testing has proven the ATI Super Damper allows the engine to make as much as 45 hp over the competition and OEM dampers.

Fluidampr, maker of high-performance dampers, says torsional vibration is not a one-time occurrence. This happens across every cylinder at varying levels, with every power stroke through one revolution of the crankshaft. These occurrences are referred to as the order. In a V-8, four cylinders fire in one crankshaft rotation, hence there are four orders of torsional vibration. In a V-6, there are three orders. In an inline four, there are two orders. Often the last order in the revolution contains the highest spike of damaging vibration. That is for one revolution! In a V-8 at 4,500 rpm, peaks of varying vibration frequency occur 18,000 times per minute. Torsional vibration and the violent twisting and rebounding of the crankshaft happens so fast, it is not visible to the naked eye.

What Fluidampr is trying to say is engines are self-destructive due to combustion pulses along the crankshaft. A good harmonic damper reduces, but will never completely eliminate, torsional twist and

429/460 Aftermarket Dampers		
Manufacturer	**Part Number**	**Additional Information**
ATI Performance	917562	Fits 429/460 with short snout for Bryant aftermarket crankshaft with key at front, hub must be honed to fit. Hub has 0.150-inch counterbore for full-length press fit.
ATI Performance	917563	Fits 429/460 with short snout for Bryant crankshaft. Aftermarket crank with key at front, hub must be honed to fit. Hub has 0.150 counterbore for full-length press fit.
ATI Performance	917564	Fits 429/460 with short snout for Bryant crankshaft. Aftermarket crank with key at front, hub must be honed to fit. Hub has .150 counterbore for full-length press fit.
ATI Performance	917620	3-ring design. 1.500 in. wide.
ATI Performance	917621	3.200-in. bolt circle pulley mount. 3-ring steel shell weight is 6.00 lbs. Steel hub average weight is 2.4 lbs.
ATI Performance	917630	3.200-in. bolt circle pulley mount. 3-ring aluminum shell weight is 6.25 lbs. Steel hub average weight is 2.4 lbs.
ATI Performance	918780	Steel hub, 3-ring, 3.90 lbs. total weight, 2.40 lbs. inertia weight.
Dorman	594-080	OEM replacement, 6.750 inches.
Ford Performance	M-6316-A460	Removable balance weight that allows use as a neutral balance unit for internally balanced crankshafts. Right-side 11 o'clock timing marks and left-side 2 o'clock timing marks for both configurations.
Fluidampr	720201	A 4-bolt pulley will need to be used and a stepped key may be required. Additional timing/degree marks at 90, 180, and 270 degrees.
Pioneer Automotive	872036	Brings the advantages of bonded rubber to high-revving race and street/race applications where an SFI-approved balancer is required.
Professional Products	80008	Must use Ford M-6359-D460 counterweight unless engine has been internally balanced. With stock keyway, and 0.250-inch keyway 180 degrees from that for dual keyway crankshafts.
Professional Products	90008	Must use Ford M-6346059-D counterweight unless engine has been internally balanced. With stock keyway, and 0.250-inch keyway 180 degrees from that for dual keyway crankshafts.
Speedmaster	PCE291-1079	Additional timing marks at 90, 180, and 270 degrees.
Summit	SUM-C4272	Summit bracket racer SFI dampers have been spin-tested to 12,500 rpm and carry an SFI-18.1 rating. Will work with internal or externally balanced engines.
Summit	SUM-B64272	Damper has two keyways, one for production size crankshafts and one for Ford SVO crankshafts. Special length spacer required on M6359-C460 crankshaft on internally balanced applications.

PRW Gold Series SFI 29.1 certified flexplates from Summit are engineered to handle the brute torque of Ford's 429/460 engines. The 4-mm-thick centerplate provides a really solid foundation for these direct bolt-ons. The ring gear is precision double-welded via robotic cold-welding processes for durability. (Photo Courtesy Summit Racing Equipment)

The Speedmaster flywheel from Summit is designed from CAD engineering and tested to limits well above the SFI ratings. When you're shopping for a flywheel, always insist on an SFI-rated piece and take note of the flywheel or flexplate you currently have. Look at tooth count and flywheel diameter. Remember, 1968–1978 is internally balanced (no offset balance weight), and 1979–1996 is externally balanced with an offset balance weight. (Photo Courtesy Summit Racing Equipment)

Dynamic balancing must always be performed on all 429/460 engine builds even if you're building a stocker. Some engine kits and crate engines get what's known as "Detroit" balance, which is the OEM approach to balancing. This is not what you want. Here, pistons, rods, rings, and bearings are weighed to determine proper bob weight for the crankshaft.

Bob weights, which simulate the weight of reciprocating mass, are hung on the rod journals before spinning. The bob weights are loaded to accurately simulate the mass. This is a very tedious process.

Just like balancing a tire, the crank is spun with the bob weights attached to each journal. The balancing machine then tells the balancer to add or subtract weight. Weight is added or subtracted from the counterweights.

In this instance, weight is removed from the counterweight by drilling out and removing metal. Mallory metal (tungsten) is added to the counterweight as necessary.

Externally balanced 460 engines have metal removed or added at the flywheel as necessary.

This ATI harmonic damper hub is balance checked and marked for drilling to remove metal to get it in balance.

vibration. The harmonic damper reduces destructive cyclic fatigue by allowing more precise pinpoint engine operation along with extending crankshaft life. Despite all the best efforts of harmonic damper manufacturers, cranks will fail from time to time, with most breaking at the fillet radius.

Dynamic Balancing

All engines, regardless of usage, should be dynamic balanced for smoothness. Dynamic balancing means getting the reciprocating mass (pistons, rings, rod bearings, connecting rods, and oil) to the exact same weight as the crankshaft counterweights. This enables the reciprocating mass and crankshaft counterweights to do-si-do around each other in perfect unison with great smoothness. No one wants an engine that shakes. Vibration is a destructive dynamic that shortens engine life.

If you're shopping for engine kits, ask if the components have been dynamic balanced. If you are told they're "Detroit balanced" or just "balanced," that's not enough. Detroit balancing is what the automakers use in production engine building, which means pistons, rods, and related parts are grouped in lots with similar weights and thrown together, which is passable with production engines but not acceptable with an expensive rebuild. You want your Ford big-block to rev smoothly and without destructive vibration.

Balancing begins with getting the reciprocating weight uniform with the lightest piston and rod assembly and all related parts. This means, if cylinder number-7 is the lightest piston and rod assembly, all reciprocating units must be shaved down to that weight exactly. Then, all crankshaft counterweights must weigh that same amount. Externally balanced 460s must have flywheels/flexplates balanced with the crank and reciprocating assemblies.

Revco Precision Balancing in Long Beach, California, has performed a lot of dynamic balancing for engine build projects I've been involved with. Larry Revis of Revco has taught me a lot about dynamic balancing, focusing on balancing, vibration analysis, and specialty machine work on engines and machines. He stresses close attention to detail in dynamic balancing, burning the midnight oil until the process is perfected. He adds that some balancing jobs can be decidedly frustrating and take much longer than anticipated. The end result is what engine builders must focus on to achieve unending smoothness.

Lubrication

Jon Kaase of Jon Kaase Racing Engines comments that the most common 429/460 oiling system issue that he hears about is loss of oil pressure. He adds that oil pressure problems are not always regarding the oil pump itself. Instead, the loss of oil pressure is normally an issue beyond the pump. Kaase comments that pumps can break off and fall into the pan or they lose relief valve parts. Pump shafts can also shear, which is why you must never use a stock pump shaft. He adds that the Kaase oil pump is a standard-volume unit with a 1.100-inch-wide rotor like the Moroso dry sump pumps in Kaase's Pro Stock engines. It more than delivers the volume necessary to keep a 460 happy.

Kaase cautions that the biggest reason for oil system failure is using incorrect roller lifters and even lifters being installed backward (yes, backward) to where the oil hole in the lifter is aligned with the main oil gallery, which causes oil to be pumped up the pushrods, flooding the top end and running the pan dry. In this case, the most important parts don't receive lubrication. Kaase employs a foolproof system of testing with his oil pumps.

"We free flow them [oil pumps], then close the pump exit [outlet] with a ball valve, then open it back up a little to where it holds 40 pounds," he said. "Deadheaded, they're always at 75 to 80 pounds."

Kaase says that they're seeing another problem with the pickup bolts and flange at the oil pump. Oftentimes the pickup leaks at this joint, draws in air, and makes the oil foamy, causing engine damage. He adds that most of the pickups have a thin flange (3/16 inch), and if a thick gasket is ever used on it, it warps and leaks when a new gasket is installed with a new pump.

Oil pressure can also suffer from excessive bearing clearances or a forgotten oil gallery plug, which will certainly affect oil pressure. A forgotten oil gallery plug will send oil pressure to zero. If the forgotten plug is external, you will wind up with 7 quarts of engine oil all over the garage floor or dyno room.

The 429/460 engine employs a pretty good oiling system to where critical parts of the engine are well fed and generously lubricated. Oil is pulled into the pump, through the oil filter, and pumped to the cam and main bearings first, then up to the valvetrain. It is similar to the 335-series oiling system, yet better in terms of oiling system priorities. It is simply a better oiling system.

Where the 385's oiling system

Whether you're building a stocker or something wildly modified, always opt for a high-volume oil pump. Melling, as one example, makes proven high-performance oil pumps.

This high-volume Melling pump has been blueprinted and safety-wired to ensure durability. Using a good thread locker on bolt threads will work just as well.

Jon Kaase suggests checking the block deck and pump contact surfaces for irregularities. These imperfections can cause leaks and pump cavitation.

can use improvement is a blueprinted high-volume pump and a cleanup of the oil galleries where possible to reduce turbulence and restriction. What you want most is volume along with good return flow to the pan. You're going to want a windage tray and a baffled pan to keep oil around the pickup in hard-corning and acceleration. Opt for the most oil pan capacity you can give your 429/460.

Pump Blueprint Recipe

The late Marvin McAfee of MCE Engines was very methodical in his approach to engine building. Marvin's stressed oil pumps must never be installed right out of the box. "Blueprinting" is an oft-abused term for rebuilding because real blueprinting means going the extra mile. Real blueprinting means taking a closer look at things engine builders don't always examine. Most install oil pumps right out of the box often assuming all bases have been covered. However, some come out of the box with all kinds of flaws and machining errors, and unless you inspect them and measure critical clearances, you're rolling the dice on more than just an oil pump.

You don't have to take your blueprinting as far as MCE Engines did; however, there are three items you need to check: G-rotor endplay, radial clearances for a full 360 degrees, and pressure relief valve function/spring pressure. If the pressure relief valve piston binds in any way, you need to chase the bore with a small ball hone until the piston glides smoothly with lubrication. If radial clearances are tight, have a machine shop examine and bore as necessary or return the pump. Rotor end clearances must fall somewhere between the minimum and maximum allowable. If there's too much clearance, you can have the housing milled to size or return the pump and hope for a better core.

These are the many parts that encompass an oil pump. This is a gerotor (pronounced "gee-rotor") oil pump (also known as a positive displacement pump), which includes an inner (drive rotor) and outer rotor (driven rotor) that rotate around one another. Oil is drawn in and carried through the pump by interaction between the inner and outer rotors.

Rotor side clearances (endplay) are checked, which should be -0.001 to -0.004 inch.

The oil pump relief valve assembly looks like this with a valve piston, spring, shim, and cup. These parts should be coated with lube during the blueprinting process for improved function and initial wear protection.

The pump cavity should be filled with engine assembly lube, which primes and lubricates the pump for a good wet start-up.

One process used by precision engine builders is a ball hone in the relief valve bore if clearances are tight. Relief valve clearances are 0.0015 to 0.0029 inch.

Once clearances have been checked, inspect the drive and driven rotors for any scoring, then give these parts a bath in engine assembly lube. Some but not all rotors have reference marks that must be in alignment.

The pump plate and housing are checked for distortion. Here, the plate is sanded on 320-grit paper on top of plate glass, which is a perfect surface. This gets the plate true. The same can be done with pump contact surfaces.

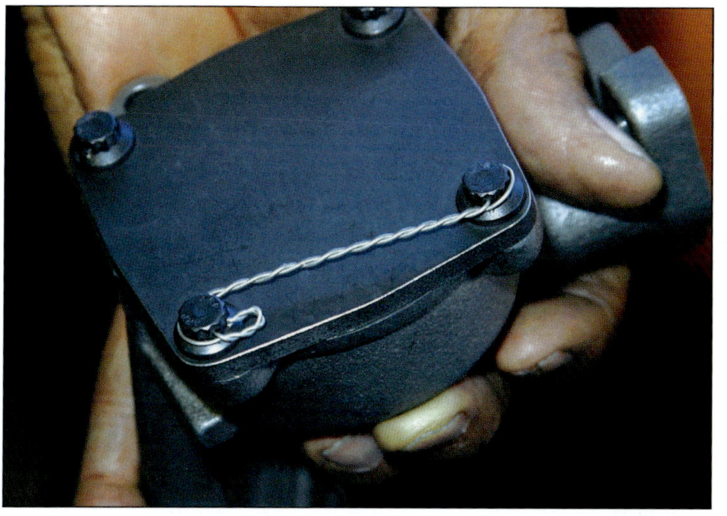

Even with stock rebuilds, MCE always safety-wired critical fasteners, such as these oil pump bolts, for security.

It is surprising how many times oil gallery plugs are overlooked and discovered during that first firing. Give your 429/460 the once-over to make sure all gallery and block plugs are installed and properly sealed.

Improved Oil Control

Although the 385-series big-block enjoys a suitable oiling system, there's always room for improvement. I suggest chamfering all oil gallery passages to reduce turbulence at transitions throughout the block. Drainback can be improved by cleaning up drain passages in the cylinder heads and lifter valley.

Jim Grubbs of JGM Performance Engineering religiously hones lifter bores to get a nice finish hone, which controls oil flow around the lifters. This, in turn, controls oil pressure. He also chamfers oil holes in the crank to improve flow across the main and rod bearings. He also carefully watches bearing clearances. One modification Jim makes with some 429/460 engine builds is an external oil line from the front oil pressure sending unit port to the rear sending unit port at the top of the block to improve oil volume until there's some evidence of oil starvation in back. Jim stresses that this is pretty much an unnecessary oil system modification, but always an option.

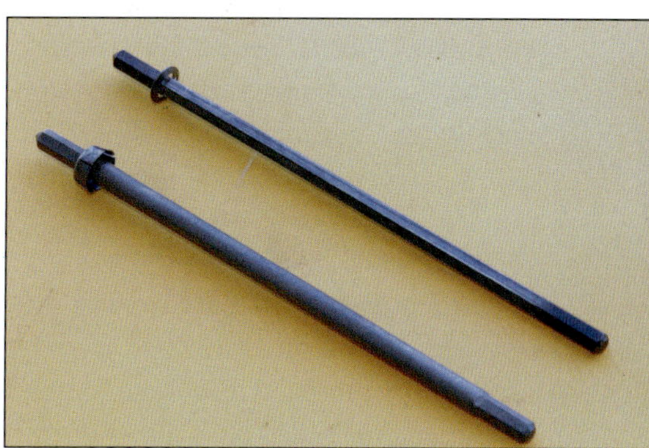

One of the best life insurance policies you can invest in is an ARP heavy-duty oil pump shaft. The factory pump shaft is not enough even in a stock engine.

To reduce turbulence and improve oil flow, all reachable oil gallery passages should be chamfered to smooth flow and improve volume.

One trick is this 0.020-inch oil hole drilled into the gallery plug to provide improved oil flow to the timing set.

Aftermarket oil pumps are not always true to mark size-wise. Pickups, particularly, are hit and miss. Opt for a Melling pump and pickup

This is a factory Cobra Jet pan, which is baffled to prevent oil windage. Spend the money on a good Milodon or Moroso deep-sump baffled oil pan, which will keep the pickup well supplied with oil.

The first order of business during pan installation, even before you install the gaskets, is to measure pan depth from the pan rails, and the pump and pickup height. The pickup must clear the sump by 1/8 to 1/4 inch.

Oil Pan

Choosing an oil pan is easy and depends on what kind of driving you intend to do. Drag racers need a deep-sump high-capacity oil pan for heat transfer and lubrication no matter how wild and crazy things become. If you're going to be cutting the apexes and rounding turns, you want a high-capacity baffled road race pan and the appropriate pickup to keep a steady supply of oil to the pump. Drag racing calls for a deep-sump oil pan capable of keeping the engine supplied at high RPM. Milodon and Canton have broad product lines that include deep-sump pans for drag racing and off-road action. You want a deep-baffled pan that will keep oil around the pickup in very demanding conditions. Even a nanosecond of pump cavitation can destroy an engine at high RPM.

If you're doing autocross, circle track, or road racing, you're going to want a pan designed specifically for extreme cornering, where oil in the sump can move left and right, putting the pump pickup in danger of cavitation. A road race pan is baffled with doors that prevent oil from leaving the pickup. Oil stays around the pickup, keeping the engine supplied with oil.

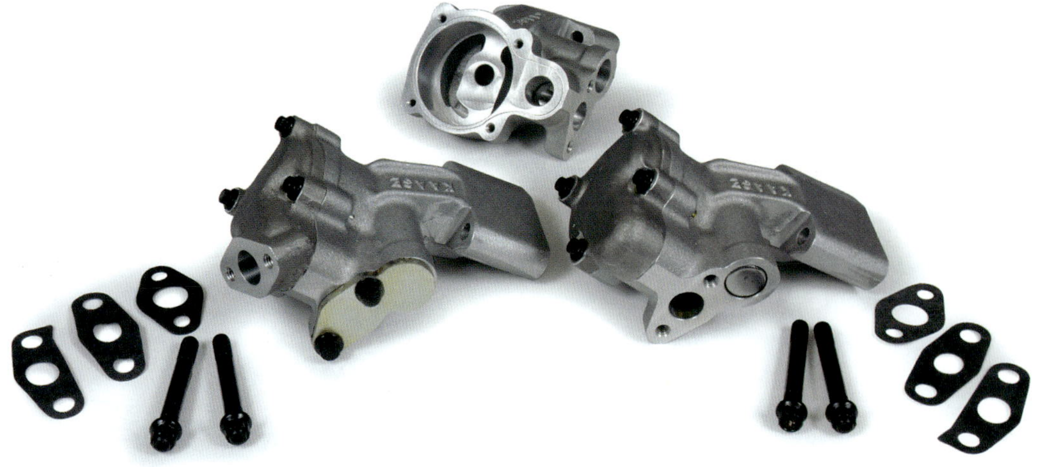

Jon Kaase Racing Engines offers an oil pump for the 429/460, which is manufactured from its own castings and machined with the latest CNC equipment. These pumps come with the original CJ-style front sump cover or the truck-style rear pickup. (Photo Courtesy Jon Kaase Racing Engines)

Drainback screening is a good preventive measure that keeps unwanted debris out of the oil pan. Moroso is a good source for drainback screening kits.

The Boss 429 sports a deep-sump oil pan with greater capacity.

The factory Boss 429 was fitted with an oil cooler. This is good medicine for 429/460 projects. The aftermarket offers an abundance of oil cooler systems for your 385-series project.

This is the factory oil cooler on a 1970 Boss 429. Aftermarket coolers can be less obtrusive when placed near the bottom of the radiator. Always place your oil cooler in front of the radiator in the slipstream.

Cylinder Heads

Cylinder head selection for the 385-series 429/460 is straightforward because there are few factory castings from which to choose. Over the lengthy 28-year production life of the 385 four basic cylinder head castings were available: the standard 429/460 head casting, Cobra Jet, Police Interceptor, and Boss 429. There's also the fuel injection truck head that came along late in the 1980s through the mid-1990s.

The Boss 429 cylinder head, with its hemispherical combustion chambers, requires no introduction. It is a standalone cylinder head and engine that very few have the good fortune to have. Due to the limited production nature of the Boss 429 engine, it is not covered extensively in this book. I can show you the most common factory castings. However, there are experimental castings out there in unknown numbers. Also available are the experimental "Blue Crescent" iron heads, very few of which made it out the back door.

Where the more common 429/460 wedge heads vary is combustion chamber shape and size. Port sizes remain virtually the same throughout this engine's production life. In truth, the 429/460 cylinder head delivers good flow and quench characteristics in all of its forms, with intake and exhaust flow numbers around 290/135–cfm intake/exhaust. When you add a good port job, these heads flow remarkably well at 320/210–cfm intake/exhaust with a nice clean-up. Ideally, you will unearth a pair of Cobra Jet or Police Interceptor castings if you cannot afford aftermarket types. The head to avoid is the Thermactor smog pump casting, which suffers from restrictive exhaust-port issues.

The most common 429/460 heads are the C8VE-A, C9VE-A, and D0VE-A, which are all basically the same cylinder head casting with 2.090/1.650-inch intake/exhaust valves and 2.180 x 1.870-inch intake ports and 1.990 x 1.300-inch exhaust ports. This is a head casting with 75- to 77-cc wedge chambers on which you can do port and bowl work and wind up with significant flow improvement, not to mention compression. Chamber size affects compression.

Another casting is the D2VE-A2A, which isn't much different than the aforementioned heads except for a larger, open 100-cc chamber, which delivers less quench and reduced compression. The D2VE-A2A head is

You can expect to see two types of rocker arm configurations with the non-adjustable 385-series cylinder head. The 429/460 head had bolt/fulcrum stamped steel rocker arms as you see on small-block Fords from 1977–up. They are no-adjust rocker arms for hydraulic lifter applications only. The C8VE heads had positive-stop rocker arms on studs.

Virtually all 429/460 chambers look like this: a kidney bean. The main differences are size, ranging from 75 to more than 90 cc. Much depends on what vintage the head casting is. Chambers grew larger with time and tougher emission standards. If you examine this exhaust valve seat closely, it is a steel insert that has been peened for security.

You can expect to see two basic 429/460 head casting types: Thermactor and non-Thermactor. This is a D0VE-C 429/460 non-Thermactor casting void of the air injector manifold port at each end of the head.

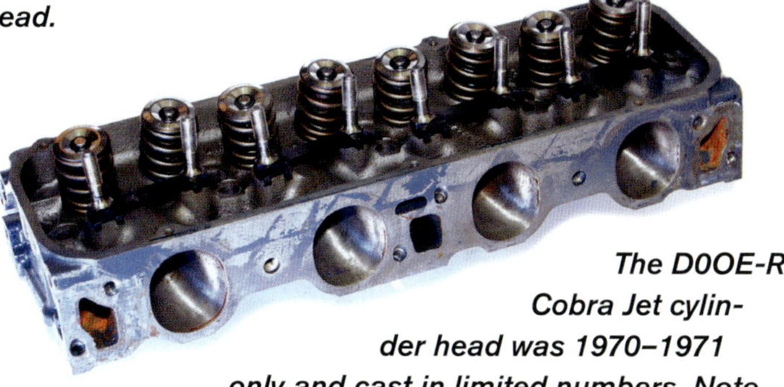

The D0OE-R Cobra Jet cylinder head was 1970–1971 only and cast in limited numbers. Note the screw-in rocker arm studs and pushrod guide plates exclusive to the Cobra Jet and Super Cobra Jet head castings. Ports are considerably larger than the C8VE-A and B, C9VE-A, D0VE-C, D2OE-AA, D2OE-AB, D2VE-A2A, D3VE-AA, D3VE-A2A, and so on, heads. All Cobra Jet cylinder heads prior to November 1969 had adjustable valvetrains. After that, only the Super Cobra Jet with mechanical lifters had an adjustable valvetrain.

This is a typical bread-and-butter 429/460 intake port, which is not as generous as the Cobra Jet and Police Interceptor head but plenty large with 2.090/1.650-inch intake/exhaust valves, 2.180 x 1.870-inch intake ports, and 1.990 x 1.300-inch exhaust ports.

This E6TE truck head (1986) has the Thermactor air injector manifold (arrow) running the length of the head. The problem with the Thermactor head is exhaust port restriction caused by the hump in the exhaust port, although it can be ground smooth.

The Cobra Jet/Super Cobra Jet head sports larger 2.240-inch intake and 1.720-inch exhaust valves in a 71- to 75-cc high-compression chamber.

This is a new-old-stock 429 Cobra Jet/Super Cobra Jet head casting. Note the provision for screw-in rocker arm studs and valve spring cups.

Don't be fooled by the screw-in studs and guide plates. This is a D0OE-C 429/460 head casting. It is not a Cobra Jet head. The screw-in studs and guide plates have been added as witness the "E7ZM" Ford Racing guide plates.

Jon Kaase Racing Engines specializes in the 429/460 as well as the 351 Cleveland. This is Kaase's P51 cylinder head for the 429/460, which is a terrific street/strip head. You get 72-cc high-quench chambers with 2.250-inch intake and 1.760-inch exhaust valves. These right-sized intake ports flow 400 cfm.

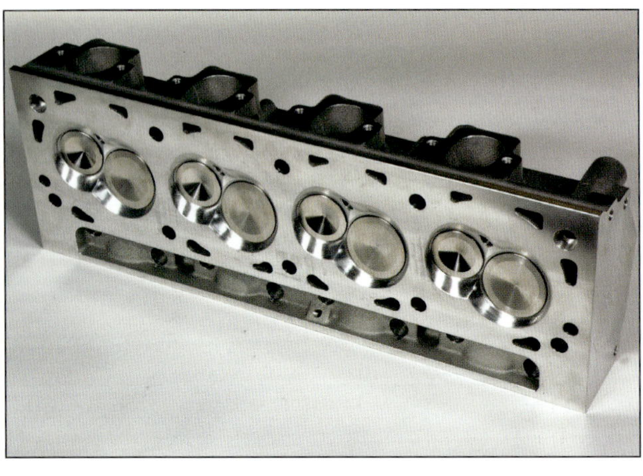

This 72-cc chamber permits experimentation with different compression ratios, allowing slightly dished or slightly domed pistons. These P51 chambers are fully CNC-machined with larger 2.250-inch intake valves. The standard 1.760-inch exhaust valves are all the 385 needs.

more prone to detonation due to its huge open chamber and poor quench. The D3VE-A, D3VE-A2A, and later head castings are emissions heads with open chambers with poor quench. They are not a good choice for performance applications.

Ford continued to cast the same basic 460 head through 1996 with the exception being the fuel injection head and Thermactor castings. When these engines were deleted from the option sheet in automobiles in 1979, they continued in Ford F-series trucks and E-series vans. These head castings show up as E7TE, E8TE, and so on, which are basically the D3VE-A casting with engineering revisions designed more for electronic fuel injection and reduced emissions.

The rarest, most desirable 429/460 wedge head is the 1970–1971 Cobra Jet casting, D0OE-R with 2.190/1.730-inch intake/exhaust valves and 2.510 x 2.110-inch intake and 2.250 x 1.300-inch exhaust ports along with 71- to 75-cc chambers. On average, these heads flow 330/160 cfm at 0.700-inch lift. Because the Cobra Jet head is rare and darned expensive, you can opt for the 1972–1974 Police Interceptor castings with the same valve sizing as the Cobra Jet head, yet with smaller ports and 88- to 91-cc chambers. These guys flow roughly the same numbers. Add good port work, and these heads improve to 380/220–cfm intake/exhaust.

Police Interceptor head port sizes are 2.200 x 1.930-inch intake and 2.060 x 1.310-inch exhaust, which means better low- to mid-range torque. Exhaust scavenging is debatable with these heads, with virtually little or no gain. The Police Interceptor heads have hardened exhaust valve seats for use with unleaded fuels, which were being introduced at the time for cleaner emissions. Three Police Interceptor castings are available: D2OE-AA, D2OE-AB, and D3AE-FA, all with 88- to 91-cc chambers. The Police Interceptor head is a nice alternative to the more expensive Cobra Jet head if you can find the CJ casting at all.

Boss 429

Because the Boss 429 engine was born for NASCAR competition, there are many variables when it comes to cylinder heads and what to do with them. The street Boss 429 is a detuned version of an all-out factory-born racing engine conceived for stock car racing. In NASCAR trim, the Boss 429 holds its own as the ultimate muscle car engine.

There are two basic Boss 429 cylinder head castings: C9AE-A and D0AE-AA. Race and experimental cylinder head castings are also circulating out there. One Boss 429 expert told me that he believes there are at least 50 different Boss 429 cylinder head castings (experimental and race) out there that haven't been documented. Some differences are subtle while others are more obvious. Although extremely rare, Blue Crescent experimental iron heads are also out there. These heads don't make a whole lot of sense for any project considering their weight and experimental status.

429/460 Cylinder Head Identification

Displacement/Year	Casting Number	Chamber Size (cc)	Valve Size (inches)	Port Size (inches)
429/460 ci (1968–1971)	C8VE-A	76	2.09 intake; 1.65 exhaust	2.18 x 1.87 intake; 1.99 x 1.30 exhaust
429/460 ci (1968–1971)	C8VE-E	76	2.09 intake; 1.65 exhaust	2.18 x 1.87 intake; 1.99 x 1.30 exhaust
429/460 ci (1969–1971)	C9VE-A	76	2.09 intake; 1.65 exhaust	2.18 x 1.87 intake; 1.99 x 1.30 exhaust
429/460 ci (1970–1971)	D0VE-A	76	2.09 intake; 1.65 exhaust	2.18 x 1.87 intake; 1.99 x 1.30 exhaust
429/460 ci (1970–1971)	D0VE-C	76	2.09 intake; 1.65 exhaust	2.18 x 1.87 intake; 1.99 x 1.30 exhaust
429 ci Cobra Jet (1970–1971 only)	D0OE-R	76	2.19 intake; 1.73 exhaust	2.51 x 2.11 intake; 2.25 x 1.30 exhaust
429/460 ci (1972)	D1VE-A	76	2.09 intake; 1.65 exhaust	2.18 x 1.87 intake; 1.99 x 1.30 exhaust
429/460 ci (1972–1974)	D2VE-AA	91.5	2.09 intake; 1.65 exhaust	2.18 x 1.87 intake; 1.99 x 1.30 exhaust
429 ci (Police Interceptor 1972–1974)	D2OE-AA	88	2.19 intake; 1.73 exhaust	2.20 x 1.93 intake; 2.06 x 1.31 exhaust
429 ci (Police Interceptor 1972–1974)	D2OE-AB	91.5	2.19 intake; 1.73 exhaust	2.20 x 1.93 intake; 2.06 x 1.31 exhaust
429/460 ci (1973)	D3AE-A2A	91.5	2.09 intake; 1.65 exhaust	2.18 x 1.87 intake; 1.99 x 1.30 exhaust
460 ci (Police Interceptor 1973–1974 only)	D3AE-FA	91.5	2.19 intake; 1.73 exhaust	2.20 x 1.93 intake; 2.06 x 1.31 exhaust
429/460 ci (1973–1974)	D3VE-AA	91.5	2.09 intake; 1.65 exhaust	2.18 x 1.87 intake; 1.99 x 1.30 exhaust
460 ci (1974–1978 Police Interceptor)	D4VE	96.2	2.09 intake; 1.65 exhaust	2.18 x 1.87 intake; 1.99 x 1.30 exhaust
460 ci (1974–1978)	D4VE-BA	96.2	2.09 intake;1.65 exhaust	2.18 x 1.87 intake; 1.99 x 1.30 exhaust
460 ci (1974–1978)	D4VE-B2A	96.2	2.09 intake; 1.65 exhaust	2.18 x 1.87 intake; 1.99 x 1.30 exhaust
460 ci (1975–1978)	D5VE-A	96.2	2.09 intake; 1.65 exhaust	2.18 x 1.87 intake; 1.99 x 1.30 exhaust
429/460 ci (1979–1985)	D9TE-FA	96.2	2.09 intake; 1.65 exhaust	2.18 x 1.87 intake; 1.99 x 1.30 exhaust
429/460 ci (1979-85)	D9TE-HA	96.2	2.09 intake; 1.65 exhaust	2.18 x 1.87 intake; 1.99 x 1.30 exhaust
429/460 ci (1985–1987)	E5TE-HA	96-97	2.09 intake; 1.65 exhaust	2.18 x 1.87 intake; 1.99 x 1.30 exhaust
429/460 ci (1985–1987)	E5TE-TA	96-97	2.09 intake; 1.65 exhaust	2.18 x 1.87 intake; 1.99 x 1.30 exhaust
429/460 ci (1986–1991)	E6TE-DA	96-97	2.09 intake; 1.65 exhaust	2.18 x 1.87 intake; 1.99 x 1.30 exhaust
429/460 ci (1986–1991)	E6TE-EA	96-97	2.09 intake; 1.65 exhaust	2.18 x 1.87 intake; 1.99 x 1.30 exhaust
429/460 ci (1986–1995)	E7TE-BD	96-97	2.09 intake; 1.65 exhaust	2.18 x 1.87 intake; 1.99 x 1.30 exhaust
429/460 ci (1988-1996)	E8TE-JA	96-97	2.09 intake; 1.65 exhaust	2.18 x 1.87 intake; 1.99 x 1.30 exhaust
429/460 ci (1988–1996)	F3TE-JA	96-97	2.09 intake; 1.65 exhaust	2.18 x 1.87 intake; 1.99 x 1.30 exhaust

Boss 429 Cylinder Head Identification				
Displacement/ Year	Casting Number	Chamber Size (cc)	Valve Size (inches)	Port Size (inches)
Boss 429 (1969–1970 only)	C9AE-AA	100	2.28 intake; 1.90 exhaust	2.36 x 2.36 intake; 2.04 x 1.680 exhaust
Boss 429 (1969–1970 only)	D0AE-AA	100	2.28 intake; 1.90 exhaust	2.36 x 2.36 intake; 2.04 x 1.680 exhaust
Note: Not all Boss 429 Cylinder Head Castings are shown here.				

Aftermarket Cylinder Heads

It can be safely said that factory iron cylinder heads have nothing on what the aftermarket has to offer. What you get from the aftermarket is extensive research and development along with the technology we enjoy today. Port and chamber technology has advanced so much since Ford was casting these iron cylinder heads a half-century ago. There's the weight advantage of cast aluminum not to mention heat transfer, thus reducing the chance of detonation. As a result, you can run more compression and have the benefit of good heat transfer via the aluminum.

The decision to opt for aftermarket aluminum cylinder heads boils down to horsepower per measure of displacement. How much horsepower and torque are you getting for the displacement you have? Factory cylinder heads aren't as finitely engineered as today's aftermarket cylinder heads. Granted, there are terrific factory cylinder heads, such as the 1970–1971 429 Cobra Jet head castings everyone building a 429/460 wants. Those huge intake ports haul in huge volumes of air and fuel. I cannot say much for the chambers because they offer little in terms of quench and compression. If you're building in displacement with a stroker kit, the factory heads will defeat any potential power gains. Port work can cost you as much as a good set of aftermarket heads.

The aftermarket offers a broad selection of aluminum cylinder heads for the 385-series engines. Air Flow Research (AFR) needs little introduction with Ford performance enthusiasts. The AFR 280-, 295-, and 315-cc BBF Bullitt 14-degree cylinder heads feature partially CNC-ported intakes, exhausts, and chambers; A356 aluminum castings; and standard exhaust port locations. The redesigned Bullitt cylinder head delivers a decreased overall runner size, a more consistent cross-sectional area, carefully massaged combustion chambers, and repositioned valves to complement the intake and exhaust ports. Together they improve engine response, providing increases in horsepower and torque. The 280-cc

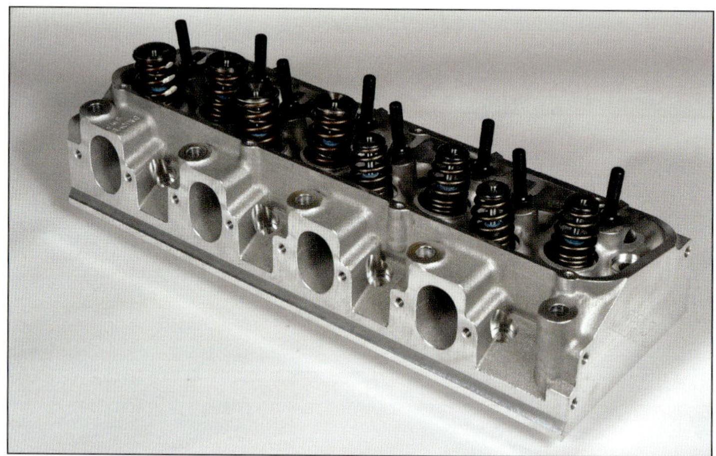

On the exhaust side, Kaase did his homework. These exhaust ports flow 239 cfm, which means plenty of velocity on the way out. This head works exceedingly well when you have a lot of valve overlap.

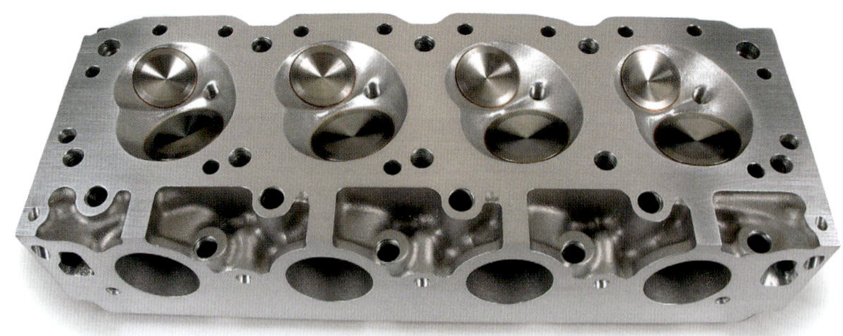

Kaase specializes in the Boss 429, offering an array of cylinder heads for this engine. In fact, you can build an entire all-aluminum Boss 429 from Kaase. "Most of the revisions applied to the Boss Nine were incorporated to make it stronger and easier to work on," Jon Kaase states on his website. Deck thickness of these cylinder heads (about 0.625 inch) is greater than the factory head. Although the valves are located in the same place, the rocker arms attach to the head in a more simplified manner.

Edelbrock, of course, offers a variety of affordable cylinder heads for the 429/460. The Edelbrock #60665 Performer RPM cylinder head is designed for all 429/460 applications. It is a terrific street/strip head for 1,500- to 6,500-rpm operation. Good for the commute, freeway acceleration, and the drag strip.

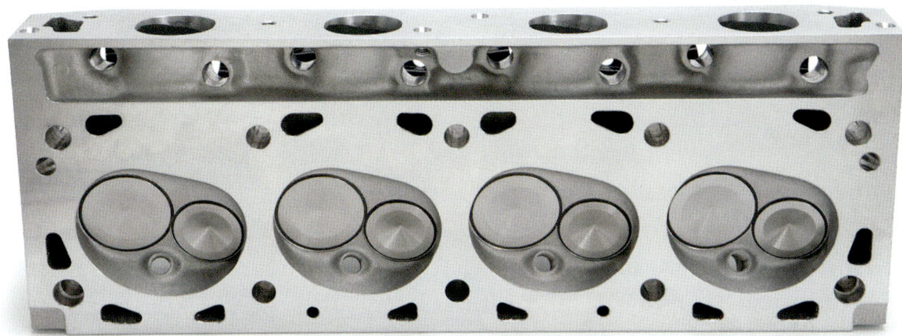

These more conventional 95-cc "kidney bean" chambers serve the Edelbrock #60665 well and give you compression options from conservative to high depending upon the piston you choose.

Bullitt heads are suggested for street, towing, or street/strip engines with displacements up to 477 ci with maximum RPM around 6,200. They're a good street/strip head for those of you who weekend race.

Ford Performance has always catered to the 429/460 enthusiast with a variety of castings. The Ford Performance M-6049-C460 Sportsman cylinder head is designed for the M-6010-A460 Ford Performance block, which is engineered for professional competition and serious Sportsman drag racers. The C460 head is made from 356-T6 aluminum with bronze valve guides and a premium valve seat insert material compatible with titanium valves. Valve angles are 7.5-degrees intake, 8.0-degrees exhaust with no side cant. It has raised intake and exhaust ports and 65-cc wedge-style combustion chambers. Ford recommends a bore size of 4.600 inches (4.500 inches minimum). Valve sizing is 2.450 inches intake and 1.900 inches exhaust, which are recommended diameters. The Sportsman head yields a port and combustion chamber design based on the successful Ford Performance 351 Yates cylinder head. This is not a head suggested for the street.

The Ford Performance Super Cobra Jet (SCJ) cylinder head is a

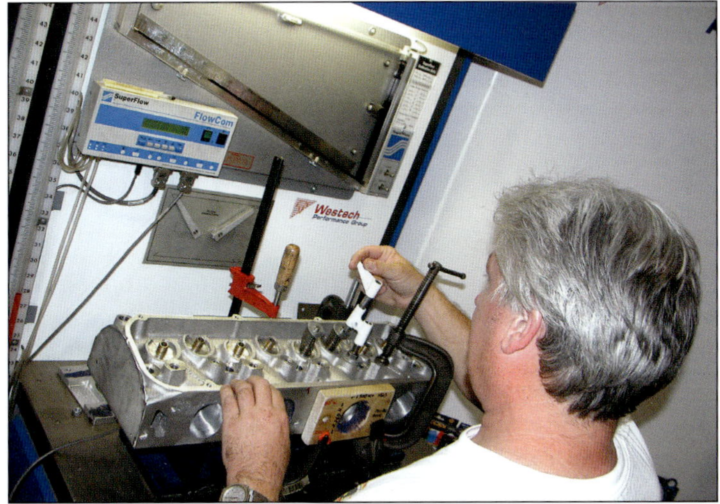

Mark Jeffrey of Trans Am Racing uses flow benches to determine his porting regimen. He works the ports beginning at the bowls. He suggests port matching on every cylinder head he does to minimize turbulence.

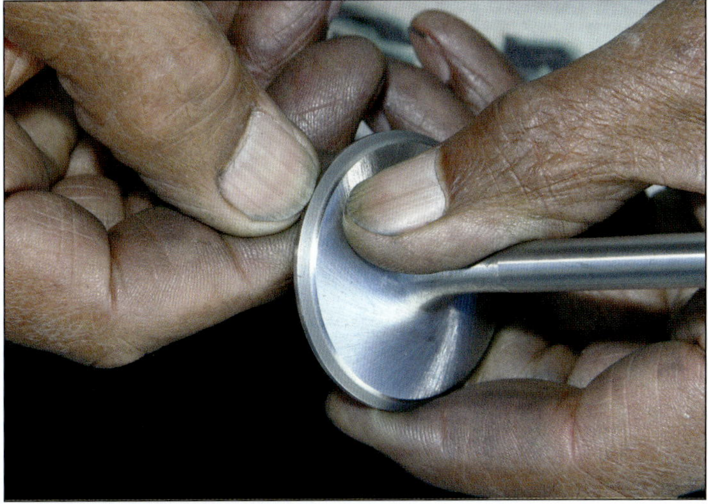

Marvin McAfee of MCE Engines in Los Angeles prefers broad valve seat contact for good heat transfer and valve cooling. This is preferable for street and road race engines.

This is what precision CNC machine work looks like. It is consistent and spot-on every time. All ports and chambers are a perfect match.

good street/strip head for 429- and 460-ci engines except the Boss 429. Valve angles and locations are engineered to reduce cylinder wall valve shrouding and improve air/fuel flow. The SCJ's combustion chambers are designed to accommodate centrally located valves in these castings. What's more, production 429 Cobra Jet intake and exhaust manifolds bolt right on these heads. They have the production Ford 429/460 valve cover bolt pattern along with 2.200-inch intake and 1.760-inch exhaust valves. The SCJ head flows 330-cfm intake and 225-cfm exhaust (290-cc intake and 148-cc exhaust). Chamber size is 72 cc. Ford assembles these heads with solid roller valve springs with closed seat pressure of 240 pounds at 1.900 inches, with open seat pressure at 625 pounds at 1.200 inches. Maximum allowable lift is 0.650 inch. Valve locks are machined at 10 degrees with steel valve spring retainers and premium valve seals. Ford says these heads call for notched pistons for valve clearance.

Jon Kaase needs little introduction with 385-series performance enthusiasts. His cylinder heads are among the best in the industry. Extensive dynamometer tests have shown average gains of at least 50 hp over the some of the best cylinder heads in the business. What's more, usable engine RPM range increases by a minimum of 500 rpm. Jon Kaase has assured me that his SR-71 wedge heads for the 429/460 will fit most engine bays and, on top of a 598-ci engine, will make over 1,100 hp and rev to 8,000 rpm. That's real power from a 385-series stroker.

Despite placing the SR-71's intake port entries 1/2 inch higher than most heads, all Super Cobra Jet intake manifolds will fit these heads. Higher intake ports are always desirable because they provide straighter, faster paths for the air-fuel mixture to reach the intake valves. Jon says raising the intake ports while preserving compatibility with conventional 385-series intake manifolds is achieved by extending the port entry face toward the valley area. This makes the SR-71 head wider. On the exhaust side of the SR-71, dimensions remain stock Super Cobra Jet/Kaase P-51. It works.

Jon adds that the SR-71's intake and exhaust bowls are deeper than stock at 0.450 inch and 0.250 inch, respectively. Intake and exhaust short-turn cross-sections, known as windows, are considerably larger than stock according to Jon. He refers to the porting system "Ported as Cast," which means the ports are shaped and sized to their best-known contours. He goes on to say that they've done their utmost to reduce the bother of additional porting, plus deeper bowls combined with easier flow around gentle short turns have improved high-RPM performance. Clearly, a lot of thought, flow bench, and dyno time have gone into the SR-71 head.

The SR-71's intake and exhaust valves are stainless steel, measuring 2.375 and 1.760 inches, respectively, with valve shapes designed for extraordinary flow. Kaase has adopted stronger rocker-stud bosses. High-end E-bronze guides are used. Valve seats in the SR-71s are of a unique Dura-Bond alloy. The SR-71's CNC-machined combustion chambers are 70 cc.

The more affordable Kaase P-51 aluminum cylinder heads for Ford 429/460 big-block engines demonstrates Kaase has corrected shortcomings in the original 385-series cylinder head. Kaase did this by relocating the valves, redesigning the kidney-bean combustion chambers, and reconfiguring the internals of the intake and exhaust ports. For the first time ever, the 385-series engine exceeded the 350-cfm peak intake flow of the desirable Boss 429 head.

Kaase took the gains made in the Super Cobra Jet heads and refined them even further. With peak intake flow ratings of around 400 cfm, the new Kaase P51 castings are available directly from Jon Kaase Racing Engines. Of perhaps greater significance is their superb mid-range flow as discussed in this chapter.

Kaase stayed with the 72-cc combustion chamber, which allows buyers to run pump gas. The Kaase chamber also permits experimentation with different compression ratios without consequence, employing slightly dished or domed pistons. The P51 chamber is CNC-machined, containing larger 2.250-inch intake valves. The standard 460 exhaust valves are retained. Kaase's P51 heads function with the original valvetrain components. However, they require longer pushrods due to revised valve geometry. Intake and exhaust port locations are unchanged, which makes the P51 head a slam-dunk.

Jon has a thirty-year history with the 385-series cylinder head. He still likes to rework them and try to improve the original 1969 design. In 2001 he redesigned the porting and valve positioning and came up with a completely new SCJ head. He partnered with JMP in California to produce the first two thousand heads for Ford. JMP has built new patterns and tooling, and Kaase has, over the last year, spent countless hours dyno testing different combinations. He has focused on the 466- and 514-ci engines with numerous cams and intake manifolds being tested.

What's the difference between this new P-51 head and the Ford Motorsport SCJ casting? First, Kaase made changes to the chamber and had them CNC-machined so they would all be the same. Then, he made changes to the water jacket to allow for more aggressive porting at the intake short turn and left-side wall. When porting the SCJs, many times he would run into water above the intake seat, close to the top of the short turn. He then set up a program to CNC under both seats, down in the bowls and to the top of the short turns. The goal was to flow about 400 cfm on the intake, 250 cfm on the exhaust. The real magic in this head, though, is the intake flow at 0.400- and 0.500-inch lift.

Jon said that one of the big complaints of the SCJ head is that some of the rocker arms don't meet the valve tip correctly in terms of geometry. In addition, if you use longer valves for more spring height, the problem is worse. Kaase has changed the rocker stud angles and positions to accommodate most rocker arms and valve lengths. New stud girdles are being made at Jomar Performance. Kaase is also having 0.100-inch-longer custom valves produced.

Jon explains that the valve guide angles and locations are the same as the Ford Motorsport SCJ's. The pistons usually don't need an exhaust valve relief with the P-51 head, while the intake relief will almost never need to be deeper than 0.150 inch. The intake face, exhaust face, and valve cover surface are also the same as the SCJ's.

"I hate flow benches," Jon added. "As you may know, most of our work is with 815-inch Pro Stock engines. On these heads the flow bench is almost totally worthless. I think it's misleading at best. You can port an older aluminum A-429 CJ head to flow 400 and 250 cfm. Then, you can have a P-51 head that flows the same. The P-51 will dyno 75 hp better than the CJ. It's all about sizes, areas, shapes, and valve placement in the bore. I think you'll find that the more an engine builder uses the dyno, the less he trusts or even uses the flow bench. There are so many flow benches out there in use that almost everybody thinks he's an expert."

Jon has a lot to say about the P-51 heads. One of his main goals in engineering these heads was to be able to deliver them with 400-cfm intake ports. Kaase has achieved that goal. In high-flowing intake ports with the port opening positioned down close to the head gasket surface, the air often breaks away from the port floor and results in unwanted turbulence.

Jon adds that this usually occurs above 0.600-inch valve lift when the air flow is high. With the P-51 head, some of the intake ports will be smooth and quiet all the way to 0.800-inch lift. He adds that those ports will usually flow over 400 cfm. Some of the ports will go turbulent at 0.550- to 0.650-inch lift. When it happens, the sound changes and the airflow drops off about 20 cfm. The flow will be the same or better than the port right up to the lift where it goes turbulent.

There are several ways to fix this, as Jon comments, all of which are not good ideas. If they raised the port entry about 1 inch at the manifold, it would be a big help because the air would not have to make such a sharp turn. He said that none of the manifolds would fit in that case. If they made the port a lot wider or taller at the short turn, that would fix the problem because the air speed would be much slower. However, Jon adds that slow is not what you want in a performance engine. When flowing some of these problem ports, sticking a butter knife or blade in the floor of the port will usually straighten it out to flow 400 cfm.

According to Jon, they have dyno tested engines with heads that flowed 400 cfm and then changed to heads where every port went turbulent to flow 375 cfm. They both made the same power. If you ran a set of heads that flowed 375 cfm because of improper porting or seat work, and then reworked them to flow 400 cfm, they would make more power.

Jon adds at the www.460FORD.com engine tech seminar in Owensboro, Kentucky, that he had a client say he replaced a set of A-429 heads (Ford aluminum Cobra Jet) with Kaase P-51s. He was thrilled to witness a 100-hp increase with the P-51s. Jon admitted that the 100-horse claim might be on the high side but thought 75 hp would be realistic if it was a good, sound engine with at least 256 degrees of cam.

Jon said that he has run enough different combinations to be able to say that a well-prepared 466-ci big-block will make about 700 hp. A 514-521 will make 800. This would be with 'as delivered' P-51 heads, at least 256 degrees of roller cam, an unmodified Edelbrock Victor 460 (or Ford counterpart), and a Dominator 1150-cfm carburetor.

Jon's assembled heads employ top-quality parts and the valves made to your specs. These valves are 0.100 inch longer than stock for greater installed height. The valve springs for the roller cam heads come from Manley (#221443). Kaase has used these springs for years on drag race, oval track, and even the Engine Masters entries. These springs are very expensive. Jon had to think long and hard about risking a cheaper spring. The best choice won out because he didn't want anyone losing an engine with Kaase saving a few bucks on valve springs. The spring locators and steel retainers and locks are from Comp Cams. The rocker studs are ARP Pro Series for added security.

What better person to chat with

When valve sizing is considered, there must also be suitable clearance between the valves and between the valves and the chamber walls. When valve shrouding is excessive, you lose airflow. You need at least 0.090-inch clearance between valves according to Marvin McAfee of MCE Engines.

Marvin is working with A460 cylinder heads right out of the box. He completely disassembles these heads and blueprints them. Valve-to-guide clearances are checked. Valve movement must be buttery smooth according to Marvin. He confirms seat contact in the process.

Prior to 1972, 429/460 iron heads had iron exhaust valve seats. With the advent of unleaded fuels in the early 1970s, Ford went to hardened steel exhaust valve seats. You have two options with early 1968–1971 heads: install hardened exhaust valve seats or opt for stainless steel valves. Here, the iron seats are cut for steel valve seats.

This is a hardened steel exhaust valve seat, which is pressed into the machined head and then cut at the same angle as the valve. The norm is a 45-degree cut. To improve airflow, it gets a multi-angle seat cut.

about cylinder head porting than Jon Kaase, who has delivered hundreds of thousands of race-proven engines throughout his career as an engine architect. Though some Kaase P51 big-block engines are driven on the street, most of them are drag-race proven through brute competition.

The big advantage of the P51 cylinder head is its convenience, Jon had commented. It fits any regular passenger car that came with a 385-series engine and it accepts store-bought exhausts and headers. Other premium race heads such as Ford's C-460 or Trick Flow's A460 won't fit in the engine bay according to Jon, especially on older Mustangs where the exhaust headers interfere with the shock towers.

You don't have to spend a lot of money porting the Kaase head because it is already done for you according to Jon. A 572-ci engine with P-51 heads will produce over 900 hp with a single carburetor without porting the intake or the heads. A 520-ci engine will make well over 800 hp. They have been an easy build and for years they have been a runaway best seller, so there are a great many out there.

Compression ratios, which vary widely from 13:1 and 14:1 down to 9:1 for street driven vehicles, are accommodated by piston design according to Kaase. Though the heads remain unchanged, the pistons can vary from dome-tops to flat-tops to dished style, depending upon compression requirements. He adds that displacements are mostly 520 to 598 ci, and the engines are normally constructed upon the original robust cast-iron block, although they are also available with an aluminum block.

Kaase P-51 Flow Numbers		
Valve Lift (inch)	Intake (cc)	Exhaust (cc)
0.100	72	52
0.200	152	107
0.300	234	151
0.400	306	183
0.500	350	202
0.600	368	215
0.700	388	229
0.800	395	239

Edelbrock offers a variety of cylinder head types, six in all, for the 429/460. The Edelbrock #61645 Performer RPM CJ cylinder head, as one example, is engineered for 1968–1987 429/460-ci engines as well as the SVO 514 engine. This is a street head designed and massaged for the daily driver and weekend racer. It does both exceedingly well. Operational range is from 1,500 to 6,500 rpm.

Speedmaster cylinder heads for the 429/460 are an affordable alternative that offer a broad power curve along with crisp throttle response and top-end performance. Speedmaster "as-cast" cylinder heads are designed for entry-level street/strip applications.

Aftermarket 429/460 Wedge Cylinder Heads

Below is a basic information table of good aftermarket cylinder heads for the 429/460, excluding the Boss 429. The information included here will lead you to each type of cylinder head without getting into too much detail. Note the manufacturer and part number, then, go to their website to get more detailed information. It is also a good idea to check out web reviews on each of these heads to see what kind of experiences others have had with them.

Brand	Part Number	Valve Size (inches)	Chamber Size (cc)	Port Size (inches)
Air Flow Research	3801; AFR 280 cc	2.250 intake; 1.760 exhaust	75	280 intake; 132 exhaust
Air Flow Research	3802; AFR 280 cc	2.250 intake; 1.550 exhaust	75	270 intake; 132 exhaust
Air Flow Research	3803; AFR 280 cc	2.500 intake; 1.760 exhaust	75	270 intake; 132 exhaust
Air Flow Research	3804; AFR 295 cc	2.500 intake; 1.760 exhaust	85	280 intake; 132 exhaust
Air Flow Research	3805; AFR 280 cc	2.250 intake; 1.550 exhaust	85	270 intake; 170 exhaust
Air Flow Research	3815; AFR 295 cc	2.500 intake; 1.760 exhaust	75	295 intake; 142 exhaust
Air Flow Research	3816; AFR 280 cc	2.500 intake; 1.760 exhaust	75	295 intake; 142 exhaust
Air Flow Research	3817; AFR 295 cc	2.500 intake; 1.760 exhaust	75	295 intake; 142 exhaust
Air Flow Research	3826; AFR 295 cc	2.500 intake; 1.760 exhaust	85	295 intake; 142 exhaust
Air Flow Research	3818; AFR 295 cc	2.500 intake; 1.760 exhaust	85	295 intake; 142 exhaust
Air Flow Research	3819; AFR 295 cc	2.500 intake; 1.760 exhaust	85	295 intake; 142 exhaust
Air Flow Research	3820; AFR 295 cc	2.500 intake; 1.760 exhaust	85	295 intake; 142 exhaust
Air Flow Research	3821; AFR 295 cc	2.500 intake; 1.760 exhaust	75	295 intake; 142 exhaust
Air Flow Research	3822; AFR 295 cc	2.500 intake; 1.760 exhaust	75	295 intake; 142 exhaust
Air Flow Research	3823; AFR 295 cc	2.500 intake; 1.760 exhaust	75	295 intake; 142 exhaust
Air Flow Research	3824; AFR 295 cc	2.500 intake; 1.760 exhaust	85	295 intake; 142 exhaust

Brand	Part Number	Valve Size (inches)	Chamber Size (cc)	Port Size (inches)
Air Flow Research	3825; AFR 295 cc	2.500 intake; 1.760 exhaust	85	295 intake; 142 exhaust
Air Flow Research	3833; AFR 315 cc	2.300 intake; 1.760 exhaust	75	315 intake; 142 exhaust
Air Flow Research	3836; AFR 315 cc	2.300 intake; 1.760 exhaust	85	295 intake; 142 exhaust
Air Flow Research	3837; AFR 315 cc	2.500 intake; 1.760 exhaust	85	295 intake; 142 exhaust
Air Flow Research	3838; AFR 315 cc	2.300 intake; 1.760 exhaust	85	315 intake; 142 exhaust
Edelbrock	60665	2.190 intake; 1.760 exhaust	95	292 intake; 100 exhaust
Edelbrock	60669	2.190 intake; 1.760 exhaust	95	292 intake; 100 exhaust
Edelbrock	60675	2.190 intake; 1.760 exhaust	75	292 intake; 100 exhaust
Edelbrock	60679	2.190 intake; 1.760 exhaust	75	292 intake; 100 exhaust
Edelbrock	61645	2.190 intake; 1.760 exhaust	75	310 intake; 100 exhaust
Edelbrock	61649	2.190 intake; 1.760 exhaust	75	310 intake; 100 exhaust
Ford Performance	M-6049-SCJA	2.200 intake; 1.760 exhaust	72	290 intake; 148 exhaust
Ford Performance	M-6049-SCJ	2.200 intake; 1.760 exhaust	72	290 intake; 148 exhaust
Ford Performance	M-6049-C460	2.450 intake; 1.900 exhaust	65	N/A
Jon Kaase Racing Engines	P51	2.250 intake; N/A exhaust	72	395 cfm @ 0.800 inch; 239 cfm @ 0.800 inch exhaust
Jon Kaase Racing Engines	SR-71	2.375 intake; 1.760 exhaust	70	435 cfm @ 0.900 inch 405 cfm intake; 297 cfm @ 0.900 inch 183 cfm exhaust
Trick Flow	TFS-53410001	2.200 intake; 1.760 exhaust	74	290 intake; 130 exhaust
Trick Flow	TFS-53410007-C01	2.200 intake; 1.760 exhaust	78	325 intake; 145 exhaust
Trick Flow	TFS-53410008-C01	2.250 intake; 1.760 exhaust	78	325 intake; 145 exhaust
Trick Flow	TFS-5341T010-C01	2.250 intake; 1.760 exhaust	78	325 intake; 145 exhaust
Trick Flow	TFS-53410002	2.200 intake; 1.760 exhaust	74	290 intake; 130 exhaust
Trick Flow	TFS-5441T801-M87	2.300 intake; 1.880 exhaust	87	340 intake; 172 exhaust
Trick Flow	TFS-5451B001-C03	18-bolt design cylinder heads are compatible with Ford Racing M-6010-A500 460 race block only	85	360 intake; 180 exhaust
Trick Flow	TFS-5451T804-C03	2.400 intake; 1.880 exhaust	85	360 intake; 180 exhaust
Trick Flow	TFS-5341T010-C01	2.200 intake; 1.760 exhaust	74	290 intake; 130 exhaust
Trick Flow	TFS-5341T010-C01	2.200 intake; 1.760 exhaust	74	290 intake; 130 exhaust
Trick Flow	TFS-5451T802-M87	2.350 intake; 1.880 exhaust	87	340 intake; 172 exhaust
Trick Flow	TFS-5451B000-C03	2.400 intake; 1.880 exhaust	85	360 intake; 180 exhaust
Trick Flow	TFS-5451B000-C04	2.400 intake; 1.880 exhaust	87	360 intake; 180 exhaust
Trick Flow	TFS-5341T003	2.200 intake; 1.760 exhaust	74	290 intake; 130 exhaust
Trick Flow	TFS-5341T008-C01	2.350 intake; 1.880 exhaust	78	325 intake; 145 exhaust
Trick Flow	TFS-5451B001-M83	2.350 intake; 1.880 exhaust	83	340 intake; 172 exhaust
Trick Flow	TFS-5441B001-M87	2.300 intake; 1.880 exhaust	87	340 intake; 172 exhaust
Trick Flow	TFS-5441T802-M83	2.350 intake; 1.880 exhaust	83	340 intake; 172 exhaust
Trick Flow	TFS-5451B001-M87	2.350 intake; 1.880 exhaust	87	340 intake; 172 exhaust
Trick Flow	TFS-5451T804-C04	2.400 intake; 1.880 exhaust	87	360 intake; 180 exhaust
Trick Flow	TFS-5451B001-C04	18-bolt design cylinder heads are compatible with Ford Racing M-6010-A500 460 race block only.	87	360 intake; 180 exhaust
Trick Flow	TFS-5451T802-M83	2.350 intake; 1.880 exhaust	83	340 intake; 172 exhaust
Trick Flow	TFS-5451T8T5-C03	2.400 intake; 1.880 exhaust	85	360 intake; 180 exhaust
Trick Flow	TFS-5341B000-C01	N/A	78	325 intake; 145 exhaust
Trick Flow	TFS-5441B001-M83	2.350 intake; 1.880 exhaust	83	340 intake; 172 exhaust
Trick Flow	TFS-5341T004	2.200 intake; 1.760 exhaust	74	290 intake; 130 exhaust
Trick Flow	TFS-5341T002	2.200 intake; 1.760 exhaust	74	290 intake; 130 exhaust
Trick Flow	TFS-53410003	2.200 intake; 1.760 exhaust	74	290 intake; 130 exhaust

Head Work

Basic cylinder head reconditioning begins with the realities of valve function. Intake and exhaust valves are there to allow fuel and air in, then seal the cylinder for compression/ignition/power cycles, then allow the egress of hot gases. To fully contain the heat energy, valves must close quickly and open in proper time with piston and crankshaft events.

A simple valve job involves first disassembly, cleaning the castings, examining the valves, guides, and seats; then determining condition, and either replacing or returning these parts to service. It is always best to replace all components with new valves, springs, keepers, retainers, and guides even if you have parts in good condition. Exhaust valves are the hottest parts in the engine. If you have 429/460 heads manufactured prior to 1972, you're going to need hardened exhaust valve seats. One option is stainless steel exhaust valves, which won't wear down or damage the iron valve seat. It is also good to consider valve seat angle and

Larger intake valves don't always yield more power. This is where flow bench testing counts. However, high-flow bench numbers don't always mean more power. You can go too large and end up losing torque. You have to look at the intake, cam profile, and cylinder head combination as a package.

JGM has also massaged the chambers and bowls but not too much because I want fuel droplets to remain in suspension for the light-off. There are a lot of opinions on what to do with the chambers. You don't want ragged edges and excessively rough casting surfaces, which can become red hot and cause preignition.

Bronze valve guide liners have been installed and are precision honed to size for a good crosshatch pattern for oil control.

You can go one of two ways on valve guides. You can replace the guide or you can install bronze valve guide liners that offer improved and controlled oil flow to the valve stems.

what it can do for or take away from flow and performance.

Another important issue is valve guides. You can ream the guides and install bronze bushings (liners), which will perform quite well and control oil flow to the valve stems. You may also replace the valve guides with steel inserts and they will be good for a long time to come.

Valve Spring Pressures

The installed height of a valve spring is the total height of the spring when the valve is seated. Valve spring height is measured from where the spring meets the bottom of the retainer to where it seats against the cylinder head. Virtually all camshafts come packaged with recommended valve spring height information. If you follow recommended spring height, you will have a spring that is not too weak (causing the valves to float at high RPM), or one that has too much spring pressure.

Valve seat pressure is the force the valve spring places on the valve head/face when it is closed. Open spring pressure is the pressure that forces the valve to close after the rocker arm opens the valve. Open pressure is greater than seat pressure because the spring is under pressure from the cam lobe and rocker arm. Seat pressure for non-roller hydraulic cams should be around 300 pounds maximum, with 350 pounds for non-roller flat-tappet mechanical cams. Seat pressure should be roughly 110 to 120 pounds maximum, with flat-tappet mechanical cams at 140 pounds. Roller cams are decidedly different.

Because a roller cam moves the valves at higher velocities, this calls for a spring with more seat pressure, which will prevent valve float at high RPM. Also, roller cams

You can replace the valve guides and opt for this steel insert durability.

Valve spring installed height is measured in preparation for valvetrain assembly. Once springs are installed and set up, springs are checked for coil bind with the valve at full open.

Shims are used to get spring height to the cam manufacturer's specifications. Sometimes, you will have to cut the spring seat to get the correct installed height.

The only valve seal to use today is the Viton seal, which controls the amount of oil that runs down the stem and guide. It also outlasts virtually every valve seal in the marketplace. This 460 head has been fitted with Cobra Jet–style spring cups.

Manley sports different duty levels of valves for an engine build: Performance and Street Series, Race Master, Severe Duty, and Extreme Duty. Most of you will need the Performance Street Series, which is engineered for street and strip. Race Master and Pro Flo, known as Race Flo valves, are manufactured of XH-426 material for the exhausts and NK-842 for the intakes targeted at the bracket, drag, and oval track racers operating below 8,000 rpm.

There are two basic Boss 429 street heads: C9AE-AA and D0OE-AA. This is a pair of D0OE-AA castings with 2.380/1.900-inch intake/exhaust valves. This Ford part number is D0AZ-6049-C. The C9AE-AA cylinder head sports 2.280/1.900-inch intake/exhaust valves. There are rare experimental and race head castings. Also, Blue Crescent iron castings may be found, but few survive.

An overhead view of the D0AE-AA Boss 429 cylinder head shows this head's true crossflow design with the most unusual monkey-motion valvetrain the Ford big-block has ever had. The Boss 429 was Ford's answer to Chrysler's 426-ci Hemi. NASCAR couldn't say no to this one.

don't have the friction associated with flat-tappet cams and lifters. As a result, valve springs with higher open pressures (around 500 to 800 pounds at peak valve lift) allow the engine to rev higher.

Spring Height

Camshafts should always be ordered in kit form. I suggest following the manufacturer's specifications. It matters little if you use matched springs, are running different springs, or are changing springs; spring height must always be checked.

Using a precision rule, measure the spring from where it meets the bottom of the retainer to where it sits on the cylinder head around the valve guide. Check installed height without shims installed. More precise than a ruler is a micrometer, which fits in place of the valve spring. Turn the dial until the valve is seated snuggly on its seat, then note the measurement on the micrometer. If the valve spring is not at the recommended installed height, you will either have to shim until it reaches the correct height or machine the spring seat in the head deeper to get the installed height needed. If you opt for a spring with a larger diameter than stock, you may have to machine the spring seats.

Whether you're reworking stock cast-iron cylinder heads or opting for a good aftermarket head, you want the best cylinder head for the money. The 429/460 has a good factory cylinder head, whether it's a bread-and-butter grocery-getter casting or the Super Cobra Jet/Police Interceptor. The 429 Police Interceptor head casting is virtually the same head as the Cobra Jet/ Super Cobra Jet. Police Interceptor castings are still widely available because so many were produced in the 1970s. Hand these heads to a good head porter and they come alive. Jim Grubbs of JGM Performance Engineering has done a tremendous amount of research and development the 385-series heads and has learned how to finesse these castings to get a lot of power.

Joe Mondello, as another excellent example, understands airflow and how it should be managed in a cylinder head port. You will want to arm yourself with the right porting tools (foot pedal controlled) so you can modulate grinder speed. Get lots of practice on a scrap iron 429/460 cylinder head. Avoid the use of an electric drill. They're more challenging to use and could damage a cylinder head. Fellow CarTech Books author David Vizard explains proper porting technique in *The Theory and Practice of Cylinder Head Modification*. Cylinder head porting is all about optimizing port shape and routing to minimize turbulence and disruption to airflow.

There are a lot of misconceptions when it comes to cylinder head porting. Larger doesn't always mean better. At the very least, you want a good port match between the intake ports and the intake manifold along with a comparable gasket port match. Any irregularities between the manifold, gasket, and intake port can be sources of turbulence.

You need to understand the relationship between pressure and velocity through the intake and exhaust ports, which changes in cross-sectional area along its path. As you increase the velocity of air and fuel or hot gases, the pressure of the air decreases. If you slow down airflow, the pressure of the air increases.

That said, how does one change the speed of the air through a port? You do this by simply making the port larger, which slows the air, or makes it smaller, which increases the air's speed. Air and gases don't like to change direction. Why? Because, when you change the airflow's direction, velocity and energy are lost in the process. Apply this logic to how heads are ported.

We've never had a better selection of great aftermarket cylinder heads than we do right now. Today, with the current CNC technology, cylinder head technology has never been better. Aftermarket cylinder heads are still limited to the design limitations of the engine.

Airflow

Few of us truly understand how a flow bench works or how airflow is measured through the ports. High air pressure always dominates low pressure for obvious reasons. As your engine draws air and atomized fuel through the intake ports, it becomes negative air pressure (a vacuum) beneath the carburetor or throttle body. Manifold vacuum is high with the throttle plates closed. As the throttle is opened, there's a reduction in vacuum until engine RPM increases.

This principle is applied to a cylinder head on the flow bench. Apply vacuum to the combustion chamber, then open the intake valve in 0.100-inch lift increments and you will get airflow numbers at each increment. Use a valve to regulate how much suction is applied along with a means of measuring the suction and the amount of flow, and you have the workings of a flow bench. Airflow measurements are normally expressed in manometers.

The humble flow bench moves air through cylinder head ports via a vacuum source, normally a vacuum cleaner motor. With that suction, it measures the amount of air moving through the port with the valve open. Increments are normally 0.100- through 0.800-inch valve lift. Flow testing is typically performed at 10, 25, or 28 inches of water. The pressure developed during flow testing should allow for the test pressure plus any losses, hence the reasoning behind these very specific numbers.

Some form of manifold is used at the intake or exhaust port to improve airflow and limit turbulence. The motor is turned on and the control valve is set at a test pressure, say 25 inches. Flow is then measured. Airflow measurements are then taken at lift increments of 0.100 inch, then 0.200 inch, and so on at 25 inches of water. Testing should be done at the same pressure using the same inlet or outlet configuration. Using a different inlet radius, valve shape, or cylinder diameter will change airflow.

The maximum flow standard through the valve is 146 cfm per square inch of valve opening. This is used to rate port efficiency. Most cylinder head porters use the valve's curtain area, which is the circumference of the valve head (3.1416 x diameter) x valve lift x 146 cfm. Then, divide the flow number by your result. This yields a percentage of the standard lift at each valve. If the port can be configured to flow up to the standard, it would be in theory achieving 100-percent efficiency. If a port only flows half as much air, it would be 50-percent efficient.

A flow bench is nothing more than a simple tool designed to measure airflow and nothing more. You get data; however, it will not instruct you how to fully understand that data. It isn't going to tell you what to do with the data. What's more, there's no guarantee that great flow numbers ensure you're going to get the performance expected.

Airflow versus Reality

You hear the words "volumetric efficiency" mentioned a lot in dyno rooms but may not understand what it means. Volumetric efficiency (VE) is the process of understanding how a cylinder bore is being filled with air and fuel in a percentage versus what it would actually be if it was filled to the same pressure as the atmospheric pressure outside the engine.

When the piston is on the downstroke away from TDC, a vacuum is created in the cylinder drawing a fresh air/fuel charge. Picture the piston as it accelerates from TDC toward the point of maximum velocity around 75-degrees after TDC. Flow then lags behind the demand, which creates a higher vacuum within the cylinder bore. The piston then slows until at BDC where it parks for a brief moment known as "dwell" before journeying back toward TDC. As the piston nears BDC, the inertia of the air from its velocity causes flow to catch up with piston demand and then finally exceed it.

After BDC, the piston is going the wrong direction to pull in air. What does that mean? It means even though you don't get 100-percent VE on the downstroke of the piston, you can still get high overall volumetric efficiency by keeping the intake valve open after BDC, in order to take advantage of that intake charge momentum and the resultant resonant tuning of the intake port. This continues the filling of the cylinder bore after the piston has reached BDC.

Loading the cylinder bore continues as the piston journeys back up the bore until the intake valve closes. It is an invisible momentum where air continues to flow into the bore even as the piston rises in the bore. This is where it becomes more complex. If everything is functioning properly, this pressure wave will arrive at the intake valve a short time after it closes. This tends to build greater cylinder pressure in the process. Were it not for the momentum of the incoming airflow along with the resonant tuning of the port, it would be impossible to achieve a 100-percent cylinder fill.

Velocity is critical on the exhaust side because it has everything to do with what happens at the intake. Exhaust pulse velocity in the port and header generates a vacuum, which creates a pressure drop in the cylinder as the piston approaches TDC on the exhaust stroke. The more valve overlap you have, the more significant it is to making power. A pressure drop from the open exhaust during valve overlap starts the intake system inducting before the piston heads downward for the intake stroke.

It has been said many times that the momentum in the air moving in and out of the engine is a function of the square of velocity, so even small changes in velocity make large changes in flow. This is affected by port dimensions and shape along with cam profile and induction. These days, there is a trend toward flow testing at much higher pressures. Peak port flow velocities can be as high as 600 feet per second (fps). However, testing a large intake port designed for high RPM use may only yield 200 fps on the flow bench, which is very different than an operational engine at high RPM.

Improving Airflow

Port work begins with what you want the engine to do. If you're building a weekend cruiser, you don't need port work. Work the heads to what you want the engine to do. For daily commute and weekend racing, minor port work is in order. All-out racing calls for a lot of port work. However, no matter what you want the engine to do, port matching is what you must do. Use the intake gasket as a template. Use Prussian Blue around the intake ports and scribe around the perimeter. Ditto for the exhaust side. Arm yourself with a flow bench or find a shop that can flow your heads. A flow bench is essential because it doesn't take much to ruin intake and exhaust ports.

Port work typically begins around the bowls and valve guides. You must be careful not to grind too deeply and get into water jackets. The greatest flow losses experienced occur as air expands and heads into the combustion chamber. You must be careful around the bowl, valve guide, and valve face. You can't always control valve shape. One of the best approaches to porting is to have an understanding of how much power you want to make. Torque comes from port velocity, which is important down low into the mid-range.

Begin port work with a flow bench to ascertain baseline flow numbers. It is a good idea to sonic check ports for wall thickness before you begin grinding. Some porters do a rubber mold port pour, allow the silicone to cure, then examine the shape of the mold to determine what needs to be done next.

Take porting one port at a time, then hit the flow bench to check your work. Count on this taking a lot of time to get it right. Get the valve seat cut and blended, then check your work again on a flow bench. Aluminum heads take less time than iron. Expect to burn up at least 100 hours doing port work, which explains why head porting is so expensive.

CNC porting is the latest technology, which makes it a lot easier for machine shops. A computer controls the predictable precision cutting. Once the heavy cutting is finished, hand-porting applies the finishing touches. In fact, most CNC port work was born from hand-porting to begin with.

CHAPTER 6

Camshaft and Valvetrain

Camshaft and valvetrain selection determine not only an engine's behavior but also how reliably and predictably an engine will perform. I'm here to dispel most of the myths and get you headed in the right direction. To understand how to select a camshaft and valvetrain for your 429/460, you must first understand how it all works and how to select components.

Selecting the right camshaft profile is rooted in how you want an engine to behave. Are you building a daily driver where low- and mid-range torque are important? Or are you building a high-revving racing engine that makes its peak torque at high RPM?

A camshaft manufacturer's catalog lists dozens of camshaft options for the same type of engine. This is where it gets mighty confusing for the novice. You see words like lift, duration, lobe separation, base circle, lobe centerline angle, and valve overlap. What does this information mean and how will it affect your engine's performance and durability?

These are all the elements of camshaft function: lift, duration, lobe separation angle, valve overlap, and the base circle. These elements determine valve function and timing. (Photo Courtesy Comp Cams)

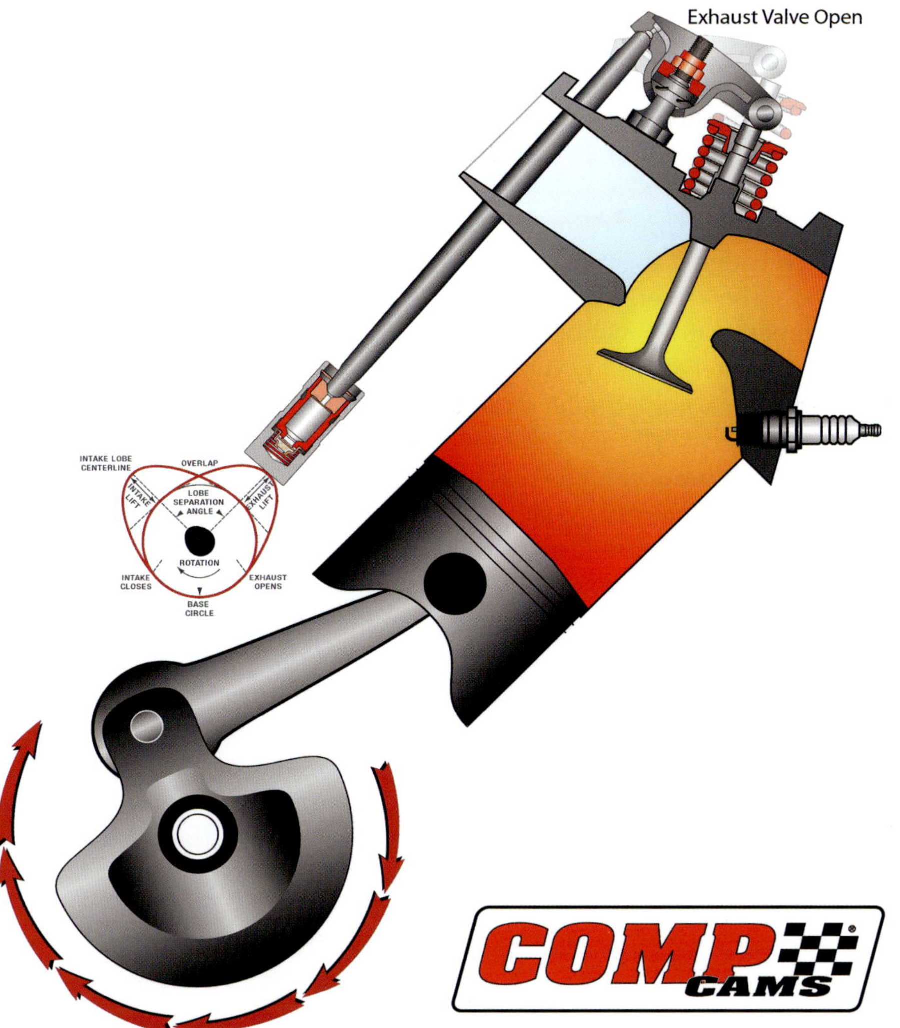

This is where valve function becomes more involved: the big picture. There's cam lobe lift and there's valve lift. Lobe lift, for example, is 0.280 inch. When we journey up the push rod to the rocker arm, the rocker arm multiplies lobe lift, which becomes valve lift. Our 0.280-inch lift at the cam lobe is multiplied by the 1.6:1 ratio rocker arm to become 0.448-inch valve lift. (Photo Courtesy Comp Cams)

Camshaft Technical Talk

Cam profile includes lobe design, dimension, positioning, when it opens the valve, when the valve closes, how long it keeps the valve open, and how far it opens the valve.

Flat-tappet camshafts work differently than roller camshafts. In truth, flat-tappet camshafts don't make much sense anymore. They limit what you can do with lobe profile. If you want an aggressive profile with flat tappets, you can only go so far or suffer with poor drivability (rough idle, low manifold vacuum) if you're seeking a hot cam. Roller cams cost considerably more than flat-tappets. However, they're worth every penny in what they do for you in terms of performance and durability.

Terminology

Lift is the maximum amount a valve-lifter-pushrod combination can be raised off the base circle. Lift is measure in thousandths of an inch (0.001 inch). Lobe profile determines how quickly this occurs. It can either be smooth or abrupt depending on lobe profile.

Duration is the amount of time the valve is open beginning when the valve unseats. By this, I mean the number of degrees the camshaft will rotate when cam lift begins. Duration typically begins at 0.004 inch of cam lift or when the lifter begins to ride the ramp coming off the base circle. "Duration at fifty" means that duration begins at 0.050 inch of cam lift. Duration at fifty is the industry standard for determining camshaft lobe duration. When you're reading camshaft specs, "Duration at fifty" is the spec you will see.

Lobe separation (also known as lobe center) is the distance (in degrees) between the intake lobe peak and the exhaust lobe peak. Lobe separation generally runs between 102 and 114 degrees (camshaft degrees).

The intake centerline is the position of the camshaft in relation to the crankshaft. For example, an intake centerline of 114 degrees means the intake valve reaches maximum lift at 114 degrees after top dead center (ATDC).

The exhaust centerline is basically the same as the intake centerline. It is when the exhaust valve reaches maximum lift before top dead center (BTDC) in degrees.

Valve overlap (lobe separation) is the period of time when both the intake and exhaust valves are open to allow for proper cylinder scavenging. Overlap occurs when the exhaust valve is closing and the piston is reaching TDC. The intake charge from the opening intake valve pushes the exhaust gases out. Camshaft grinders can change valve overlap to modify the performance of a camshaft. Sometimes they do this rather than change lift or duration.

Adjustable valve timing is being able to dial-in a camshaft by adjusting valve timing at the timing sprocket. By adjusting the valve timing at the sprocket, you can increase or decrease torque. Advance valve timing and you increase torque but lose horsepower. Retard valve timing and you lose torque but gain horsepower.

Street Camshafts

The best street performance cams are those ground with a lobe separation between 108 to 114 degrees. When you keep lobe separation above 112 degrees, you improve drivability because the engine idles smoother and makes better low-end torque. There's also more vacuum at idle for accessories. Any time lobe separation is below 108 degrees, idle quality and streetability suffer. However, there's more to it than just lobe separation.

Compression and cam timing must be considered together because one affects the other. Valve timing events directly affect cylinder pressure and ultimately working/dynamic compression. Long intake valve duration reduces cylinder pressure. Shorter intake duration increases cylinder pressure. Too much cylinder pressure can cause detonation (pinging). Too little pressure and you lose torque. You can count on cam manufacturers to figure stock compression ratios into their camshaft selection tables, which makes choosing a camshaft easier than it's ever been. Plug your application into the equation, and you will be pleased with the result most of the time.

It is best to be conservative with your cam specs if you want reliability and an engine that will live a long time. Stay with a conservative lift profile (0.500-inch lift). High-lift camshafts are hard on a valvetrain. They put valve-to-piston clearances at risk. Watch duration and lobe separation closely, which will help you be more effective in camshaft selection. Instead of opening the valve more (lift), you want to open it longer (duration) and in better efficiency with piston timing (overlap or lobe separation).

Always keep in mind what you're going to have for induction, heads, and exhaust. The savvy engine architect understands that in order to work effectively, an engine must have matched components. Cam, valvetrain, heads, intake manifold, and exhaust system must all work as a team or you're just wasting time and money. If you're going with stock cylinder heads, the cam profile doesn't need to be too aggressive. Opt for a cam profile that will give you good low- to mid-range torque. Torque doesn't do you any good on the street when it happens at 6,000 rpm. Choose a cam profile that will make good torque between 2,500– and 4,500 rpm.

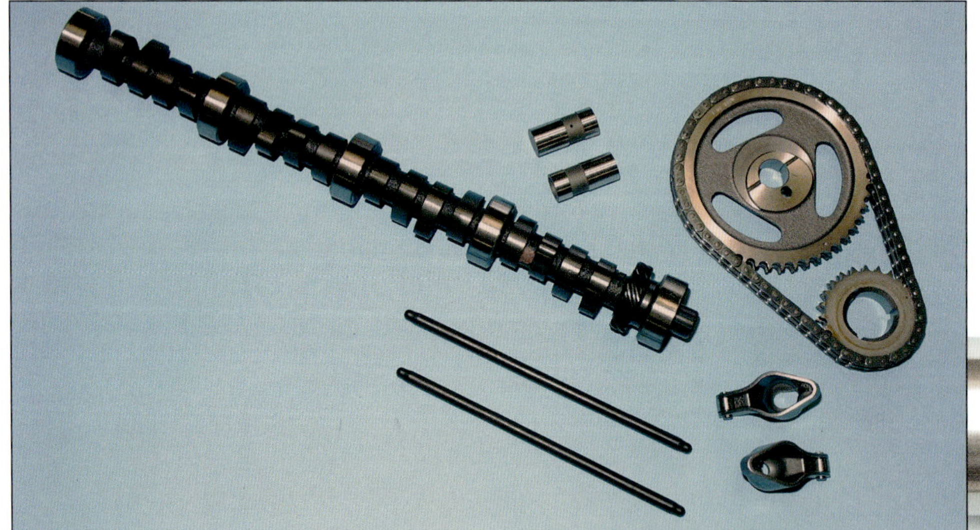

These are the basics of camshaft and valve function. Before you is a hydraulic flat-tappet camshaft, which is a good choice if you're on a limited budget. There are friction-reducing components shown here: a dual roller timing set and roller-tip stamped steel rocker arms. Spend the money on one-piece thick-wall pushrods.

Flat tappets don't sit squarely on the cam lobes but instead offset to where the cam lobe spins the lifter for even wear.

One thing to remember with camshaft selection is how the cam will work with your cylinder heads. Some camshafts will actually lose power with a given head because there's too much lift or duration. This is why you want to research a cylinder head before choosing a camshaft.

When you're shopping for cylinder heads, it can become overwhelming because there are so many types. First, you have to treat your engine build as an entire package, the sum total of what your engine is. You need to consider actual displacement, the type of vehicle, the way it will be driven most of the time, compression ratio, axle ratio, camshaft profile, and any modifications you may have made or will make such as boost or nitrous.

Cylinder heads, though important to performance, are but a part of the picture. Some aftermarket companies, such as Edelbrock and Trick Flow, offer complete packages where they've done all of the thinking for you. Cam, heads, and intake manifold are hand-picked to work together. Set a game plan for your engine and stick with that plan. Resist the temptation to jump around and mix it up with different performance parts that may not be compatible.

When you're evaluating cylinder heads, don't get hyper-focused on flow numbers. Flow numbers are but a part of a cylinder head's success. They may flow well on a flow bench and perform below par on an engine. Flow numbers impress at 0.600-inch lift on a bench. However, street engines don't always call for that much valve lift. You want to know what a cylinder head will do on your engine in a broad range of valve lifts.

Remember, bigger isn't always better when it comes to cams, heads, and intake manifolds. On the street, you want more conservative port and valve sizing for better low- to-mid-range torque for good traffic light-to-traffic light performance. If you're going road racing, you want heads that will bring you out of the turns and into the straights with an attitude. This is where torque becomes paramount because you need it when engine RPM becomes low.

Smaller intake port volumes will get you better low-end torque and snappy throttle response, while larger intake ports allow greater flow at higher RPM. As a result, smaller intake ports deliver better performance for street and weekend race vehicles. Large ports will cause low-end torque numbers to suffer. By the same token, large intake runners benefit high-revving and greater displacements.

Port volume is evaluated by port length and cross-sectional area. Matching the correct cross-sectional area to the engine's demand is the trick to choosing the right cylinder head. A proper-size intake runner will create the correct balance between airflow volume (how much) and airflow velocity (how fast). Large ports don't always win the performance shootout. What's more, swirl and tumble in the combustion chamber are also critical. You want to keep atomized fuel in suspension in the chamber just prior to light-off, which spreads a more even flash across the top of the piston. You must consider cam profile in choosing a cylinder head; also valve overlap, lobe centers, duration, and valve lift when they come off the seats.

Flat-tappet camshafts are a machined iron alloy casting and therefore have to be properly work-hardened when they're installed. Work-hardened is another way of hardening the lobes via lifter compression on the lobe. You must have zinc in the oil with any flat-tappet camshaft. When the engine is first fired, it must be run at 2,500 rpm for at least 30 minutes to work-harden the cam lobes.

Flat-tappet lifters are made of steel alloy and of a similar hardness as the cam. (Photo Courtesy Comp Cams)

Hydraulic lifters, as their name implies, have an inner plunger on which the pushrod rides. The plunger rides on oil pressure. They self-adjust as the cam wears and do not require regular adjustment like a solid tappet does.

Flat-tappet camshaft installation requires extra care. Cam lobes and lifter faces get molybdenum grease to lubricate them and to assist the work-hardening process. Journals get engine assembly lube; they never get moly lube.

The type of fuel you intend to run also affects camshaft selection. You can actually raise compression if you're running a mild camshaft profile or using a higher octane fuel. Camshaft timing events must be directly tied to compression ratio. The longer the duration, the lower the cylinder pressure and working compression is. The shorter the duration, the less air you're going to bring into the cylinder, which also affects compression. The objective needs to be the highest compression possible without detonation. You want the most duration possible without compression extremes.

Valve overlap, as stated earlier, is the period between exhaust stroke and intake stroke when both valves are off their seats. This improves exhaust scavenging and cylinder filling. It improves exhaust scavenging by allowing the incoming intake charge to push out remaining exhaust gases via the closing exhaust valve. Were the exhaust valve completely closed, you wouldn't get scavenging. The greater the overlap in a street engine, the less torque the engine will make down low where you need it most.

Street engines need 10 to 55 degrees of valve overlap to be effective in making torque. When valve overlap goes beyond 55 degrees, torque down low falters. A powerful street engine will need greater than 55 degrees of valve overlap, but not much greater. To give you an idea of what I'm talking about, racing engines need 70 to 115 degrees of valve overlap because this is what you need at high RPM.

Lobe separation angle (LSA) is another area of consideration in street cam selection. This dynamic is chosen based on displacement and how the engine will be used. Consider lobe separation based on how much displacement and valve sizing you're going to be using. The smaller the valves, the tighter (fewer degrees) lobe separation should be. However, tighter lobe separation does adversely affect idle quality. This is why most camshaft manufacturers spec their cams with wider lobe separations than the custom grinders.

Duration in a street engine is likely the most important dynamic to consider in your selection process. You increase duration whenever less lift is desired. Why? Because you get airflow into the cylinder bore two ways: lift and duration. You can open the valve more and for less time to get airflow. Or you can open the valve less and keep it open longer via duration to get airflow. Each way will have a different effect on performance. Duration is determined by how much cylinder head and displacement you have, and how the engine will be used. Excessive duration hurts low-end torque, which is what you need on the street.

You have to achieve a balance by maximizing duration without a loss in low-end torque. You do this by using the right heads with proper valve sizing. Large valves and ports do not work well for street use because velocity and torque are lacking.

What does this tell you about duration? You want greater duration whenever displacement and valve

If you can afford it, roller-tappet camshafts are a great long-term investment. They deliver a broader range of performance features including a more aggressive profile without consequence. Because they are a steel roller, there's virtually no cam lobe wear.

This is a small base circle roller cam, which is normally employed for a stroker big-block in order to clear the connecting rods.

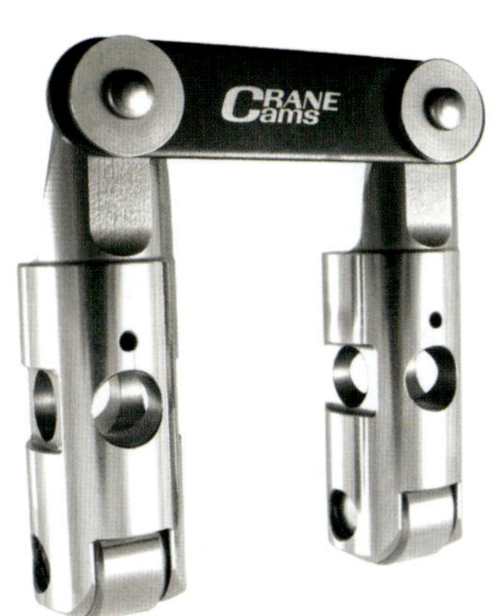

Roller tappets are great friction reducers and money well spent. Because the marketplace is long on different camshaft manufacturers, you have a lot of shopping to do in order to find the right grind for you. (Photo Courtesy Crane Cams)

Use engine assembly lube on roller tappets; never use molybdenum. Molybdenum's only purpose, aside from lubrication, is to help work-harden mating surfaces, such as flat-tappet cam lobe and distributor/oil pump drive gears.

Molybdenum, also known as moly lube, is used primarily for the work-hardening of cam lobes and gears.

sizing go up. Increasing duration falls directly in line with torque peak and RPM range, and this does not mean you necessarily gain any torque as RPM increases. It means peak torque comes at a higher RPM range. For example, if the engine is making 350 ft-lbs of torque at 4,500 rpm and you increase duration, peak torque will come at a higher RPM range.

Compression has a direct effect on what duration should be. When you're running higher compression, you have to watch duration closely because it can drive up cylinder pressures. Sometimes you can curb compression and run greater duration depending on how you want to make power. When you have greater duration, the engine is going to make more power on the high end and less on the low end.

Higher compression with a shorter duration helps the engine make low-end torque where you need it most on the street. The thing to watch for with compression is detonation and overheating. Detonation can do significant engine damage when you're at wide-open throttle. Maximum street compression should be 10.0:1 depending on the cylinder head and cam you've selected.

Valve lift is an issue you must think about as it pertains to an engine's needs. Small-blocks, as one example, generally need more valve lift than big-blocks. As you increase lift, you generally increase torque. This is especially important at low- and mid-range RPM where it happens most on the street. Your objective needs to be more torque with less RPM if you want your engine to live longer. Revs are what drain the life out of an engine.

To make good low-end torque with a 429/460, you need a camshaft that will offer a combination of effective lift and duration. You will want to run longer intake duration to make the most of valve lift. You get valve lift via cam lobes to be sure. However, rocker arm ratio is the other half of the lift equation. The most common rocker arm ratio is 1.6:1, which means the rocker arm gives the valve 1.6 times the lift you have at the cam lobe. When you go with a 1.7:1 ratio rocker arm, valve lift becomes 1.7 times what you find at the lobe.

It is best to spec a cam on the side of conservatism, especially if you're building an engine for daily and weekend bracket racing. When you opt for an aggressive camshaft with a lot of lift, you're putting more stress on the valve stem, guide, and spring. The constant hammering of daily use with excessive lift is what makes engines fail.

Dual-Pattern Camshafts

You've undoubtedly heard the term "dual-pattern" camshaft. This type runs different profiles on the intake and exhaust sides to meet a need. Typically, a dual-pattern camshaft will run longer exhaust valve duration as a means to improve scavenging and exhaust flow through poor cylinder head exhaust port designs, restrictive factory manifolds, and stock exhaust systems. (This is also beneficial whenever you're running nitrous or supercharging/turbocharging.) If you have opened up exhaust flow with better cylinder heads, a good set of headers, and a less restrictive exhaust system, running a dual-pattern camshaft doesn't make much sense because it bleeds off torque at low- and mid-RPM ranges, often attributed to "over-scavenging" on the exhaust side.

Historically, drag racers have favored dual-pattern cams because the reduction on low-RPM torque often helped with traction. Other types or racers, such as road course oval track racers, often preferred single-pattern cams because they simply made more power on modified engines. Modern cylinder heads, with excellent intake-to-exhaust flow ratios eliminate the need for dual-pattern cams in most performance applications.

Racing Camshafts

If you're building an engine for racing, it is a different situation than you find with street engines. Camshaft profile in a racing engine depends upon the type of racing you're going to do, vehicle weight and type, even the type of transmission and rear axle ratio.

Drag racing mandates a different camshaft profile than road or circle-track racing. A short-track racing engine will need to be able to produce huge amounts of torque in short order, for example. The same is true for a drag racer. These issues teach us something about engine breathing. Breathing effectiveness is determined by camshaft profile.

Lobe separation for the drag racing camshaft should be between 104 and 118 degrees, which is a broad range because drag racing needs can vary quite a bit. This is where you have to custom dial-in your application with a camshaft grinder. Most camshaft grinders have computation charts that show the right cam for an application. As needs change, so must the camshaft profile.

If you're going road racing, lobe separation becomes more specific in the 106-degree range. Some cam grinders push lobe separation higher for the circle-track engine, depending on conditions. Generally, the higher the lobe separation, the broader the torque curve (more torque over a broader RPM range).

Why Degree a Camshaft?

Making power isn't just about adding displacement, large-port heads, a big carburetor, and a lumpy camshaft, it is about the physics of packaging and tuning your engine properly. Why do you degree camshafts after they're installed in an engine? What does it accomplish?

Degreeing a camshaft is a quest to learn the truth about power and

JGM Performance Engineering does a minor hone, ever so slight, to cut a crosshatch pattern for oil control and bore snugness.

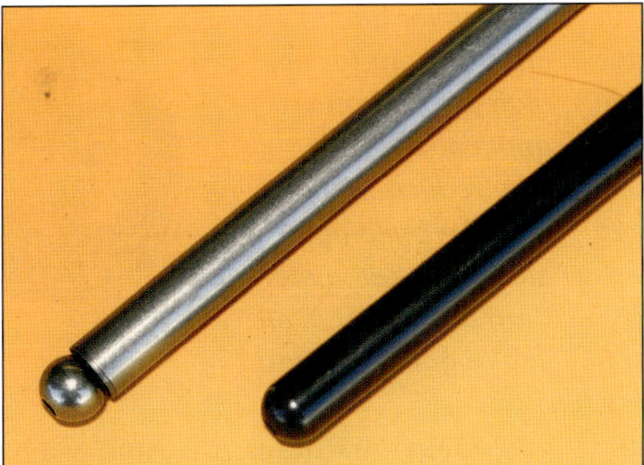

There are two types of pushrods you can expect to find out there. On the left is the budget ball-style pushrod, which is fine for street cruisers and occasional weekend racers. Good life insurance is the one-piece, thick-wall pushrod on the right.

These are adjustable pushrod checkers used to confirm proper valvetrain geometry. Adjust to where the rocker arm tip is centered on the valve stem with the valve closed. Tip travel should always be centered on the valve stem.

how to get more. The most basic reason for degreeing a camshaft is to determine that you have the correct grind for the job and that your cam matches the card. Camshaft grinders today employ the most advanced technology available. As a result, very few faulty camshafts ever make it to the consumer. However, camshafts do get mispackaged and improperly ground at times, which means you could receive a completely different grind than appears on the cam card and packaging. This is why you should fact check during cam installation.

When you degree a camshaft, you're determining valve timing events as they relate to crankshaft position. The crankshaft makes two complete revolutions for every one revolution of the camshaft. One full revolution of each is 360 degrees. This means the crank turns 720 degrees and the cam turns 360 degrees. Think of rotation as a pie. A half a turn is 180 degrees. A quarter of a turn is 90 degrees.

Duration is the number of degrees of rotation the camshaft will make from the time the valve begins to open until the time it closes. When you see 244 degrees of duration, this means 244 degrees of camshaft rotation from valve unseat to valve seat. Overlap or lobe separation is the number of degrees between maximum valve lift intake and maximum valve lift exhaust. With all this in mind, you can degree the camshaft timing events in time with piston travel.

You degree a camshaft by bolting a degree wheel to the crankshaft, cranking the number-1 piston to TDC, finding true TDC, and installing a timing pointer. You can get a degree wheel (#SUM-G-1057) kit from Summit Racing Equipment.

You find TDC with a Summit bolt-on piston stop (#SUM-900188) that bolts to the deck or screws into the spark plug hole (#SUM-900189). I suggest doing this with the cylinder head removed, which provides the greatest accuracy because you want true TDC. Begin this process by turning the crankshaft clockwise until the number-1 piston comes up to TDC and you are smack in the middle of crank rollover with the rod at 12 o'clock. With the cylinder head installed, hold your thumb over the spark plug hole and listen to the air being forced out by the piston.

At this point, both timing marks on the crank and camshaft sprockets should be in perfect alignment at 12 and 6 o'clock. Install the degree wheel next and align the bolt-on timing pointer. With all of this accomplished, the number-1 piston should be at TDC, with the degree wheel and pointer at zero degrees. This is what's known as true TDC and becomes your base point of reference. Everything from here on out becomes BTDC or ATDC. The intake valve will open at a given number of degrees ATDC and close at a given number of degrees BTDC. The exhaust valve will open at a given number of degrees BTDC and close a given number of degrees ATDC.

Dual-roller timing sets are optimum for any high-performance application. They also reduce friction. If you're building a stone stocker, a standard timing set is all you're going to need.

Cam degreeing begins with getting piston number-1 at true TDC. Use the dial indicator to sense and measure piston movement. Rotate each side of perceived TDC to gauge piston movement. Slowly turn the crank each way until you achieve dead center via the dial indicator.

Timing Components

The aftermarket offers a wide variety of timing sets and belt drives for the big-block Ford. The choice tends to be simple depending upon what you want the engine to do. If you're building a stocker, a standard OEM-style set will be all you need. A dual-roller timing set reduces friction and makes valve timing more precise. You can run a dual roller with a stock 429/460. They wear better and reduce internal friction. If you're concerned about valve timing, opt for an adjustable timing set with an adjustable crank sprocket. There are also adjustable cam sprocket timing sets from a wide variety of sources.

Another option for avid racers is the belt drive. Jon Kaase Racing Engines offers at least four different options. Belt drives generate less friction, effectively dampen adverse harmonics before they reach the valvetrain, maintain precision valve timing, particularly at high engine speeds, and they're convenient when it comes to fast turnaround valve timing adjustments.

An adjustable drive-belt idler is included on the Innovators West drive to allow for precise adjustment of drive-belt tension. This is important when taking into consideration the production tolerances of new belts and the re-tensioning of used belts. A cam retaining plate is provided with two encased roller bearings: one between the camshaft and plate, and the other between the cam pulley and plate. Optional high-vacuum seals, alloy steel drive hub, and camshaft drive adapter are available.

Both Summit Racing Equipment and Comp Cams offer degree wheels in various sizes. If you're going to build your own 429/460, having a degree wheel, dial indicator, and a pointer is essential. This is Summit #SUM-G1056-16.

An adjustable timing set is a good investment if you're concerned about cam specs and valve timing. You can advance or retard valve timing as needs warrant. Compare the cam card to your findings.

This is the Innovators West belt-drive from Jon Kaase Racing Engines engineered specifically for the big-block Ford. (Photo Courtesy Jon Kaase Racing Engines)

Grab power any way you can get it via friction reducers, such as a fully rollerized valvetrain. This is a cam thrust rolling bearing at the sprocket.

Lifters

Four basic lifter (tappet) types are used in 429/460 engines: flat-tappet hydraulic and mechanical, and roller hydraulic and mechanical. Flat-tappet lifters were original equipment in all 385-series engines. Roller tappets found use more and more in Ford factory V-8 engines after 1985, which is when the aftermarket got involved. More and more engine builds are witnessing the use of roller tappets because there's less friction, smoother operation, and the ability to run a more aggressive profile without the drawbacks of a radical flat-tappet camshaft.

Roller tappets are more costly than flat tappets due to tighter tolerances and a greater number of parts. Their cost puts them outside of the budget engine category, but they're worth every penny in what they save in wear and tear. They also give you the advantage if your desire is to run a more aggressive camshaft profile.

Although hydraulic lifters saw more widespread use beginning in the 1960s, their use dates back to the 1920s. Hydraulic lifters don't require periodic adjustment as a mechanical or solid lifter does. As the camshaft and valvetrain wear, hydraulic lifters expand with the wear via oil pressure to take up clearance. This keeps operation quiet and reliability sound.

Lifter and cam lobe wear and failure, are rarely caused by a manufacturing defect. They fail because you don't give them a good start when it's time to fire the engine in the first place. Flat-tappet camshafts must be broken-in properly or failure is inevitable. Molybdenum lube must be applied to the cam lobe and lifter face. The engine must then be operated at 2,500 rpm for 20 to 30 minutes after the initial fire-up to properly wear in the lobes. You must also use ZDDP zinc additive in the oil for proper break-in.

Roller tappets don't require break-in because rollers and cam lobes enjoy a good low-friction relationship to begin with. Flat-tappet mechanical camshafts are good for high-revving engines where the inaccuracies of hydraulic camshafts (lifter collapse) are unacceptable. Mechanical camshafts give you accuracy because there's nothing left to chance. Lift moves with the cam lobe with solid precision. Given proper valve lash adjustment, mechanical lifters do the job very well. Thing is, mechanical flat and roller tappets have to be adjusted periodically, which can be annoying on a daily-driven street engine. This is where you will need to do some soul searching before selecting a camshaft.

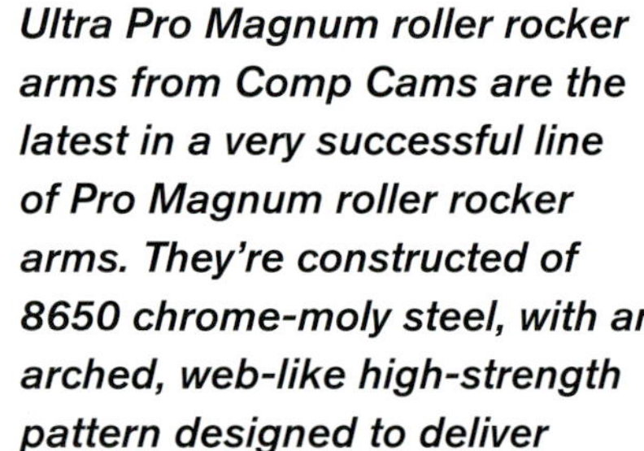

Ultra Pro Magnum roller rocker arms from Comp Cams are the latest in a very successful line of Pro Magnum roller rocker arms. They're constructed of 8650 chrome-moly steel, with an arched, web-like high-strength pattern designed to deliver increased strength and rigidity. Their unique black oxide exterior finish helps prevent corrosion and increases durability. (Photo Courtesy Comp Cams)

The aftermarket is a wealth of familiar time-proven roller rocker arms for a variety of applications. Rocker arm ratio is valve lift-to-cam lobe lift. If you have a 1.6:1 rocker ratio, you're taking lobe lift and multiplying it 1.6 times. If you want to increase valve lift, opt for 1.7:1. Check valve-to-piston clearances first. (Photo Courtesy Crane Cams)

Trick Flow rockers have been employed on a number of projects, and I've never been disappointed. They feature heat-treated CNC-machined rockers, premium needle-bearing fulcrums, roller tips, and a machined relief for improved valve spring clearance. Best of all, you can buy one or a complete set.

If you have the budget, this is how you build a valvetrain. Jesel Sportsman Series rocker kits will bolt onto any cylinder head without modifications and still fit under a stock 429/460 valve cover. Jesel valvetrain components stay adjusted and offer a precision fit.

A 429 Super Cobra Jet head with factory screw-in studs, guide plates, and Crane Classic roller rockers. All moving parts have been dressed with engine assembly lube.

You can take a standard 429/460 head and ditch the bolt/fulcrum or positive-stop rocker arm configuration with Manley screw-in rocker arm studs and guide plates. This makes your valvetrain fully adjustable and solid.

Valve adjustment can be approached in several ways with the 385-series engines. This Super Cobra Jet gets its valve lash adjusted with a thickness gauge because it is fitted with mechanical tappets. With hydraulic tappets, adjustment can be with an adjustable rocker stud, positive stop, or bolt/fulcrum. The latter two are adjusted by confirming pushrod length and lifter compression.

Rocker Arms and Pushrods

The pushrod and rocker arm transfer the cam lobe's energy to the valve stem. Think of the rocker arm as the camshaft's messenger because the rocker arm multiplies lift, which makes the valve open farther than the camshaft's lobe lift. Rocker arm types range from stock cast affairs all the way up to extruded and forged pieces with roller bearings and tips. Forged or extruded roller rocker arms are quite costly, which generally leaves them out of a budget engine program. However, this doesn't mean you have to settle for stock cast or stamped steel pieces either.

Stock cast or stamped steel rocker arms don't perform well under the heavy demands of radical camshaft profiles. An aggressive camshaft profile will break a stock rocker arm. This is why it is always best to err on the side of heavy-duty whenever you're building an engine. Stamped steel, ball-stud, roller tip rocker arms are a good first step toward valvetrain durability whenever you opt for an aggressive camshaft. The roller tip reduces the stress you experience with stock rocker arms. Thing is, when you increase lift and valve spring pressures, a stamped steel or cast roller tip rocker arm doesn't always stand up to the test, especially when spring pressures climb to more than 350 pounds. Even the best stamped steel, roller tip rocker arm will fail when overstressed.

When lift and spring pressures go skyward, you're going to want a roller pivot, roller tip forged rocker arm for your budget engine build. Going that extra mile with a super-durable rocker arm ensures longer engine life, especially if you're going to drive it daily. For the weekend racer, stepping up to a better rocker arm is like writing a life insurance policy because marginal rocker arms will not stand up to the high-revving task. Roller pivot, roller tip rocker arms also ensure valvetrain precision and accuracy when the revs get high.

I suggest looking to Crane Cams, Comp Cams, or Ford Racing for your rocker arms and pushrods. These companies have a lot of valuable experience with valvetrain components and offer wide selection. A good rule of thumb is to run the same brand of rocker arm and camshaft. See your favorite camshaft company or speed shop for more details.

When it comes to valvetrain adjustment, 385-series engines have flexibility in adjustable aftermarket studs where adjustable studs were not originally used. From 1968 to 1977, 385-series engines received no-adjust positive-stop rocker arm studs, which are undesirable for the performance buff. From 1978 to the present, the rocker arm stud was replaced with a new-design stamped steel rocker arm, fulcrum, and bolt that mount atop a boss much like the small-block Fords have in the years since. The exception to all of this was the screw-in stud and adjustable rocker arm employed on the Cobra Jet and Super Cobra Jet 429 engines in 1970–1971. Only the Super Cobra Jet had adjustable mechanical tappets.

Valvetrain Geometry

It is important that you confirm proper valvetrain geometry first, which is the centering of the rocker arm tip on the valve stem tip when you're doing valvetrain setup. This happens by using the correct-length pushrod for your application. Purchase a Comp Cams pushrod checker at your favorite speed shop if ever you're in doubt, and use it to properly configure your 385's rocker arm tip-to-stem geometry.

A pushrod checker is little more than an adjustable pushrod that you can use to confirm rocker arm geometry. If the pushrod is too long, the tip will be under-centered on the valve stem, causing excessive side loads toward the outside of the cylinder head. If the pushrod is too short, the rocker arm tip will be over-centered, causing excessive side loading toward the inside of the head. In either case, side loads on the valve stem and guide cause excessive wear and early failure. This is why you want the rocker arm tip to be properly centered on the valve stem for smooth operation.

One accessory that will reduce valve stem tip wear and side loading is the roller tip rocker arm. Roller tip rocker arms roll smoothly across the valve stem tip, virtually eliminating wear because there's little internal friction. Stamped steel roller tip rocker arms are available at budget prices without the high cost of extruded or forged pieces.

Rocker-Arm Adjustment

If you're building a bolt/fulcrum rocker 429/460, there is no valve lash adjustment. Tighten the fulcrum to the proper torque specifications and that's the end of it. If you have valve lash issues with a bolt/fulcrum rocker pivot, adjustment sometimes calls for pushrods of varying lengths to get lash into proper adjustment. If you have a noisy rocker arm, confirm the lifter status before doing anything else. A collapsed lifter will cause excessive rocker arm noise due to excessive lash. Ford says to allow 5 to 55 seconds of lifter leakdown time. A damaged or excessively worn rocker arm can make noise. So will a damaged or excessively worn fulcrum. Ford suggests a 0.060-inch-longer pushrod to help take up excessive clearance. Again, use a pushrod checker.

Most of you will opt for an adjustable stud-mounted rocker arm with mechanical or hydraulic tappets. There's endless discussion about how to adjust valve lash with hydraulic lifter engines with stud-mounted rocker arms. Hydraulic lifter plungers have a limited amount of travel or preload, 0.020 to 0.060 inch at the most. On top, that means approximately 1/4 to 3/4 turn at the rocker arm adjustment.

Everyone has their own approach to valve lash adjustment with hydraulic lifters. Here's one approach I picked up from a prominent California engine builder. Begin with the first cylinder on each bank and work your way aft one cylinder at a time. This way, you won't miss any. Valve adjustment is best taken one cylinder at a time with the cam lobe on the base circle of the valve you are adjusting. Twirl the pushrod with your fingertips while slowly tightening the rocker arm adjustment nut. When the pushrod becomes harder to turn with your fingertips, you are at zero valve lash and the lifter is not compressed.

When the intake valve is almost closed, adjust exhaust valve lash. When the exhaust valve begins to open, adjust intake valve lash. This ensures the valve you are adjusting is fully closed and you are on the base circle of the cam lobe. How you intend to use the engine determines valve lash. High-revving engines should get zero lash or 1/8 to 1/4 turn once you hit zero lash. This allows room should the lifter pump up at high RPM. Daily drivers and weekend cruisers can go as much as 1/2 turn. My personal approach to valve lash is no more than 1/4 turn. I have also seen engines that will tolerate only zero valve lash. Anything more and you will experience misfire and roughness because the valve (or valves) is not seating.

You won't know if you've been successful at valve lash adjustment until you fire the engine and it's at operating temperature. If you have significant rocker arm chatter, there's excessive lash. If there's roughness, valve lash is too tight. Some aftermarket rocker arms, such as the Comp Cams Pro Magnum or Ultra Pro Magnum, make a soft clicking sound on a par with what you would hear with mechanical tappets, which makes a 429/460 sound more like it has mechanical tappets but is of no consequence.

Proper valve adjustment is crucial to both performance and durability. A valve that doesn't seat properly from a tight lash adjustment will ultimately burn and fail. Valves need contact with the seat not only for the obvious (compression) but also for heat transfer to the seat and water jacket. According to Lunati Cams, valve lash for the 429/460 with a flat-tappet mechanical cam is 0.024/0.026-inch intake/exhaust. The same could be said for a mechanical roller.

When you're checking pushrod length, you want the rocker arm tip to be close to center on the valve stem tip and dead center with the valve fully open. Remember, the rocker arm tip is going to walk across the valve stem tip when you come up on the high side of the cam lobe. Take a black felt-tip marker and darken the valve stem tip. Then, install the rocker arm and pushrod. Hand-crank the engine and watch the valve pass through one full opening and closing. Get down alongside the rocker arm and valve spring and watch how the rocker arm travels. Then, inspect the black marking for a wear pattern. This will show you exactly where the rocker arm tip has traveled across the valve stem tip. The pattern should be centered on the valve stem tip. If it runs too much toward the outside of the valve stem tip, the pushrod is too short. If it runs toward the inside of the valve stem tip, the pushrod is too long.

INDUCTION

Aside from camshafts and cylinder heads, few things affect performance more than induction, which begins with carburetion. There are two basic types of performance carburetors from which to choose: Holley and Carter AFB/AVS-based carburetors.

Edelbrock has taken the time-proven Carter AFB/AVS and refined it to being the best the AFB/AVS has ever been. The beauty of the AFB/AVS is serviceability. You can remove the air horn and not spill one drop of fuel. Jet and metering rod swaps are easy. Most AFB/AVS issues can be solved on the engine.

Holley has been the heart and soul of racing and street performance for six decades, which is one heck of a track record for any performance product. Performance buffs search high and low for dusty old vintage Holley carburetors. I personally admit to being partial to the older Holley castings from the 1960s and 1970s because they are more predictable and of better quality. However, these old castings are also a crapshoot because they shift and also become clogged with debris. Take your chances at the swap meets and online auctions. Most of the time, you will be delighted with the find.

What makes Holley performance carburetors so appealing is service and tunability. Jet, power valve, and metering block swaps are easy but, admittedly, messy at times because you must remove the fuel bowls. Accelerator pump adjustment is simple. Vacuum and mechanical secondary dial-in takes a little practice. Tuning a Holley carburetor takes a lot of practice yet becomes second nature in due course.

The popular Holley 1850/4150/4160 has been atomizing fuel and air since 1957 when Ford used it for its high-performance 312-ci Y-block V-8 to replace the problematic Teapot "Fire Box" carburetor. The reinvented Holley was a simple, easy-to-tune 4-barrel carburetor. In fact, it was so versatile that it became the most popular performance carburetor in history. What's more, Holley continues to sell a bunch of them today with no end in sight.

There are also Ford's own carburetors, which in the 28 years of 385 production aren't much to talk about. All 420/460 engines were

The Autolite/Motorcraft 4300 4-barrel carburetor was more of an emissions carburetor than it was a performance carburetor. When it was introduced in 1967, it was just 441 cfm (not nearly enough for a 429/460). Ford enlarged it to 600 cfm in 1968.

GM's Rochester Quadrajet was the standard carburetor for the 429/460 engines in the early 1970s. If you're shopping for a Ford Quadrajet, don't get it mixed up with the GM version, which is an easy mistake to make, even though it is different than the Ford. Look for the Ford-style fuel filter, which employs a hose (not a hard line).

This is the GM Rochester Quadrajet. Note the integral fuel filter, which is located in the inlet and hard-lined from the fuel pump.

equipped with Autolite/Motorcraft 2100-series 2-barrel carburetors, the 4300/4150 4-barrel, or the Rochester Quadrajet.

The 2100/2150 has always been a reliable carburetor; however, it is in no way a performance carburetor. The 4100, which was never offered on the 429/460 and discontinued in 1966, is a solid and reliable 4-barrel carburetor. However, at a maximum of 600 cfm, it's just not enough carburetor for the 429/460. The 4300 was designed from scratch with a focus on emissions reduction and was never really intended to be a performance carburetor.

The 4300/4150, introduced in 1967, has always struggled with drivability problems: surging, hesitation, and flat spots. At first, the only size available was an engine-choking 441 cfm; then, later, it was 600 cfm. The late Jon Enyeart of Pony Carburetors knew and understood the 4300 and 4300D carburetors. Despite their poor reputation for performance, Jon always knew how to get them working properly. But, unless you're building a concours-restored stone stocker, the 4300 should never be a consideration because they're too problematic.

Carburetor Selection

It is easy to buy into believing that a larger carburetor, more aggressive camshaft, and large-port heads will make more power, but this isn't always true. Sometimes, you can have too much carburetor. Induction, camshaft, and heads should always sync with your driving agenda. If you're building a driver, you're going to have to compromise to some degree in terms of performance if you want reliability and some level of fuel economy. Few people want a "rumpity-rump-rump" temperamental muscle car for their daily commute.

You compromise because radical engines don't do well for the commute or vacation trip. They also struggle to pass a smog check depending on where you live. Radical camshaft profiles give the engine a rough idle, which can be frustrating in traffic and make it virtually impossible to pass a smog check. A high-compression ratio can cause overheating when traffic comes to a stop. It can also cause destructive spark knock and detonation. Too much carburetion fouls spark plugs and pollutes the air. Radical cams also produce low manifold vacuum at idle, making vacuum-assisted power brakes dangerous.

This brings me to another valid point: emissions. Environmentalists and performance enthusiasts don't get along very well, but it is your responsibility as a performance enthusiast to build and tune your engines for cleaner emissions where possible. I hear a collective big sigh out there, but it really does pay to run cleaner. This doesn't mean you have to go out and buy catalytic converters. It does mean you need to package your induction and ignition systems for cleaner emissions at the tailpipe.

You want carburetor size and driving agenda to be compatible for optimum performance and cleaner emissions. If you think this clean emissions thing is a lot of bunk, consider the last time you were behind a hopped-up vintage muscle car or street rod in traffic. The obnoxious exhaust gases high on hydrocarbon emissions made your eyes water. If your vehicle falls under the guidelines of state emission laws and smog checks, the law doesn't give you a choice. Clean up your exhaust emission or face revocation of your license plates in some states.

This is a common mistake: insufficient fuel line sizing. The 429/460 must have at least a 3/8-inch diameter from the fuel tank and pump. As power demands increase, so must fuel line diameter. Note the 5/16-inch-diameter fuel hose from the tank and the huge 1/2-inch line to the carburetor. This means we have 5/16 inch maximum, which is not enough.

Carburetor Size

Carburetor sizing boils down to this. A carburetor that's too small will become apparent quickly in the absence of power at high RPM. Large carburetors give you more torque on the high end. Smaller carburetors do well at low RPM because velocity translates to torque.

Carburetor sizing is something few of us get right. However, it is important to performance and durability. Before you can determine what size of carburetor you need, you have to know the maximum airflow your engine is going to require. This may seem to be a simple task, but it isn't. When you do the math of computing carburetor size, you've only scratched the surface. Then, you need to know how the engine will be used, the engine's operational window, and the number of cylinders. This is where it gets even trickier. According to author Dave Emanuel, you should use the following formula.

Flow Rating (cfm) at 3.0 in/Hg ÷ 1.414 =
Flow (cfm) at 1.5 in/Hg

Flow Rating (cfm) at 1.5 in/Hg ÷ 1.414 =
Flow (cfm) at 3.0 in/Hg

These formulas are based on presumed maximum vacuum attainable under load at wide-open throttle, according to Emanuel. In theory, an engine won't realize manifold vacuum of more than 1.5 in/Hg with a 4-barrel carburetor, nor more than 3.0 in/Hg with a 2-barrel carburetor. Let's face it, carburetor manufacturers and car magazines can suggest carburetor sizing based on loose information. However, each and every engine is different even if both are identically equipped.

Carburetor airflow ratings don't always match how much a given carburetor will flow. That said, carburetor sizing guidelines aren't always absolute but instead are suggestions to get you close. Sizing also depends on displacement and volumetric efficiency according to Emanuel. It also depends on vehicle type, weight, and size not to mention transmission gearing and axle ratio. Let's keep it simple. You want to know what your big-block's maximum RPM range will be coupled with where it's going to be, RPM-wise, most of the time.

Try this basic formula and see how it fits your plan.

460 ci x 6,500 rpm ÷ 3,456 =
865 cfm

This means your average high-performance street big-block needs 850 cfm. It is when you get into high RPM and greater displacement, the more you need CFM, a larger carburetor. Let's say you're working with a 460 and it is going to make most of its power in the form of torque between 2,000 and 5,000 rpm. You're not going to need much more than 750 to 850 cfm. If you're going to take your 460 above 6,000, you're talking 850 cfm.

When you get on the dyno, you start thinking of air/fuel ratio and volumetric efficiency (VE). Volumetric efficiency is the percentage of the theoretical maximum amount of air and fuel you can draw into an engine during two complete crankshaft revolutions. What does this really mean? It means if you take a 460-ci engine and turn the crank two revolutions, you should get 460 ci of air. This doesn't happen in the real world. In fact, volumetric efficiency varies a lot throughout RPM ranges under load in dyno testing.

It is true most engines experience a VE number of 70 to 80 percent at maximum engine speed. Racing engines at high revs average 85- to 90-percent VE. If you're really on top of your game as an engine builder and tuner, you can achieve 90 to 110 percent at high RPM with a racing engine.

To figure potential VE numbers, here's the math.

460 ci x 6,500 rpm =
2600000 ÷ 3456 =
865.16 x 1.1 VE = 951.678

In theory, a 900- or 950-cfm carburetor would be the right size; however, there are other variables you experience in the real world that either raise or lower this number. Header tube size and length, collector size, exhaust pipe size, intake manifold type, cylinder heads, ambient temperature and humidity, engine temperature are just a few.

I can sit here and tell you all day via math formulas what you can expect when it's time to load your 460 on a dyno. However, absolute truth happens when you spin that engine and place it under a load. If you're operating under hot conditions, these math formulas don't mean anything because you will undoubtedly experience disappointing numbers. At high elevations, they mean even less because you haven't considered these elements.

Keep proper carburetor jetting in mind too. Jets that are too large will make the engine run rich or "fat," watering the eyes of those who have to follow you. Jets that are too small can be harmful if you're leaning on it hard, and lean detonation burns a hole in a piston. Again, fine-tune the carburetor and size the jets for best results. Always err on the side of slightly rich versus lean for longer engine life.

If you really want to make a lasting impression on the community, go for a smog sniffer each time you make a carb/jet change and see what it does for emissions. A true measure of mixture is more wide-open throttle versus light throttle. Light to normal throttle doesn't give you an accurate measure of mixture.

Holley Carburetors

Holley was founded by George M. Holley and his brother Earl in 1899 as the Holley Brothers Company. By 1904, the Holley brothers were seriously in the carburetor business with the original Iron Pot 1-barrel carburetor. In time, Holley carburetors were original equipment on a wide variety of new automobiles, in particular Fords.

The Holley 4150 has been around since 1957. In 750- and 850-cfm sizes, it is a perfect fit for your street performance 429/460-ci big-block. Vacuum secondaries are better for the street because they cycle-in smoothly as needed. (Photo Courtesy Holley)

The Holley HP-series carburetors have been the racing standard for nearly two decades. Classic HP carburetors are available from 390 to 1,000 cfm. They feature a contoured venturi inlet for balanced airflow, screw-in air bleeds for precision tuning, high-flow metering blocks, and Dominator-style fuel bowls. (Photo Courtesy Holley)

Holley's first 4-barrel carburetor was the 2140 in 1953 on Lincolns, then the infamous 4000 Teapot firebox in 1955. It was nicknamed the "Firebox" because Holley placed the fuel bowl over the throttle bores. When an engine would backfire through the intake during a lean condition, it tended to set the fuel bowl on fire.

The traditional Holley 4150 twin-bowl 4-barrel performance carburetor dates back to 1957 when it was first installed on new Fords as original equipment. Holley's relationship with Ford is well documented because Holley was long Ford's choice for carburetion through the 1980s.

Most of you are probably going to go with an aftermarket intake manifold designed for the Holley 1850/4150/4160 square-flange carburetors or similar aftermarket replacements like the AFB and AVS. If you're going with Holley carburetion, you

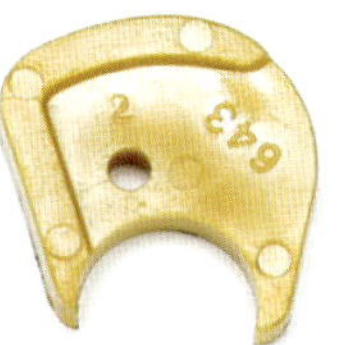

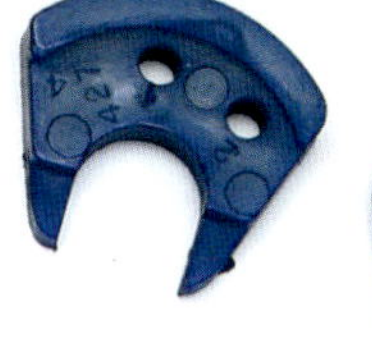

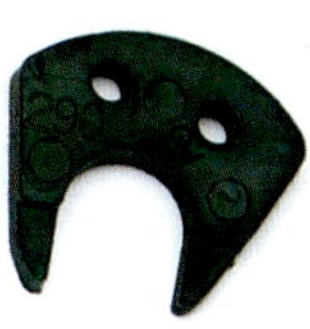
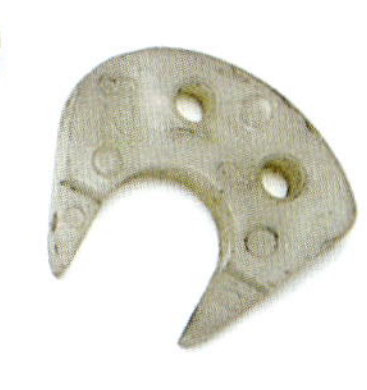

Keep an assortment of Holley accelerator pump cams on hand for carburetor tuning. They determine how much pump shot you're going to get.

If you're running a Holley carburetor, you need to keep an arsenal of parts on hand because you're going to need them. Keep a jet kit, a variety of secondary springs, gaskets, accelerator pump diaphragms and cams, power valves, and more odds and ends depending on the Holley you're running.

Holley makes light work of float adjustment, which is one reason these race-proven carburetors have sold so well for more than 60 years. You will want to arm yourself with a float sight glass, which eliminates fuel spillage.

The huge Holley dominator calls for a larger flange than the 1850/4150/4160 carburetors because it is strictly a racing carburetor. It has a contoured venturi inlet for balanced airflow and increased horsepower, screw-in air bleeds, and a high-flow metering system with race calibrations and annular boosters.

need to understand the differences. The 4150 carburetor has adjustable metering blocks for both primary and secondary circuits.

The 4160 carburetor has an adjustable primary metering block and a non-adjustable secondary metering plate. Single pumpers have a primary accelerator pump; double pumpers have both primary and secondary accelerator pumps.

Vacuum secondaries are found mostly on street performance Holleys, while mechanical secondaries are race oriented. Vacuum secondaries come into play as you lean on the throttle under hard acceleration. Mechanical secondaries open immediately with a wide-open throttle.

You will likely never see mechanical secondaries without a secondary accelerator pump. Vacuum secondary operation depends on spring pressure and intake manifold vacuum at wide-open throttle. Too much spring pressure and your secondaries will loaf or not open at all. Too little and they will open too quickly, causing a significant flat spot.

The 4150/4160 carburetors have undergone a lot of changes since the 1950s and 1960s. Each has been offered as original equipment on a variety of factory high-performance engines including Ford. When you're searching for a good used period Holley 4150/4160 from the good old days, it pays to know what you have in your hands. Swap meets are loaded with all kinds of 4150/4160 carburetors from Holley's good old days. Recommended reading is David Vizard's *How to Super Tune and Modify Holley Carburetors* from CarTech Books, which covers these legendary atomizers in great detail. Another terrific Holley book is Mike Mavrigian's *Holley Carburetors: How to Rebuild*, also from CarTech Books.

The anatomy of the Edelbrock carburetor demonstrates just how easy they are to service whether you're in the garage on a Saturday or at the track looking to improve the tune. Metering rods and swappable jets make tuning a snap and do so without spilling fuel. Available sizes range from 500 to 800 cfm.

Edelbrock Carburetors

Edelbrock carburetors are based on the time-proven, easy-to-tune Carter AFB and AVS. These carburetors perform well in street/strip applica-

The Edelbrock 1407 Performer Series 750-cfm manual choke carburetor is a proven unit that can handle the rigors of daily driving while delivering consistent, reliable street performance from day to day. You can commute with it and you can race with it. Metering rods are utilized to transition between circuits instead of a power valve. The Performer has the unique ability to hold a tune.

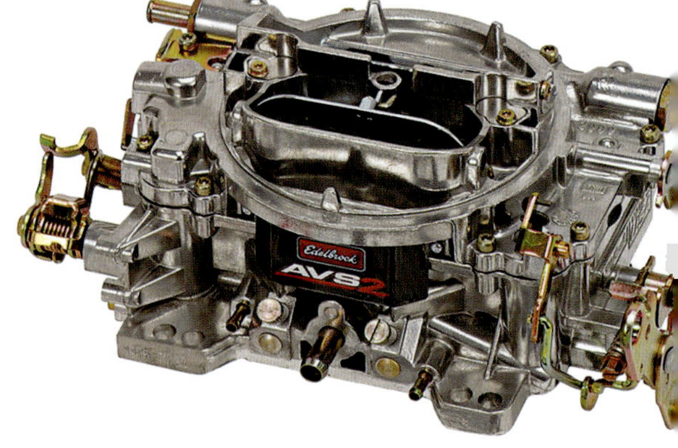

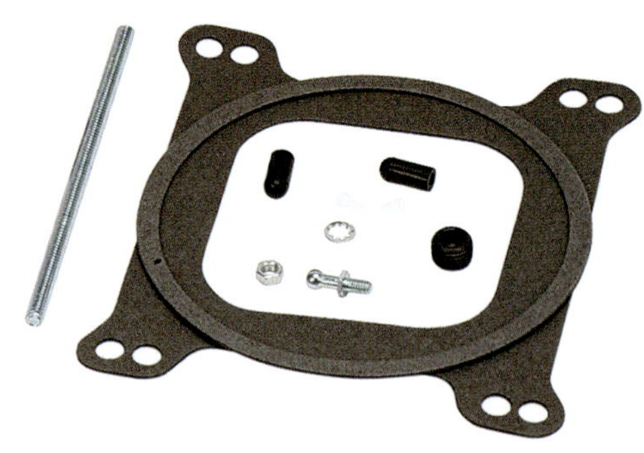

Edelbrock's Annular Flow Booster technology gives you superior fuel atomization for any 429/460 with the AVS2 800-cfm Manual Choke Carburetor. Fuel distribution is refined by eight equally spaced orifices in the booster rings that replace down-leg boosters. This means no flat spots. The real beauty of these Edelbrock carburetors is that they're easy to service and tune, and without fuel spillage.

tions along with Edelbrock's own performance intake manifolds. Edelbrock carburetors function with metering rods and jets like the classic Carters do. There are two basic types of Edelbrock carburetors: the Performer Series and the Thunder AVS Series. Sizing ranges from 500 to 850 cfm.

Because these are Carter-based designs, they're among the easiest carburetors to tune on an engine. The 1400 Performer Series carburetor with electric choke is a good, reliable street performance carburetor in day-to-day driving because it tolerates today's fuels. Metering rods deliver that transition between idle and power circuits. What's more, metering rods can be changed in minutes. The Performer has the unique ability to hold a tune. You're not constantly underhood making adjustments.

Edelbrock's Thunder AVS allows for a smooth transition from primary to wide-open throttle thanks to the Qwik-Tune vacuum secondary air valve, which delivers more precise throttle response. Primary and secondary booster clusters offer the most accurate and up-to-date calibration available for today's persnickety fuels and lame octane levels.

The fuel sender/pickup can be no smaller than 3/8 inch for the 429/460. If you're running big power, you're going to need larger.

Not only must fuel line size meet the demand, so must the fuel pump. Fuel pump capacity and line size must be able to keep up with demand, being able to deliver enough fuel for the amount of power expected. A good rule to follow is if your fuel pump flows at 50 gph it should be able to feed a 500-hp engine.

Carter Carburetors

The Carter AFB and AVS 4-barrel carburetors have also been around since 1957. The AFB and AVS were not only original equipment in a lot of automobiles but they also became something of a performance standard for racers and street enthusiasts alike, much as the Holley did. Carter Carburetor has been gone since 1985; however, there are untold millions of Carter AFB and AVS carburetors everywhere. They remain very popular.

Chrysler and GM employed the AFB/AVS on a lot of vintage muscle cars, but Ford never did (with Lincoln being the only exception). That doesn't mean you can't run it on your 429/460. The appeal of the AFB and AVS is how easy they are to service and tune on the engine. Like the popular Edelbrock Performer and Thunder AVS Series carburetors, the Carter AFB/AVS carburetors work on metering rods and jets for

Carburetor spacers are an interesting study because they can make a difference in power. Start with a 1-inch spacer and see what it does for power.

ease of tuning. There's no concern about fuel spillage when service is performed because these carburetors are like a bathtub. You can swap jets and metering rods without spilling a drop. There's also no power valve to sweat out either.

Federal-Mogul acquired Carter Carburetor in 1986 and manufactured the AFB and AVS along with other popular Carter models. That continued until 2013 when Carter was sold to a private equity firm. In 2018, Carter was acquired by Trico.

Demon Carburetors

Demon Carburetors, a division of Holley, remains uniquely Demon with a wide variety of performance carburetors for a broad spectrum of budgets. Street Demons and Road Demons are both Holley- and Carter-based atomizers in terms of design but are actually quite different in terms of performance and function.

The Street Demon, architecturally, is Carter based and available in 625- and 750-cfm sizes. The Road Demon is Holley based and available in 650- and 750-cfm sizes. All have suitable Ford throttle and kickdown linkages and are among the easiest carburetors to tune.

The Screamin' Demon, Mighty Demon, and Speed Demon kick it up a couple of notches in terms of performance. Holley says these race-oriented Demon carburetors are available in a wide range of sizes and options for a street/strip car. You get a billet-aluminum metering block, billet-aluminum baseplates, large-capacity fuel bowls complete with dual-sight glasses, dual-threaded inlets on each side, and internal baffling to prevent fuel slosh when you are on the track. All-aluminum polished construction with billet metering blocks and base plate makes them 40 percent lighter than the original Demons. Secondary fuel bowls include notched floats and jet extensions to prevent fuel starvation during hard launches

Quick Fuel Technology

Quick Fuel, also a division of Holley, are simply great carburetors. You never have to wonder if they're okay out of the box because they are factory tested. Quick Fuel's Slayer series of street carburetors sport changeable air bleeds and power valve channel restrictions. It is fully tunable with a secondary metering block with swappable jets and all-aluminum construction for weight savings.

What I like about Slayer carburetors is fitment. They are equipped with universal throttle linkages to accommodate Ford mechanically-modulated automatic transmission kickdown linkages. Slayer carburetors are available in 450-, 600-, and 750-cfm vacuum-secondary models.

The Hot Rod (HR) Series QFT carburetor is another truly versatile performer for a broad spectrum of engines with lightweight die-cast aluminum components, tunability you might expect from more expensive racing carburetors, including changeable bleeds, idle feed, power valve channel restrictions, and four-corner idle adjustment.

This is an older Speed Demon carburetor with automatic choke and vacuum secondaries, which is a good street/strip carburetor. The Speed Demon line offers a wide range of sizes with vacuum and mechanical secondaries. Expect to see a range of sizes from 650 cfm to 850 cfm.

Weber Carburetors

I almost forgot about this carburetor because it isn't necessarily mainstream, especially with 385-series engines. The Weber IDA, IDF, and DCOE carburetors have seen use on everything from Ferraris to Volkswagens. For one thing, these are good-looking twin-bore carburetors that have experienced great success as performance pieces around the world. However, they are not for everyone. You must know what you're doing, otherwise you can count on a frustrating experience trying to tune them. Webers do not come cheap nor do the intake manifolds that support them.

Exotic Weber carburetion elevates the cool factor. Blue Thunder makes the 429/460 manifold to accommodate the IDA Webers.

The aftermarket offers a wealth of bolt-in retro electronic fuel injection systems ranging from simple throttle-body systems to port injection. Holley's Sniper EFI is available as a bolt-on throttle body for your carbureted 429/460. It hides nicely beneath the air cleaner or you can show it off with an open-element air cleaner.

The beauty of Webers is how well they mix fuel and air before it all reaches the venturi. Another positive is how tunable the Weber is with a wide variety of jets and venturis available to get it right where you want it. Although the Weber really is a racing carburetor, it can be operated on the street. It has never been a practical carburetor for street use and is quite temperamental.

Weber caught the close attention of the late Carroll Shelby, who decided to place a quartet of these carburetors on top of Ford's 260-ci V-8 in the early 1960s, giving Ford's small-block a 30-hp advantage. Since that time, Webers have seen widespread use on most Ford V-8s. The nice thing about the Weber is air/fuel distribution because each bore has its own bore (or eight throttle bores for eight cylinders) offering perfect fuel distribution.

The Weber carburetor works much the same way as any carburetor with a float bowl and main metering jets. Once fuel passes through jets, it then passes through emulsifier tubes where it is mixed with air and atomized into the venturi. At this point it passes through the throttle bore. There is an idle circuit function when throttle plates are closed.

Weber carburetors do not have a choke but instead have a fuel enrichment system that functions when the engine is cold. Like most carburetors, Weber have an accelerator pump, which sprays raw fuel into the throttle bore when the throttle is advanced. The trick with Webers is getting them in sync with each other.

Bolt-On EFI

Retro bolt-on throttle-body electronic fuel injection (EFI) has been quite the evolution and for a long time. It has had its share of issues and frustrated a lot of enthusiasts. It has taken manufacturers decades to perfect this process. All of the fuel and ignition system players have been involved: Edelbrock, Holley, F.A.S.T., Summit Racing, FiTech, and MSD. The result has been incredible bolt-on, self-tuning EFI systems that have made it easier to shelve your carburetor.

The beauty of bolt-on EFI is ease of installation and operation once you get it up and running. Once it's running, it is always a good idea to see a professional tuner to get both spark and fuel curves on the beam. Once your engine is in proper tune, you can enjoy twisting the key for an instant cold start.

Which system you choose is a matter of personal choice. I've had great personal success with Holley Sniper and the FiTech systems, which are similar and easy to work with. Summit's Max-EFI system is an easy bolt-on and self-learning.

These retro systems are excellent for street and strip. What makes them great for the commute and a weekend getaway is ease of operation. There's no warmup or a choke to sweat out. If you're embarrassed by EFI, don't be. It hides beneath the

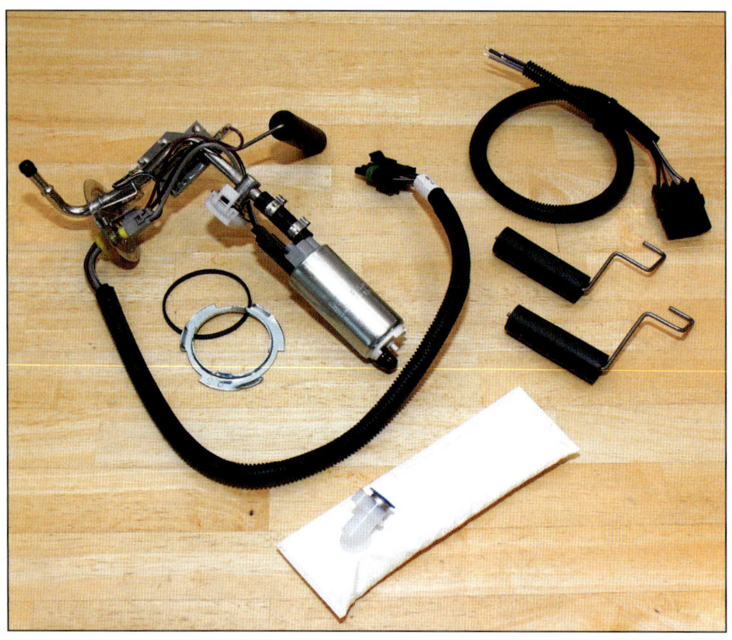

Holley offers fuel delivery options from inline external pumps to easy-to-install non-return in-tank sender/pump systems. This in-tank Sniper EFI in-tank system combines both the pump and sender and you don't have to worry about a return line.

Here's an external inline EFI pump system on a classic Mustang that's easy to access and service.

It is always best to hard-line the fuel system and keep hose usage to a minimum. Today's fuels have harsh additives that are hard on fuel system soft parts. Opt for hard lines and/or braided stainless fuel system hoses in the interest of safety.

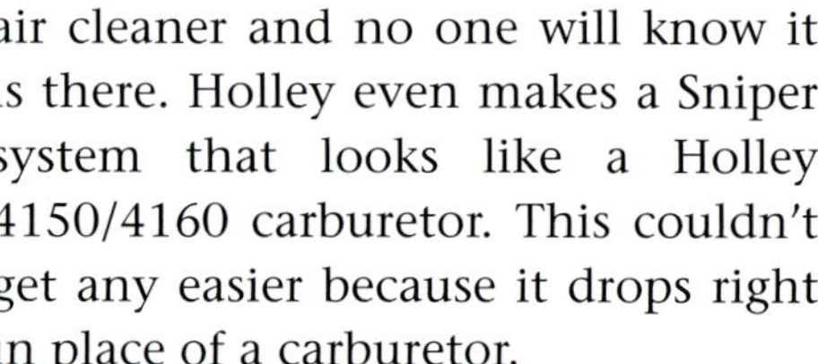

air cleaner and no one will know it is there. Holley even makes a Sniper system that looks like a Holley 4150/4160 carburetor. This couldn't get any easier because it drops right in place of a carburetor.

Bolt-on EFI does require a support system, the oxygen sensor in your exhaust system, coolant temperature sensor, power sources, electric fuel pump, and your patience. You will find as you install this system that it's easy to do and will pay dividends in ease of use.

Intake Manifold

The 429/460 induction story is a simple one sporting the Autolite/Motorcraft 2100/2150 2-barrel carburetor with huge 1.230-inch throttle bores for grocery getters. With 4-barrel carburetion, the 429 was equipped with the 605-cfm Autolite/Motorcraft 4300. It was never fitted with the Autolite shoebox 4100. Later on, it was fitted with the emissions 4350 spread-bore carburetor. There was also the 4300D, a spread-bore carburetor specifically for the Boss 351 in 1971 only. There's no legitimate reason to even consider any of the 4300/4350 carburetors for your 429/460 project. They are in no way considered performance carburetors.

When it comes to factory iron intake manifolds for the 385-series engines, there were two basic 4-barrel manifolds: the Holley square-flange and the Quadrajet flange. The spread-bore Quadrajet flange was short-lived in 1970–1971 for Ford-spec 715-cfm Quadrajet carburetors only.

Ford opted for the use of GM's Rochester Quadrajet carburetor due to tougher federal emission standards until it could get the Autolite/

Motorcraft 4300 dialed-in from an emissions and drivability standpoint. The 4300 was used on some Ford and Mercury Division 429 engines beginning in 1969. Quadrajet filled the gap for 1970–1971 until Ford went back to the 4300 in 1972 to meet tough federal emissions standards.

The 429 Cobra Jet available in 1970–1971 only was fitted with the 715-cfm Rochester Quadrajet. The uprated 780-cfm 429 Super Cobra Jet with mechanical tappets was fitted with the Holley 4150. The Boss 429 for 1969–1970 was fitted with a 780-cfm Holley 4150.

Where the 460 induction system changed dramatically was when Ford went to sequential electronic fuel injection (SEFI) in the late 1980s. None of them were passenger car applications because the 385-series big-block became for truck and van only at the end of the 1970s. The 460's SEFI induction package consists of a lower intake manifold set up for port injection coupled with an upper intake manifold and twin-bore throttle body. This induction system didn't change much in the course of production, which ended in the 1990s.

Common Ford 429/460 Intake Manifolds		
Model Year	**Ford Part/ Casting Number**	**Description**
1968–1969	C8SE-9425-B	Cast-iron 4V, square flange
1969	C9VE-9424-A	Cast-iron 4V, square flange
1969–up	C9XE-9424-G	Aluminum racing 4V; Dominator flange
1970	D0OE-9425-B	Cast-iron 4V, square flange; also super Cobra Jet
1970	D0OE-9425-C	Cast-iron 4V, square flange; also Super Cobra Jet
1970	D0OE-9425-D	Cast-iron 4V, spread bore; Quadrajet flange
1970	XE-152211	Cast Iron 4V, spread bore; Quadrajet flange (Experimental)
1970	D0VE-9425-B	Cast-iron 4V, square flange
1971	D1AE-9425-BA	Cast-iron 4V, spread bore; Quadrajet flange
1976	D6VE-9425-A3A	Cast-iron 4V, spread bore; Quadrajet flange
1987–1997	E7TE-9K501	Lower SEFI intake manifold
1987–1997	F2TZ-9E926-H	Twin-bore throttle body

This is the D0OE-9425-C iron intake for the Holley 4150/4160 square-flange carburetor.

Intake manifold selection depends on how you intend to use your big-block. The single plane is for high-RPM racing, dual plane is for street, and in between are some single-plane manifolds for the street. The single-plane Edelbrock Torker has never really been a street manifold nor has it ever been long on torque even at high RPM. The same can be said for Edelbrock's Streetmaster single-plane intake manifold. The Streetmaster has longer intake runners for mid-range torque and high-RPM operation. Low-end torque is still compromised with the Streetmaster. The dual plane remains the best choice for the street.

Yet, in my many experiences with intake manifolds and dyno rooms, there are the ironies. Single-plane intake manifolds with long runners have been proven to be successful on the dyno depending on camshaft and cylinder head selection. The Edelbrock Streetmaster is a single-plane manifold as previously stated. Yet it has yielded broad torque curves in dyno testing.

Dual-plane high-rise manifolds don't always have to be new ones either. Vintage Edelbrock, Weiand, and Offenhauser dual-plane high-rise manifolds yield the benefits of low-end torque and high-RPM breathability, and they can be found at swap meets all over the place. They do well on the street in stop-and-go driving, and they yield plenty of power when it's time to get it on.

Single-plane intake manifolds such as the Edelbrock Torker, Torker II, and Tarantula are not always good street manifolds because they're designed to make peak torque at 3,000 to 7,000 rpm, yet I see them on street engines where a good dual-plane manifold would work much better. The 429/460 yields great low- and mid-range torque by design thanks to good bore and stroke physics. They make a tremendous amount of torque no matter what you do with them.

Long intake runners and a dual-plane design are but two reasons why you can achieve good low- and mid-range torque from a carbureted engine. You also want cool air both ahead of the carburetor and beneath it. To get cool air before the carburetor, you need to source cool air from outside. Underhood air is much hotter than ambient air. If you can drop the intake air temperature by 50 to 80°F, this will make a considerable difference in thermal expansion inside the combustion chamber.

Cooler air comes from a hood scoop or a ram-air scoop at the leading edge of the vehicle. Ram air can be sourced through the radiator support or beneath the front bumper. Ram-air kits can be sourced from Summit Racing Equipment, Speedway, or your favorite speed shop. The choice is yours.

Getting cool air induction air after the carburetor takes closing off the manifold heat passages from the exhaust side of the cylinder head. Unless you use your big-block for a

The quickest way to identify Ford castings, such as this intake, is via the casting number and casting date code.

Rochester Quadrajet carburetors call for this spread-bore intake if you're doing a restoration. It also accommodates the Holley spread-bore carburetors. This particular intake has a Ford experimental casting number: XE-152211.

The Edelbrock Performer 460 dual-plane manifold is an excellent street/strip manifold. It enables the morning commute and weekend bracket racing to live peacefully side by side. (Photo Courtesy Edelbrock)

The Edelbrock Victor 460 single-plane intake manifold is engineered for the 429/460 competition engines with the factory cast-iron Cobra Jet, SVO Cobra-Jet aluminum (M-6049-A429), and Edelbrock 460 CJ aluminum heads. This is what you want for drag racing, marine use, or any application requiring high-RPM power up to 8,000 rpm. It does not fit 1988 and later 460 engines. (Photo Courtesy Edelbrock)

For street and weekend strip racing, the Edelbrock RPM Air-Gap 460 intake manifold is a terrific dual-plane manifold designed for square and spread-bore carburetors. What makes the Air-Gap design superior is an open-air space that separates the runners from the hot engine oil resulting in a cooler, denser charge for more power. The Air-Gap 460 will not fit 1988 and later model 460 engines. (Photo Courtesy Edelbrock)

Getting a good port match is the easiest form of porting there is. You want a nice blend between the intake manifold and cylinder heads for reduced turbulence and even distribution of the air/fuel mix.

The Weiand Stealth (part number 8012) dual-plane intake manifold is your classic dual-plane high-rise manifold with high-ceiling runners, which makes it suitable for street and strip action along with your choice of square-flange Holley, Edelbrock, Demon, and Quick-Fuel carburetors. (Photo Courtesy Holley/Weiand)

cold-weather commute, there's no need for manifold heat. To stop unproductive heat, install the manifold heat block-off plates included in most intake manifold gasket kits. Manifold heat is needed only when the outside air is cold. A cold-intake manifold does not allow the fuel to atomize as well as it does in a hot manifold, which causes hesitation and stumbling.

You want a low-restriction air cleaner that will effectively filter out dirt while allowing healthy breathing at the same time. K&N air filters meet the mission effectively, but they don't come cheap. They can be washed and reused, which actually saves you money in the long term because K&N claims these filters are expected to last a million miles. What's more, they outperform the nearest competitor by a wide margin. A K&N air filter is money well spent in terms of performance and longevity. The new K&N filter with a separate filter in the lid improves breathing even more. This isn't a paid product endorsement, but a fact proven many times and with untold thousands of users.

One of the biggest mistakes that enthusiasts make is having too much carburetion. It may surprise you to know that engines don't need as much carburetion as you might think. The formula is simple and without a lot of complex engine math. Over-carburetion on a street engine is a waste. It wastes fuel and it pollutes the air. Too much fuel can be as bad for an engine as not enough fuel. Too much fuel washes precious lubricating oil off the cylinder walls and fouls spark plugs. Your performance objective should also include being environmentally responsible. Plan and tune for cleaner air, not just power. Performance today has two parts: efficiency and power. With efficiency, you get power and cleaner air.

Popular 429/460 Aftermarket Intake Manifolds		
Manufacturer	**Part Number**	**Description**
Blue Thunder	IM-429CJ-4V	429/460 CJ high-rise 4V
Blue Thunder	IM-429CJ-4VC	429/460 CJ high-rise 4V; Competition
Blue Thunder	IM-429CJ-D	429/460 CJ high-rise; Dominator flange
Blue Thunder	IM-429S-D	429/460 Standard Port; high-rise; Dominator flange
Blue Thunder	IM-429-8V	429/460 8V high-rise
Blue Thunder	IM-429CJ-8V	429/460 8V CJ; Port matched
Blue Thunder	IM-429B-4V	Boss 429 4V; Reproduction
Blue Thunder	IM-429B-8V	Boss 429 8V; Reproduction
Blue Thunder	IM-429 CJ-I	429/460 race injection
Blue Thunder	IMW-429-S	429/460 IDA 8V straight
Blue Thunder	IMW-429-A	429/460 IDA 8V Angle
Edelbrock	7166	Performer RPM 460 (satin)
Edelbrock	71661	Performer RPM 460 (polished)
Edelbrock	7566	Air-Gap 460 (satin)
Edelbrock	75661	Air-Gap 460 (polished)
Edelbrock	5066	Torker II 460 (satin); Single Plane
Edelbrock	50661	Torker II 460 (polished); Single Plane
Edelbrock	50665	Victor 460 EFI; Needs 3645 fuel rail
Edelbrock	2966	Victor 460 (satin); Square flange
Edelbrock	29661	Victor 460 (polished); Square flange
Edelbrock	2965	Victor 460 (satin); Dominator flange
Edelbrock	29651	Victor 460 (polished); Dominator flange
Ford Performance	M-9424-C460	Single Plane 4V; Dominator Flange
Trick Flow	TFS-5340012	R-series single plane; Dominator flange
Trick Flow	TFS-55400111	R-series PowerPort; Single plane; Dominator flange
Trick Flow	TFS-53400111	Track heat; Single plane; Square bore
Weiand	8012	Stealth 4V dual plane
Weiand	8021	Stealth 4V dual plane

Quick Power

Nitrous oxide or "squeeze" is popular for those looking for quick and easy power (50 to 150 hp) on demand. It makes boatloads of power at the touch of a button. However, all this power at the touch of a button isn't free. Nitrous can be harmful to an engine that isn't properly prepped and tuned. It hammers rod bearings and piston rings. It can do extensive engine damage. It is also hard on main bearings.

No matter what the nitrous crowd tells you about "laughing gas," nitrous shortens engine life because power is not free. Don't be drawn into believing it's a magic horsepower pill without consequences. If you're going to be running nitrous oxide, be prepared for shorter engine life.

What is nitrous oxide and what does it do? Nitrous is a physics lesson in how to generate greater amounts of power from the air/fuel charge you introduce to the combustion chambers. Nitrous oxide is a very simple gas composed of two nitrogen atoms attached to one oxygen atom. Its chemical formula is N2O.

Contrary to what you may believe about N2O, it is not a poisonous gas nor is it harmful to the atmosphere. Because N2O is an asphyxiant, it can suffocate you if inhaled in heavy quantities. It would have a similar effect on you as carbon dioxide (CO2), called oxygen deprivation. Nitrous Oxide is available in three basic grades: medical, commercial, and high purity. The medical grade is what's commonly known as laughing gas used by dentists and surgeons. It has to be very pure for human consumption.

You must be licensed as a medical professional to get it. Commercial-grade nitrous oxide is used in engines for performance gains. High purity is also a medical-grade nitrous oxide that is extremely pure and priced and controlled accordingly.

Commercial-grade nitrous oxide is marketed as Nytrous+ and sold by the Puritan-Bennett Corporation. You can find it all across the country. It is a mix of 99.9-percent nitrous oxide and 0.01-percent sulfur dioxide. Puritan-Bennett adds the sulfur dioxide to give its N2O gas some odor just as you experience with natural gas.

When you buy nitrous oxide, it is pumped into a storage tank that you provide the supplier. You need an appropriate tank capable of holding at least 1,800 pounds per square inch (psi). To play it safe, your tank(s) must have a visible certification date within the past five years. Inside the tank, nitrous oxide exists in liquid form. As it leaves the tank, it becomes a gas. When it leaves the tank quickly, it leaves very cold, just like refrigerants and propane. To be a liquid, there has to be enough pressure inside the tank to turn the nitrous oxide into a liquid. Unpressurized, nitrous oxide exists as a gas. For nitrous oxide to become a liquid in an unpressurized environment, the ambient temperature has to be –127°F. At 70°F, nitrous oxide needs to be pressurized to 760 psi to become a liquid. Warm things up to 80°F and you need 865 psi to make nitrous oxide a liquid.

The use of nitrous oxide to make power is nothing new. In World War II, it was used to help aircraft engines make power. The principle then was much the same as it is now. Nitrous oxide was stored under pressure in tanks, much as it is today. Nitrous oxide stored under pressure must be anchored securely in the interest of safety. I stress safety because a carelessly handled nitrous bottle with nearly 1,000 psi of pressure behaves like a bomb if the bottle fails. To get the nitrous you need for performance use on demand, you meter this gas from the bottle via electrical solenoids that are fired when you hit the go button. Nitrous oxide should be administered on demand at a time when it is safe to do so. For one thing, nitrous should never be administered to the intake ports unless the throttle is wide open. Set up properly, the throttle should close a nitrous solenoid switch when in the wide-open position. Closing the switch activates the nitrous oxide solenoid, releasing the nitrous oxide into the intake manifold.

So, how do you get nitrous oxide into the intake ports? You can do in it a number of ways, depending on how the engine is set up. Carbureted engines get their nitrous diet through a fogger plate located beneath the carburetor. Pin the butterflies and the nitrous oxide "fogs" the intake plenum, assisting the air/fuel mixture en route to the chambers. Carbureted engines may also use nozzles at each intake port to administer the nitrous. The nice part about this design is being able to tune each cylinder bore based on the needs of that cylinder. On carbureted engines, the center ports typically receive more fuel and air than the perimeter ports. The outers tend to run leaner than the centers, which is critical when you are running nitrous oxide.

Port fuel-injected engines also use nozzles from a common tube manifold to administer nitrous oxide at each port. Like its carbureted counterpart, the port-injected nitrous arrangement can be port-tuned for better performance. This is especially true when you think of your V-8 engine as eight separate engines operating on a common crankshaft.

One popular misconception is that you get power from the nitrous oxide itself. This isn't true. Nitrous works hand-in-hand with the air/fuel mix to make power in each cylinder bore. Nitrous oxide brings out the best in the fuel. Not only is the nitrous oxide mist cold (good for thermal expansion) it is also loaded with oxygen, which gives the igniting air/fuel mix a bad attitude. It makes the air/fuel mix burn faster, which creates a powerful thermal expansion experience in each combustion chamber.

Where you have to be careful with nitrous is how you feed it to the engines. Perhaps this isn't the best parallel, but nitrous oxide has to be thought of in the same way you would cocaine, crystal meth, or nicotine. The more powerful the nitrous oxide experience, the more an enthusiast wants. So, you keep feeding the engine more nitrous oxide in your quest for power until it fails under

Nitrous oxide seems the magic pill for power. However, with nitrous comes responsibility. Horsepower and torque are not free. If you're running nitrous, your nitrous system must be in a perfect state of tune including the engine. A lean mixture or any interruption in fuel spells disaster. (Photo Courtesy Summit Racing Equipment)

the stress. You must recognize your engine's limits before even getting started on a nitrous diet.

Compression is thought of two ways: static and dynamic. Static compression is the ratio you often think of. This is the swept volume above the piston, with the piston at BDC, versus the clearance volume left when the piston is at TDC. If you have 100 cc of volume with the piston at BDC and 10 cc left with the piston at TDC, then you have a static compression ratio of 10.0:1, or 100 cc to 10 cc.

Dynamic compression is what happens with the engine operating. This is the kind of compression that happens with pistons, valves, and gases in motion through the engine. You get dynamic compression when you are huffing lungfulls of air through the engine during operation. With the engine running, you are pumping more volume through the cylinders and chambers than you would by simply hand-cranking the engine. This actually increases the compression ratio, which means dynamic compression is higher than static compression. So, what does all of this mean for your engine? It means you need to consider the dynamic compression ratio as your engine's actual compression figure when you're planning for nitrous oxide.

On the exhaust side of nitrous, duration is an important issue. Because the air/fuel/nitrous charge coming in expands with fury during ignition, it needs a way to escape when the exhaust valve opens. You need a longer exhaust valve duration with nitrous for good scavenging and thorough extraction of power, which is why nitrous cams are ground differently.

While you're thinking about exhaust valve duration, you must also remember overlap in all of this. Less overlap, more dynamic compression. More overlap, less dynamic compression. Overlap is that process in the power cycle where the exhaust valve is closing and the intake valve is opening. The incoming charge helps scavenge the outgoing hot gases through the overlap process. What this means is simple. It means the exhaust valve needs to open earlier in the cycle and stay open longer for adequate scavenging.

Fuel octane plays into the power process because you need to understand when and how the fuel will ignite. The higher the fuel octane rating, the more slowly it ignites and burns, which reduces the chances of detonation and preignition. With a higher octane rating, you get a smooth, more predictable light-off in the chamber. When you opt for a lower fuel octane rating, you get a more unstable fuel that will light quickly and cause pinging. When you throw nitrous oxide into the equation, you can count on a quick light-off that can be violent in nature. This is why a higher octane rating is so critical to a cohesive performance package.

If your tuning effort involves a carburetor, you have to get jet sizing down to a science that will help your engine live on nitrous oxide. As a rule, carbureted engines live happily with an air/fuel ratio of 12.5:1 to 13.0:1. This is where you have just the right amount of air and fuel to make power. If you go any leaner, you can cause engine damage. You will also lose power. Any richer and you lose power as well.

When you're working with a fuel-injected engine, you can control fuel mixture by reprogramming the electronic control module or changing injector size. With nitrous, tuners typically go up on injector size and fine tune from there. Too large is better than too small. Factory fuel injection systems run a fuel manifold pressure of 30 to 45 psi. If you're running nitrous oxide, you're going to need a lot more fuel pressure to get the job done safely. Around 80 psi is considered the norm for nitrous and electronic fuel injection.

Ignition timing is the next big hurdle because it can kill an engine as quickly as a lean fuel mixture or too much compression when you're running nitrous. You want the spark to occur in advance of peak cylinder pressure because it takes time for the air/fuel/nitrous mixture to ignite. Under normal circumstances, without nitrous, you want full spark advance around 36 to 41 degrees BTDC. Exactly where the spark occurs depends on how the engine is equipped and how it performs at full spark advance at 3,500 rpm. Because each engine is different, full advance is going to vary from engine to engine.

When you throw nitrous into the equation, you get an air/fuel/nitrous mixture that is going to ignite more rapidly than the conventional air/fuel mix. The pros suggest retarding the ignition timing to approximately 12 degrees BTDC because the air/fuel/nitrous mixture ignites much more quickly. With the full spark advance at 36 to 41 degrees BTDC, you would waste the engine in short order. Retard timing to 12 degrees BTDC and go from there. Twelve degrees BTDC at 3,500 rpm needs to be your baseline, then slowly advance ignition timing from there. Test it out at wide-open throttle under a load, beginning at 12 degrees BTDC, then advance from there 1 degree at a time.

With those basics out of the way, there are other points to consider when running nitrous. To be effective, fuel has to atomize (vaporize) properly. This means the fuel has to "mist" as it enters the intake manifold and, ultimately, the combustion chamber. The problem here is that nitrous comes out of the fogger or nozzle ice cold. This makes it very difficult to atomize the fuel effectively. When nitrous oxide comes out of the fogger or nozzle at a frigid –100°F, fuel tends to exist as large droplets, rather than the mist you need for good ignition and combustion.

Nitrous oxide system manufacturers have dealt effectively with the issue of fuel atomization by designing systems that allow the gasoline to atomize with the nitrous fog or mist. The finer you can get the mist, the more power you're going to make.

Supercharging and Turbocharging

Supercharging, like nitrous oxide injection, was conceived a long time ago to extract as much power as possible from a given displacement. Unlike nitrous oxide, supercharging is more involved, yet easier to tune and manage. It's easier to tune because you know you're getting into trouble before getting there. Knowing you're in trouble comes from the sound of detonation. Superchargers and turbochargers don't come on as strong as quickly as nitrous. For the most part, they cannot damage the engine as quickly as nitrous because you can come off the power in time to prevent engine damage. There is also a safety device, called a waste-gate, designed to prevent overboost with superchargers and turbochargers. With nitrous oxide, damage and certain engine death are instantaneous if you deliver too much of it without enough fuel, or with too much ignition timing.

Supercharging and turbocharging both accomplish the same objective. They each force air into the cylinders to make the most of a combustion power cycle. They mechanically increase cylinder pressure, which, given enough fuel, makes more power. Superchargers are driven by the engine's crankshaft. Turbochargers are driven by exhaust gas pressure. A supercharger's compressor, driven by the crankshaft, moves the air you're feeding into the intake manifold. A turbocharger's compressor, driven by exhaust gas, does the same thing.

Superchargers give the engine nearly immediate power. The power comes on stronger with RPM. With the increase in RPM, the compressor turns faster, forcing more air pressure into the intake manifold, which gives you the power. You prevent overpressure by fitting the supercharger with a waste-gate, which vents excessive pressure.

Turbochargers take a certain amount of time to give you induction pressure when you step on the gas. This is called turbo lag. Because it takes the turbocharger time to spool up during acceleration, there is a certain amount of lag before you get the boost or pressure and the resulting power. Turbochargers have a waste-gate, which also bleeds excessive boost pressure, which prevents engine damage.

There are six basic different types of superchargers: centrifugal, rotary, axial flow, Roots (two-lobe and three-lobe), vane, and Lysholm screw. Probably the most common type on small- and middle-block Fords are centrifugal and Roots lobe types. Centrifugal types are typically hung on the front of the engine,

Supercharging and turbocharging, like nitrous oxide, call for precision tuning and common sense. If you're going to run higher cylinder pressures, extensive prep must go into your engine build. Compression must be appropriate for artificial aspiration or you wind up with engine failure.

driven by the crankshaft pulley. Roots blowers, also driven by the crankshaft pulley, are normally an integral part of the intake manifold, with the carburetor mounted immediately upwind of the blower. With fuel injection, the throttle body is mounted in any number of locations before the Roots blower's intake. Fuel injectors are positioned in each of the intake ports, downwind of the Roots blower.

Which type of supercharger should you choose and why? This is hard to answer because everyone has different expectations and needs. Which supercharger you choose is going to depend on your needs. Roots and centrifugal superchargers both have significant purposes. You choose the Roots blower for different purposes than you choose a centrifugal huffer. Let's talk about the Roots blower first.

The Roots lobe-type supercharger has served many purposes during its service lifetime. Probably the most common Roots supercharger duty has been to feed hungry Detroit two-stroke diesel engines. You've undoubtedly heard the term "6-71 blower" in hot-rodding circles. Detroit two-stroke diesel engines, once manufactured by General Motors, are named based on displacement, number of cylinders, and cylinder arrangement. The Detroit 6V-71, for example, is a V-6, with 71 ci of displacement per cylinder. A Detroit 8V-92 is a V-8 with 92 ci per cylinder. The Detroit 6-71 is an inline six with 71 ci per cylinder. So, when you see a huge 6-71 blower atop a well-fed small-block Ford, it's a blower originally designed for huge heavy-duty Detroit diesels that power semi-trucks.

What makes a Roots blower quite effective is its positive displacement design, which a Detroit two-stroke diesel engine needs for proper ingestion of air and scavenging of exhaust gases. This kind of positive displacement design ascertains plenty of cylinder pressure when and where it counts in a high-performance V-8 engine.

When I speak of positive displacement in a Roots blower, this is because its very design doesn't allow much, if any, air to escape en route to the chambers. Roots blowers have two- and three-lobe rotor designs where rotors interlock to ensure consistent airflow, under pressure, into the engine.

Ford has been using the Roots design on factory production engines for many years, beginning with the 1989 3.8L Essex V-6 Thunderbird SC. Today, it is used atop the 5.4L SOHC V-8 engine in the Lightning and Harley-Davidson F-150 trucks, just to name two variations. This reliable, highly successful supercharger will work quite well on your small-block Ford.

A more common type of supercharger is the centrifugal type you see and hear at a lot of Ford events on newer 5.0L and 4.6L Mustangs. It's that familiar whistle associated mostly with the Vortech and Paxton superchargers. Instead of the interlocking rotors used in the Roots positive displacement supercharger, centrifugal superchargers employ a fan that draws air into its center and rings it outward into a duct where it enters the intake manifold. Centrifugal force is defined by The American Heritage Dictionary as "the component of an apparent force or a body in curvilinear motion, as observed from that body, that is directed away from a curvature or axis of rotation."

In other words, centrifugal force is the energy of a spinning object that tends to throw the object, or parts of the object, outward. In this case, air is the object you sling outward from the spinning fan (compressor). The compressor takes the air in through its center and blows it outward with the whirling blades or fins that thrust it outward into the shell into the intake tube. Not only does the compressor move the air outward from its center but it also squeezes the air in the shell, feeding it to the intake tube.

Think of the centrifugal-style blower like your hairdryer where air is drawn into one side and blown out the other side. A hairdryer is a compressor of sorts. Even the humble blower in your Ford's air conditioning system compresses air to some degree before it exits your dashboard outlets. So does your home vacuum cleaner, where most of them are of a centrifugal blower design. The best vacuum cleaner example I can think of is an old-fashioned Kirby upright vacuum cleaner with a centrifugal blower.

Turbochargers are like a centrifugal supercharger because they work much the same way. Instead of being belt-driven, they're driven by a turbine that is propelled by hot exhaust gases. As you accelerate, hot exhaust gases drive the turbocharger's single-stage turbine, which drives the centrifugal compressor.

IGNITION

Ignition systems have to be pinpoint accurate with potent spark timing to ensure a lighted mixture and power. It's easy to light the air/fuel mixture at low RPM. It gets tricky at high RPM, where conditions change dramatically. When you're first taught about how engines work, you think it is the simple four-cycle process: intake, compression/ignition, power stroke, and exhaust. However, it really is more complicated. Because the physics is more involved, it is the finite timing of these four events that determines how reliably your engine will perform.

Fuel and air ignite in a quick fire, which is a light-off across the piston dome that begins where the ignition source is. The ignition of air/fuel begins at the ignition source whether it's a spark plug or a red-hot piece of carbon. As the air/fuel mix ignites, it flashes and expands across the chamber at a rate of about 700 feet per second and acts on the piston, rod, and crank.

Because fuel and air ignite in something of a quick fire, you need to allow time for this thermal reaction to happen. Your spark plug doesn't fire when the piston reaches TDC, but rather it fires BTDC because fuel needs time to ignite and act. This ignition process happens in a nanosecond even at idle. At high RPM, it happens in a fraction of a nanosecond and must happen earlier in the compression/ignition cycle. Under optimum conditions, you get a smooth light-off and a generous outpouring of power.

Where this becomes even more complex is cam profile, combustion chamber size and shape, valve size and shape, and both dynamic and static compression ratio. Even more confusing is when you have identical engines, yet ignition timing doesn't offer the same reaction or power. That's because no two engines are exactly the same. There are just enough variables that each engine mandates its own tuning agenda even if you're working with identical engines.

The single-point Autolite/Motorcraft distributor wasn't much even in its day. They suffered from poor shaft support (a single bushing), which caused point bounce at high RPM. Ford later compensated with a second shaft bushing, which didn't change the dynamics much.

Ford took the same basic distributor and made it a dual-point for high-performance engines. It did a good job in its day. However, the aftermarket answered the call with better high-performance ignitions.

Each Autolite/Motorcraft distributor is identified with a Ford part number and a date code. Both tell you a lot about application and engine type, plus advance curving.

When you adjust ignition timing, it must be performed with a timing light and an accurate harmonic damper. Your harmonic damper timing marks must be properly indexed. Even a new harmonic damper must be examined for proper indexing. I've seen them as much as 11 degrees off.

Find true TDC at cylinder number-1, which should be midway in the crank rollover point for the crank journal. Install and index the distributor at number-1. This is static timing and where you begin tuning.

When you get the engine fired, be ready to set ignition timing right off the bat with the engine at 2,500 to 3,500 rpm to learn total timing. With the vacuum advance connected at 3,500 rpm, you must know where your ignition timing is. Ignition timing should be checked two ways at 2,500 to 3,500 rpm: vacuum advance connected and disconnected. Total ignition timing with vacuum advance connected should be no more than 36 degrees BTDC. At idle, it should be around 6 to 12 degrees BTDC.

When you're dialing-in total timing, begin conservatively at 30 to 34 degrees BTDC and observe

Beginning in 1968, Ford went to an advance/retard distributor known as IMCO (improved combustion), which either advanced or retarded the spark depending upon throttle position, manifold vacuum, and coolant temperature. A thermal vacuum switch at the thermostat housing controlled vacuum direction depending upon coolant temperature.

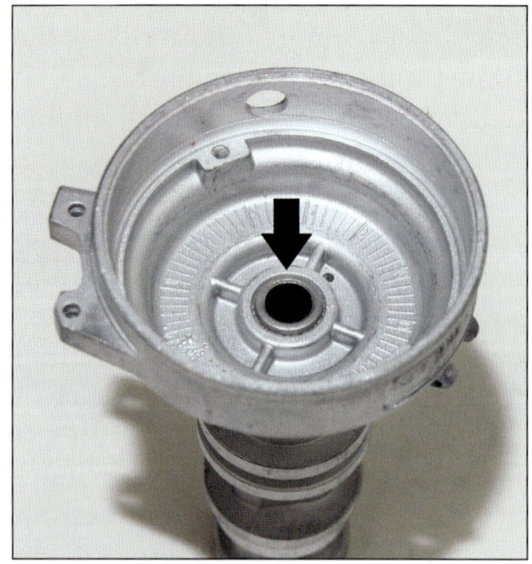

The Autolite/Motorcraft distributor's weak link was this single-shaft bushing. Because oil distribution to the bushing is decidedly poor, bushing wear is severe. Shaft wobble causes point bounce and irregular ignition timing.

Breaker plate function in these Ford distributors gets dicey at best. The original breaker plate (far left) worked quite well. Ford and aftermarket breaker plate replacements (center and right) tend to be terrible. They do not work smoothly and tend to weaken at the pivot point.

You can expect to see two types of vacuum advance units for old Ford distributors. On the left is the early-style advance unit, which is curved via shims and spring pressure. To slow the rate of advance, add shims. To speed up advance, remove shims. On the right is an aftermarket advance unit, which is adjusted with an Allen wrench through the vacuum port: clockwise to slow advance and counterclockwise to speed it up.

Beneath the break plate are the centrifugal advance weight and springs, which go to work as RPM increases. The flyweights work against spring pressure to control the rate of advance. Swapping springs of different tensions controls the rate of advance.

Ford's Duraspark ignition arrived in 1974 and has been an excellent, reliable factory ignition system. Both the vacuum and centrifugal advance mechanisms work the same way as the older Autolite distributors.

operation. Push it as far as 36 to 38 degrees BTDC but no higher. Under hard acceleration or loaded on a dyno, listen for spark knock. If you have spark knock, retard ignition timing 1 degree at a time.

When you're checking ignition timing, not only do you want to know total ignition timing (advance) but also the rate of advance when the throttle is opened. When you goose the throttle, how quickly does spark advance occur? Does it occur too early at lower RPM, or is it slow to come on as the throttle is opened and RPM increases? You want spark advance to roll with RPM increase and throttle movement. If you don't have a vacuum advance, spark advance should increase in linear fashion with RPM, more slowly.

Ultimately, at 2,500 to 3,500 rpm, total timing should never be more than 36 degrees BTDC. Of course, you can push it to 38 or even 40 degrees BTDC, but it is risky even if you don't get spark knock. Conditions change when it is hot and you're roaring around a road course at wide-open throttle, which is when you can get pinging (spark knock) and not be able to hear it, which is when the damage occurs. This is why you want to start conservatively with ignition timing and work it 1 degree at a time. Expected total timing also depends on the cam profile, octane rating, and induction.

Spark Knock

Spark knock, detonation, pinging, and preignition are common terms for basically the same thing. Spark knock happens with early ignition timing, a red-hot piece of carbon or ragged edge, overheating, fuel octane rating too low, compression too high, a cam profile harboring too much cylinder pressure or working compression, or ambient air being too hot. The rattling or knocking is abnormal combustion resulting in a strong shock wave across the piston dome, which acts on the piston pin and skirts causing the metallic sound you hear under hard acceleration.

To eliminate spark knock during tuning, you must first establish why there is spark knock. What do you have for fuel octane? Have you confirmed both static and working compression? Do you have carboned-up combustion chambers? What is the known cam profile? Is the ambient temperature extraordinarily hot?

Breaker Point Ignition

Point-triggered or breaker point ignition is a simple on/off switch that opens and closes the primary ignition circuit to charge-up the coil and reduce a brief discharge of high-energy current to fire a spark plug. It can be debated as to who invented the breaker high-energy discharge ignition system, but who cares? What you're interested in knowing is how it works and how to make it better.

When you turn on the ignition switch, power travels to the primary ignition circuit to energize the coil and breaker points. Current travels through resistance wire in a Ford to the primary circuit. If points are closed, current flow across the contact points tends to burn the contacts. As current flows through the primary side of the ignition coil, it creates a strong magnetic field, which in turn induces a huge surge of current on the secondary side to the distributor. The condenser is there to take up the surge of high-energy electricity, which would arc violently across the open point gap were it not for the condenser. This action would quickly burn and pit the contacts. But there's more. The condenser allows the ignition system to build an electrical momentum where a steady clip of 20,000 to 30,000 volts to the secondary side to fire spark plugs.

The average garage mechanic will tell you an engine will run without the condenser. However, engines generally don't run very well without condensers because the condenser acts as an electrical cushion, a shock absorber for high-energy electricity. Without it, electricity returns to ground, arcing across the points and being of little value to operation.

Dwell Time

Ignition points are a rotary cam-actuated switch that operates in time with a 429/460's firing order. The opening and closing of points turn electricity on and off through the ignition coil. Dwell time is the amount of time the distributor shaft rotation in degrees that points are closed. Each time the points open, a spark plug fires.

With a dual-point distributor, you increase dwell time to build more coil saturation and a more potent spark. You also eliminate the limitations of a single set of ignition points. The keys to improved performance is increased dwell time and a stronger spark. When you widen the point gap, you increase dwell time.

Electronic Ignition

Despite a point-triggered ignition's time-proven ability to fire spark plugs with precision accuracy, there are shortcomings. As you increase engine speed, there's less dwell time to build adequate current, which reduces spark potency. This causes misfire at high RPM because you need a powerful enough spark to overcome high cylinder pressures. At high RPM, points tend to bounce and flutter also causing misfire. This is where transistorized ignition and, later, Hall Effect electronic ignition came from. There has also been capacitive discharge ignition with a very potent spark triggered by ignition points.

Ford was among the first to use transistorized ignition in the early 1960s, and Duraspark did in 1975. Chrysler was the first U.S. automaker to go with mass production electronic ignition in 1974. Somewhere in there was GM's first shot at mag-triggered electronic ignition, then HEI (high-energy ignition) in the late 1970s. HEI was a great idea because it eliminated the external ignition coil.

There have also been light-triggered electronic ignition systems with shutter-wheel triggers and light-emitting diodes (LEDs) such as Mallory's Unilite ignition in the 1970s, which is still in production today. Light-triggered ignitions have performed well and with great reliability. Most electronic ignition systems since the 1970s have been Hall Effect (magnetic trigger) systems, which are the most reliable. In fact, even in this age of coil-on-plug fuel-injected engine control systems Hall Effect is still used in crank trigger capacity.

The main reason automakers went to electronic ignition in the 1970s wasn't so much for performance but for reducing emissions because every misfire is unburned hydrocarbons and increased emissions. If you listen to new cars and trucks today, they don't misfire. That comes from a potent high-energy spark and the precision of electronic fuel injection.

Earlier, I mentioned capacitive discharge ignition. When you combine electronic ignition with capacitive discharge, you allow an inductive-type ignition system to build tremendous amounts of electricity for the secondary side to fire spark plugs. When you get right down to MSD's ignition boxes, this is exactly what they are on a more high-tech scale. They pack a huge wallop and discharge huge amounts of electricity for each spark plug firing. In fact, these systems are designed to handle up to 12,000 rpm, which 385-series engines will never see.

The key to performance and cleaner emissions is a potent spark. How you get that potent spark depends on your support system and what you use for spark enhancement. MSD, as one example, has a variety of ignition enhancement systems, most of which are based on capacitive discharge. The MSD 6A-series ignition enhancers are based on this principle, and they do an outstanding job of keeping the fire lit at high RPM. One MSD enhancer, the 6 BTM (Boost Timing Master) allows you to control spark timing if you're running a supercharger or nitrous, which helps keep you out of trouble when the heat is high and your foot is in it.

Ignition Coils

Most factory Ford ignition coils from the early 1970s make approximately 20,000 to 30,000 volts. This makes them less than adequate for high-performance use. Stock ignition coils work fine for normal driving at low- to mid-range RPM. However, when you start spinning a Ford big-block upward of six grand and higher at wide-open throttle, a factory coil cannot keep up. It will continue to fire spark plugs, but not at the intensity they need to light the mixture. This is a combination of dwell/saturation time and spark potency.

At high RPM under great cylinder pressures, a weak spark gets snuffed out, hindering its ability to light the mixture. If you add supercharging or nitrous, it becomes overwhelming quickly. Therefore, you want a powerful ignition coil coupled with an ignition enhancer, such as capacitive or multi-spark discharge. You want the most spark your ignition system can pack even with a street engine.

Distributor Types

The good news here is that there are a lot of distributor types available for the 385-series engine family. There's not much good to say about Ford distributors because they're just not up to the task of high-RPM use. The Autolite/Motorcraft distributors consist of bronze bushings on a steel shaft, with some having only one bushing and others having two. Because oil distribution is so poor, bushings and shafts wear out quickly, causing side play (wobble) and point bounce at high RPM. This problem also exists with Duraspark distributors to some degree. So, unless you're building a stealthy stocker, avoid using Ford distributors.

As with Holley carburetors mentioned earlier in this book, I tend to go with what I know works. MSD Ignition is another one of those things I know works without a hitch. The same can be said for PerTronix, Mallory, Crane, and Performance Distributors ignition components. These are exceptional systems. I've had good experiences with these ignition systems, and when they're installed and tuned properly, they offer outstanding performance.

Because the 429/460 engine family uses the same distributor as the 335-series 351C/351M/400-ci engines, there's a lot out there to choose from. Choice boils down to street or race or a combination of both. Street engines should be equipped with distributors that have a vacuum advance for good off-idle response. Street/strip engines are more centrifugal advance depending upon how much time is spent at high RPM. Again, how is your engine operated most of the time? This determines what type of distributor you're going to choose.

MSD Ignition

There's a reason why you see the MSD name out there more than any other in racing, and that's because so much research and development go into its products. MSD ignition

Street 460 engines do a better job with the MSD Street Pro Billet distributor with vacuum advance. The diameter of the special MSD cap and housing are 5/8 inch smaller than stock Ford Duraspark distributors providing room at the front of the engine. I like the special MSD cap, which features male terminals and is firmly screwed down to the cap. MSD provides everything you need to get it installed and curved.

The MSD Pro Billet distributor incorporates MSD's race-proven mag' pickup and precision reluctor to deliver accurate trigger signals to the MSD ignition box throughout high RPM. The reluctor assembly is turned by a hardened steel shaft, which rides in a sealed ball bearing for high-RPM stability and endurance. This is a terrific street/strip distributor.

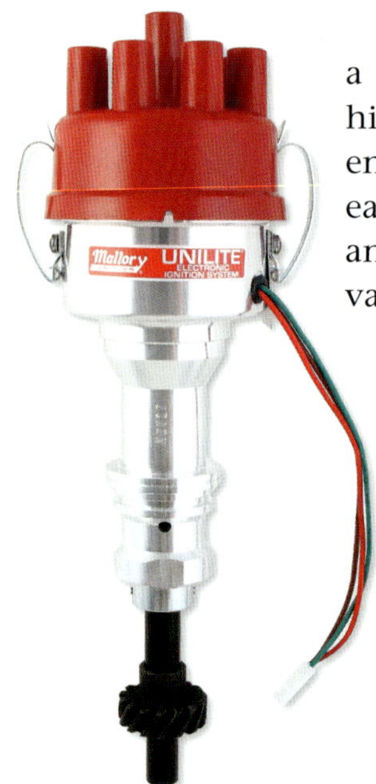

Mallory Unilite ignition was introduced at a time when enthusiasts wanted precision performance and were tired of ignition points. Unilite became the standard for solid, reliable electronic ignition systems. You can still get Unilite today from Mallory. Go to www.holley.com for more detail.

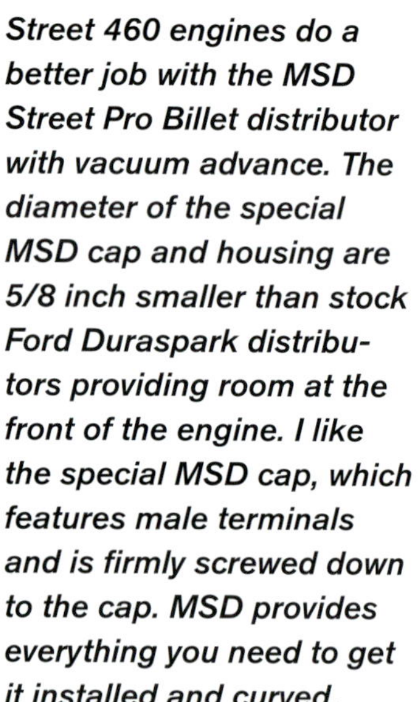

Ignition amplifiers such as the MSD 6AL intensify the spark to overcome high cylinder pressures and high RPM.

products are tested in tough, grueling environments where they're subjected to the worse conditions imaginable. Again, this is not a paid endorsement, but a fact based on feedback from people in the industry. If MSD Ignition products weren't up to the job, you wouldn't see them on racetracks everywhere.

There are three basic choices for those who want MSD: billet, billet with a vacuum advance, and electronic programmable units. For the street, you want the MSD #8477 Pro-Billet distributor with a vacuum advance. The #8477 is a high-performance street distributor engineered and manufactured for ease of use with an easy-to-access and adjust mechanical advance and a vacuum advance you can adjust with a simple Allen wrench. Mechanical advance is based on Delco distributors of long ago, which were easy to tune because the advance was right under the rotor. It's a matter of changing spring tension and and/or bushings. The #8477 is C.A.R.B. approved.

There are two MSD distributors designed for racing: #8577 and #8569. The #8569 crank-trigger distributor fits low in the block if you're running a tunnel ram or blower. The #8569 must be used with a crank trigger and MSD's ignition control. The #8577 billet distributor is mechanical advance only and designed for high-revving applications. You can tune the #8577 with ease using provided advanced springs and bushings.

Mallory Ignition

Another name that has held its own through the years is Mallory, with the same level of reliability and performance it has long had through Unilite technology. There are Mallory Unilite distributors available for the 385-series engines: #4756701 dual-advance distributor with mechanical and vacuum advance, which is primarily for street use.

The Mallory #8556701C HEI distributor is a coil-in-cap unit that is all self-contained. Fit may be tricky with the Mallory HEI depending on your 429/460's induction system. The #8556701C can be converted for racing with an advance lockout. For those of you who choose to tune your Mallory HEI, both mechanical and vacuum advances are programmable and easy to access.

The Mallory #3756701 is a mechanical advance–only unit with Unilite for pinpoint accuracy. What makes the Mallory #3756701 a great distributor is reliability and its maintenance-free disposition. Aside from the occasional cap and rotor replacement or wiping the optics, it requires no attention. This is the distributor you want for high-RPM use.

Performance Distributors

Performance Distributors in Memphis, Tennessee, is located within spitting distance of Comp Cams and enjoys a great reputation for building affordable high-quality ignition systems for Ford applications. Founded by the late Kelly Davis, Performance Distributors is still a family-owned and -operated business. When you get on the phone with these folks, it's like chatting with an old friend. There's nothing you can't ask of them.

There are two basic types of electronic ignition systems available from Performance Distributors for Clevelands and 385-series engines: Ford's time-proven Duraspark ignition and the revolutionary D.U.I. (Davis Unified Ignition), which is based on GM's HEI system with a self-contained ignition coil in cap. Either way, you get factory-style reliability and easy-to-get parts. If you want more of a stock appearance for your 385 project, Performance Distributors is very helpful with Duraspark. If you want a clean appearance without clutter, the D.U.I. system is your best choice.

Here's a word to the wise on distributor gears. If you're running an old-fashioned flat-tappet camshaft, which is made of iron, you can run a distributor right out of the box with an iron-driven gear. If you're running a steel billet roller cam, you must run a bronze or steel gear with the same hardness as the camshaft. If given a preference, choose the steel gear instead of the bronze.

When you order a Duraspark distributor from Performance Distributors, you're getting a custom calibrated piece curved for your application. That's why Performance Distributors wants to know all about your engine when it takes your order. Performance Distributors blueprints every distributor with a full-length bronze bushing, new hard parts, and precision calibration for a seamless advance as RPM increase. Each Duraspark distributor is capable of 10,000 rpm, although I suggest not going there. Please specify flat-tappet or roller camshaft with your order.

Duraspark	#32720
D.U.I.	#32820
Racing D.U.I.	#328211 (with vacuum advance)
Racing D.U.I.	#328212 (without vacuum advance)

The racing D.U.I. system can handle up to 9,000 rpm. Because it delivers a greater dwell angle, it delivers a hotter spark enabling you to widen spark plug gaps to 0.050 to 0.055 inch. Because these distributors are already curved to your custom application, all you do is install and go.

Ignition Wires

Although there are lots of aftermarket ignition wires out there, I go with what I know and what has worked well for me. MSD Ignition wires stand up to extreme heat and get electricity to its destination without a hitch. Because you can get MSD ignition wires in black as well as red, they render a more stock appearance if that's what you desire. MSD wires have an 8.5-mm outer extrusion that stands up to heat. Inside this jacket is extra-heavy glass braid, then a high-dielectric insulator. Next, a helically-wrapped copper alloy conductor. Inside of that is a ferro-magnetically impregnated core to get current to spark plugs at autobahn speed.

It isn't only about the spark plug leads you choose but how you

Before you install a new distributor, make sure you have the correct drive gear for the camshaft you have. Flat-tappet cams call for an iron gear. Roller cams call for a bronze or steel gear. Check the installed endplay as shown, which should be 0.005 to 0.010 inch.

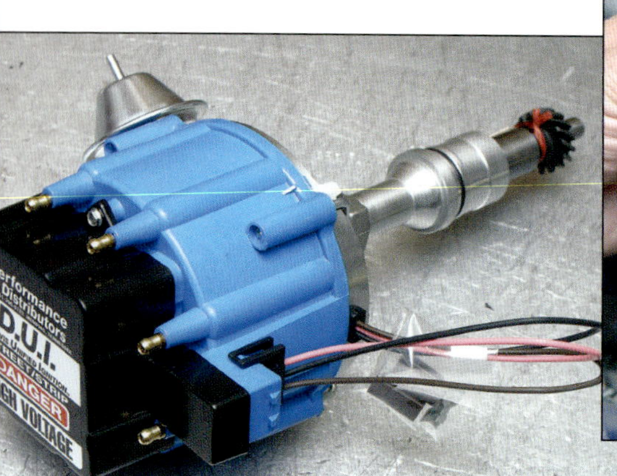

A long-time player in the ignition business has been Steve Davis at Performance Distributors. This company creates terrific ignition systems. The all-in-one D.U.I. applies GM's HEI ignition to Ford engines. No external coils, modules, or spark boxes are needed.

Easily one of the greatest innovations has been the PerTronix Ignitor series retrofit for vintage distributors. The Ignitor I, II, and III each has its purpose depending on what you want your engine to do. They install in less than 30 minutes. Don't forget to install the ground lead inside your Ford distributor.

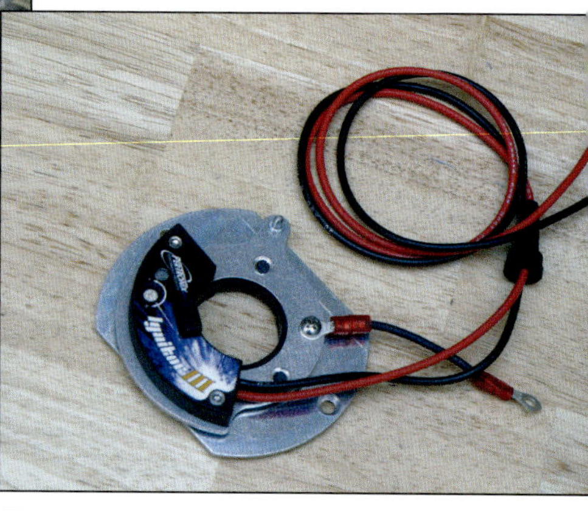

The PerTronix Ignitor III delivers five times more spark energy than a typical point-triggered system. It sports an integrated digital rev limiter with LED feedback for a precise RPM setting, memory-safe function, and adaptive dwell that maintains peak energy throughout the entire RPM range reducing misfires while improving engine performance. It is smog legal in all 50 states.

route and locate them. Ignition wires should be routed parallel where possible at least 1/4 inch or more apart to minimize the risk of crossfire. You also want to keep wires at least 1/4 to 1/2 inch from metal surfaces to prevent arcing to ground and misfire. Crossfire, which is when a spark plug receives current intended for another, can destroy an engine at high RPM.

Because high-energy electricity is very unpredictable in nature, it travels unexpected paths at times and for reasons you don't always understand. You can have the most ironclad ignition system and experience stray current, crossfire, and a blown

Performance Distributors makes these cool LiveWires ignition harnesses for a variety of engines including the 429/460. Performance Distributors LiveWires are a high-quality, extreme low-resistance spark plug wire with a high-temperature sleeve that protects the plug wire from the extreme underhood temperatures. Inside this high-temperature sleeve is an 8-mm spiral core wire with a durable and lasting silicone jacket.

Jon Kaase ignition wires are available for both Boss 429 and wedge 385-series engines in Light Blue, Dark Blue, and Black. They are a low-resistance wire for high-energy ignition systems with a silicone wrap for heat resistance. Because they are custom-cut wires, you can get them to the required length with a clean installation.

engine. Sometimes, current travels across exhaust gases or even coolant in a water jacket, causing crossfire or misfire, even more than one spark plug firing at the same time, reducing the effectiveness of the one that was supposed to fire. This is why you need to eliminate any potential pitfalls going in. Go with the best ignition parts and set them up with the precision of an aircraft electrical system.

Finally, distributor caps and rotors. Never buy these components on the cheap. Go with the best insulation and brass terminals name brands such as MSD, Accel, Mallory, and original equipment where possible. If you're committed to the use of a Ford distributor, opt for the Duraspark system. Use the Duraspark distributor cap with terminals spaced more widely apart. Make sure you have a vented cap to help keep ionized air levels to a minimum inside.

One more thing: take note of how much air gap there is between the rotor tip and terminal. Too much gap and you run the risk of crossfire inside the cap. Once your engine has been in operation, be wise to carbon tracking inside the cap, which can also cause crossfire and misfire.

The MSD Blaster ignition coil is a productive drop-in replacement for a factory coil. You get a hotter spark from this guy, which ensures a complete light-off at higher RPM. This is an affordable upgrade you can install in minutes.

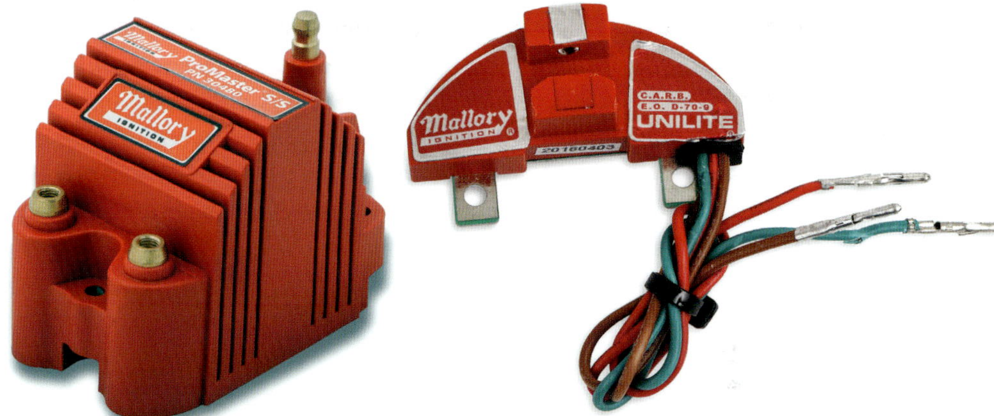

When you use this Mallory coil with the HyFire Ignition and the ProMaster S/S, you get 300 milliamps of electricity and a maximum voltage output of 40,000. It features an efficient winding design and assembly for a compact size. Primary and secondary windings are encased in polyurethane for durability.

Mallory's Unilite ignition really is the original aftermarket system. It offers solid reliability and is easy to install.

Spark Plugs

Spark plugs have become a very complicated subject in recent years because there are so many different types, not to mention marketing angles. The best advice I can offer is to stick with what has worked for generations: the humble cross-electrode spark plug. Platinum-tip spark plugs work best with high-energy ignition systems because they last. Outside of that feature, stick with simple resistor or non-resistor spark plugs in your big-block.

Your greatest concern when choosing a spark plug is heat range. How quickly does your spark plug get rid of heat? If a spark plug's heat range is high, it doesn't get rid of heat quickly, which can cause pinging (spark knock). Even if there's no spark knock, the firing tip can run hotter than it should, causing premature failure. Heat range depends on how long the insulator is, which determines how quickly heat transfers to the head. Ideally, your spark plug's heat range will keep combustion temperatures somewhere around 800 to 1,500°F. Your best indication of heat range depends on spark plug insulator color after a wide-open-throttle blast and shutdown. Tan to a light tan is what you want to see. Sooty black indicates you're running too cold, not to mention rich. Snow white means you are too lean and heat range is too high. Small dots of aluminum on the insulator indicate bigger troubles, such as piston damage.

Heat range is also determined by cam profile and how much cylinder pressure will be made as a result. Cylinder pressure is a product of dynamic or working compression, which affects spark plug heat range selection. Another issue you want to consider is how far the center electrode extends into the combustion chamber. Will it clear the piston?

This can be checked when you are checking valve-to-piston clearances during mock-up. This logic falls in line with heat-range selection. The longer the center electrode, the greater risk of piston contact. If your heads are already installed, this is something you do carefully by slowly hand-cranking the engine, feeling for resistance, then pulling the spark plug and checking for contact.

Yet another item to consider is spark plug indexing. Though some will say this doesn't matter, others live by it. Thread spark plugs where the anode (cross electrode) doesn't block the spark where the firing tip is open to the chamber. Mark each spark plug with a felt-tip marker and go for it.

Charging System

The 429/460 engines were fitted with a variety of Autolite and Motorcraft alternators, both externally and internally regulated. Although these charging systems were adequate in their day, they're not much to write home about today. If you're performing a concours restoration where authenticity is important, you're going to want a factory charging system. There are companies that can restore your factory alternator with all of the correct markings and infuse more charging power in the process.

Powermaster has an alternator for every need. This is the Powermaster 1G Ford alternator, which delivers 75 amps of charging power. This is a good choice for restomods and concours restored vehicles.

The Motorcraft 2G alternator is a poor design used as original equipment in the 1980s. It is a troublesome alternator and should be avoided. A popular swap is the newer 3G alternator with greater amperage and durability.

A number of charging options are available from Summit Racing and Powermaster. You can replace the factory alternator in your vintage Ford while keeping with its original look. These retro 1G externally regulated alternators make 75 amps, which is all most vintage Fords, Mercurys, and Lincolns need. These reproduction Powermaster alternators conform to the proper size and appearance of original equipment while incorporating today's technology. They utilize OEM finishes and wiring connections for ease of installation and durability.

Ford's 2G alternator from the 1980s is never a good choice. It is known as the "fire starter" alternator because it tends to short out at the connector. Most with the 2G replace it with a 3G or 4G alternator. Your best option, of course, is a good internally regulated aftermarket alternator, such as the Ford 3G, which delivers a lot of power (up to 200 amps) without the hassle of those dated factory charging systems. The 3G (Summit #477591) Ford alternator is a simple one-wire alternator you can easily adapt to any vehicle's electrical system. Painless Performance makes a kit that enables you to install a 3G or 4G (single-wire) alternator in your vintage externally regulated Ford, Mercury, or Lincoln.

Here's the very popular Motorcraft 3G alternator, which bolts right in place of the 1G and 2G alternators. The Powermaster 3G comes with a serpentine pulley. However, you can swap to a V-belt pulley with ease. This particular 3G packs 200 amps of charging power.

Starters

The 429/460 engines were fitted with the direct-drive Autolite/Motorcraft starter. It was a good, serviceable starter for its time but very much out of date, especially if you've built a high-compression 385. That's when you need a modern, lightweight, high-torque, reduction-gear starter. There are dozens of high-torque starters in the marketplace. With their gear-reduction drives, heavy-duty PowerMaster Mastertorque starters from Summit make the power necessary, 180 ft-lbs of torque, to crank your 460. That said, they handle engines with compression ratios as high as 14.0:1. If your stock Motorcraft starter clears the oil pan, these mini-starters will as well.

You will want to invest in a high-quality proven starter solenoid. Some of the cheaper off-shore solenoids can stick and continue cranking the engine once it has started. One reason for sticking solenoids is overtightening the terminal nuts. They just need to be snug, not overtightened. Use your Ford solenoid in conjunction with the Powermaster's onboard solenoid for best results.

TCI Automotive offers a number of terrific high-torque starters for the 429/460. Ditto for MSD, which offers a line of high-torque starters. If you're running long-tube headers and even shorties, you will want to protect the starter from destructive heat. A number of options are available for starter protection. Most of these aftermarket high-torque starters are fully adjustable to where you can adjust the angle to suit your installation.

Senders

Sending units (senders) keep you in close touch with an engine's vitals. Never operate a 429/460 without instrumentation to keep you in touch. Few things are more devastating than discovering you didn't have oil pressure or had an overheat and didn't know it. It is always a good idea to have mechanical gauges handy to confirm what your electric instruments are telling you.

When you first fire your big-block, screw a mechanical oil pressure gauge into the block for confirmation. Ditto for coolant temperature. Then, compare numbers with the electrical instruments.

Quite a few of us know what senders do but not how they do it. This is a coolant temperature sender. It works on the principle of resistance to ground. Power flows from the voltage limiter on the back of the instrument cluster through the gauge to the sender to ground. With high resistance, the gauge reads low. With low resistance, the gauge reads high.

This is an oil pressure sender for a gauge. With high resistance, the gauge reads low. With low resistance, the gauge reads high.

Keep in mind electrical instruments aren't always linear. They read high. They read low. Most electrical instruments can be calibrated to match the mechanical gauges. As long as readings are in the "normal" range, you should be okay.

Electrical instruments function on resistance to ground from the sending unit. The greater the resistance to ground, the lower the gauge will read. As resistance falls to ground, the higher the gauge will read. This applies to oil pressure, coolant temperature, and fuel level. Within the coolant, fuel, and oil gauges is a heating element. Heat affects the watch spring–style needle movement. With high resistance to ground, the spring moves the needle very little because the heating element isn't very warm. As resistance falls and current flow becomes aggressive, the heating element warms, which affects the movement. The needle registers higher.

This type of oil pressure sender is a simple on/off switch. With no oil pressure, you have a closed circuit and the oil light is on. With oil pressure, the circuit to ground is open and the light is out.

The oil pressure sender is a diaphragm unit, which moves from high resistance to low resistance as oil pressure climbs. Coolant temperature works the same way. Engine cold, high resistance to ground, and very little current flow. As the engine warms, resistance becomes lower to ground and the gauge moves higher. The fuel gauge works the same way. Empty tank, high resistance, and no needle movement. Full tank, low resistance to ground, and the needle roars to the Full mark. Make sure all sending units and instruments are in good working order. Engine life depends on it.

Exhaust

It is remarkable how many of us build engines and give very little thought to the exhaust system. Did you know how far reaching the exhaust system is in terms of performance? The exhaust system typically crosses your mind when the engine is reinstalled and ready to fire. Headers and the exhaust system are just as important to power as induction, camshaft profile, and cylinder heads.

We think of induction, cylinder heads, cam profiles, compression, stroke, bore size, valve spring pressures, carburetors and injectors, throttle bore size, ignition system, and more. However, we rarely consider the advantages of good exhaust scavenging. There's very little that is glamorous about exhaust systems aside from awe-inspiring sound.

Not enough attention is paid to how the exhaust system affects performance. It is just as important to performance as induction, camshaft selection, and cylinder heads. Exhaust scavenging is everything to how your engine will perform.

System Sizing

A wide variety of information and opinions are available online on how headers should be selected for a specific application. Header and exhaust system modifications add value to your efforts to make more power. The size of the primary tube must meet the requirements of the engine and the vehicle's intended use. Length of the header tubes and collector design/sizing must meet your maximum RPM requirements and vehicle use. Headers must fit the vehicle without ridiculous modifications to the vehicle.

Primary tube sizing right off the cylinder heads is your first consideration. Engine displacement, horsepower output, average RPM, vehicle use most of the time, plus any power-adders (nitrous or supercharging) planned come next. What type of cylinder heads do you expect to use? Bore and stroke? Camshaft specifications (lobe centerline, exhaust opening, lobe lift), rocker arm ratio, port configuration, and exhaust valve size? What about the rest of the exhaust system? What is pipe sizing, muffler type and sizing, and where will the exhaust exit? How about vehicle weight, rear axle ratio, and transmission type?

Smaller primary tube diameter helps velocity, which enhances torque. Larger primary tube size is better for high RPM (above 6,500 rpm) but hurts low- to mid-range torque. If header tubes are too small for the amount of power your engine makes, it will cause restriction and make the engine run hotter. Too large and you lose torque along with the possibility of exhaust gas reversion.

You have to think of your engine as an air pump. It draws in cool air and atomized fuel, which are compressed and ignited to make power. Torque comes from air velocity, meaning how fast you can move air and hot gases through the engine. Horsepower at high RPM comes from the volume of air/fuel you can move through the engine. The faster the air enters and exits through the chambers, the more torque the engine will make. The more volume of air you pass through the engine, the more horsepower the engine will make. Ideally, you will have both.

Designing an exhaust system begins at the header flanges, knowing what you want the engine to do. Most factory exhaust systems don't offer sufficient scavenging because they are so restrictive. Automakers have always compromised on the basis of noise. Pipe sizing tends to be small for cabin quiet. Factory exhaust systems are more about cabin noise levels and the economics of mass production.

What you want from your 429/460 is deep breathing and scavenging. With restriction comes excessive backpressure and the contamination of fresh air/fuel charges and poor performance depending upon cam profile and RPM range expected. As RPM increases, the worse this phenomenon becomes because spent gases tend to back up into the combustion chamber to contaminate the mixture. The more backwash you have on the intake stroke from spent gases, the more contaminated your engine's chambers become at high RPM, which causes serious performance issues from a tainted air/fuel mix. Contaminants take up precious space that could be better utilized by fresh air and fuel mass.

The first order of business is header design and both primary and secondary tube sizing. You might ask what you stand to gain from headers versus factory iron exhaust manifolds or short-tube versus long-tube headers. Based on experience more than anything, I will say you stand to gain at least 20 to 30 hp and comparable torque from long-tube headers. Much depends on how you choose and size the headers.

Headers allow hot gases to roar from ports into the exhaust system more quickly than you will see with exhaust manifolds. Unless you're restoring a Lincoln, Country Squire

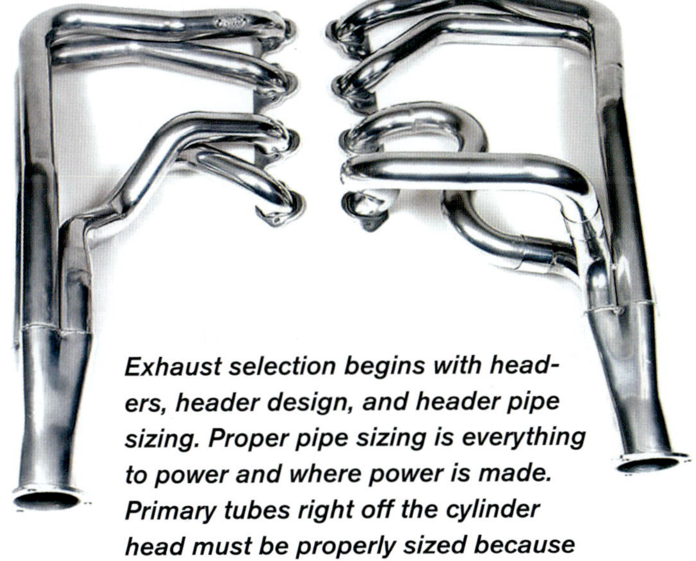

Exhaust selection begins with headers, header design, and header pipe sizing. Proper pipe sizing is everything to power and where power is made. Primary tubes right off the cylinder head must be properly sized because this is where exhaust scavenging begins. What counts is primary tube diameter and length. Longer primaries reduce the possibility of exhaust reversion. Most common primary tube sizes include 1½-, 1⅝-, 1¾-, 1⅞-, 2-, 2⅛-, 2¼-, and 2⅜ inches.

The best headers I've ever used come from Ford Powertrain Solutions (FPS) in Western Washington. Headers are all these people do and they turn out an incredible product. They fit perfectly and they are dyno developed. I like the ball-and-socket collectors, which have been copied by a number of header manufacturers. No worries about collector leaks.

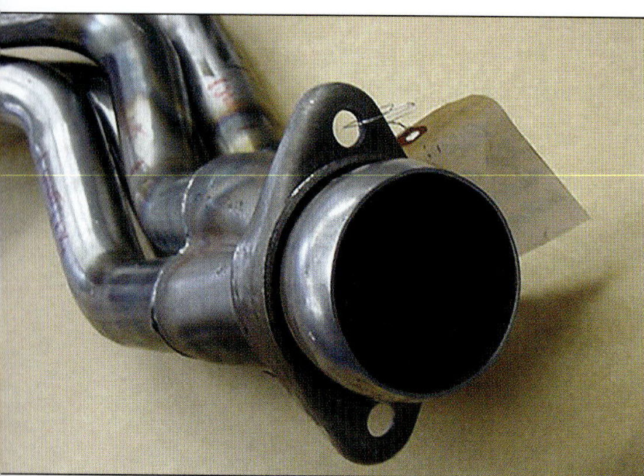

These FPS headers yield easy-fit exhaust collectors that dovetail into virtually any exhaust system. They do not leak.

station wagon, or a 429 Super Cobra Jet Mach 1, headers are going to be on your shopping list. Because most exhaust manifolds are designed more with space considerations in mind than gas flow, you will find rough cast iron inhibits flow terribly. Therefore, any kind of header, shorty or long tube, offers better flow than a rough cast-iron manifold. Rough cast surfaces create turbulence and restriction.

Begin planning with primary tubes right off the header flanges. Then, look at secondary tubes and collectors down under. Primary tube size and length are determined by where you want your torque curve. The smaller the primary tubes, the better low- to mid-range torque will be. However, if they are too small for the amount of power, things get too hot and you lose horsepower on the high end. If they are too large, you lose low- to mid-range torque. Primary tube length moves the torque and horsepower curves up or down depending on length. You either broaden or narrow the powerband (torque curve) based on primary tube length. You also move the torque peak up or down depending upon primary tube length.

Primary tube diameter and length are important considerations, which can make it tricky to choose

Three Formulas for Header Selection

1. Peak Torque RPM = primary tube size x 88,200 ÷ displacement of 1 cylinder bore.
2. Primary tube area = peak torque RPM ÷ 88,200 x displacement of 1 cylinder

The displacement of 1 cylinder is then multiplied by eight.

3. Displacement of 1 cylinder = primary pipe area x 88,200 ÷ peak torque RPM.

Formulas 1 and 2 provide a method for determining peak torque RPM (as contributed by the primary pipes) if you have already selected headers and know engine size. Formula 3 applies where primary pipe area can be determined if the desired peak torque RPM and engine size are already known.

This is an excellent example of how to execute an exhaust system. Long-tube headers clear the undercarriage by a wide margin and segue into a streamlined exhaust system with a crossover tube for balance. The main issue with any exhaust system is proper pipe sizing. You can go too large and lose precious torque or go too small and lose horsepower.

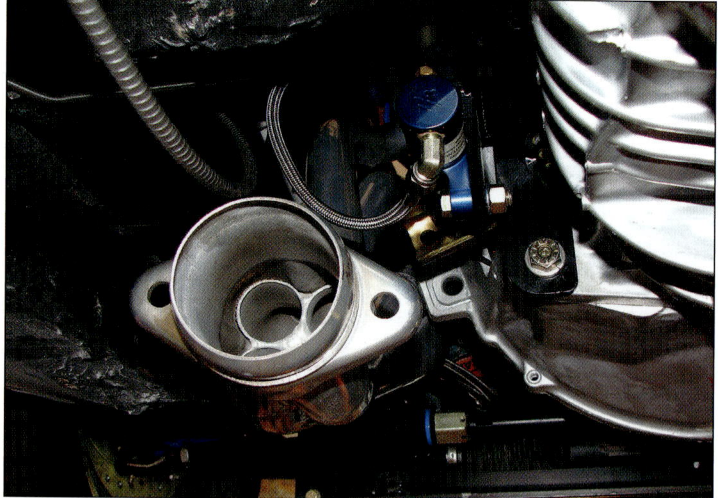

There are different approaches to header collectors. It seems every header manufacturer has a different approach to collectors. The collector should be free of ragged edges that can cause turbulence. I'm not certain that fire cones have been proven to improve power. Some manufacturers believe in them.

Equal-length headers are more effective with an open exhaust system at high RPM yet make virtually no difference through mufflers on the street. Because they consume a lot of space, and because you're working with a big-block, they're not worth the trouble.

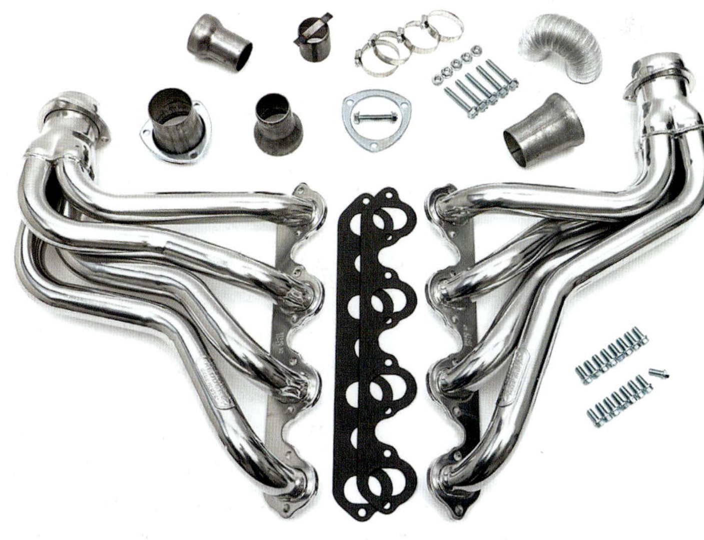

I like this complete Hedman installation kit (#89146) for the 429/460. Hedman street headers are available in black-painted or polished HTC thermal ceramic-coated finishes for corrosion resistance. What's more, Hedman includes all hardware and gaskets. (Photo Courtesy Hedman)

the right header for your application. So, with the knowledge of how primary tube size and length affect torque peak and below torque peak, you're ready to make an educated header purchase decision.

Here's a good formula from *Car Craft* magazine.

The magazine's example was a 350-ci Chevrolet; however, you can easily apply this formula to your 429/460–ci Ford. When you divide displacement (350 ci) by eight cylinders, you wind up with 43.750 ci per cylinder. Let's say you want peak torque to come on board around 4,000 rpm. Primary tube size choices are 1⅝, 1¾, and 1⅞ inches with a 0.040-inch wall thickness. That becomes 0.080 inch when you figure in 360 degrees of tube cross-section.

It goes like this: Area = (3.1416) x (ID radius) x (ID radius). It is through this formula you wind up with 1⅝ inches = 2.07 square inches. With a 1¾-inch tube, you get 2.19 square inches. With 1⅞ inches, you get 2.53 square inches.

If you plug each of these values into Equation 1, peak torque becomes 4,173, 4,416, and 5,100 rpm consecutively. This means 1⅝-inch primary tubes are optimum for this application. Of course, when you add displacement or want to push RPM/hp higher, you will have to go up a size or two. Apply this formula to your 429/460 project.

Another element not often addressed enough is primary tube length. Long-tube headers make more power, period. This has been

These Patriot Tight Tuck shorty headers for street rods offer nice fit and segue right into a custom exhaust system. They provide answers to many problems associated with engine swaps in street rods. Tight Tucks are manufactured from durable 16-gauge tubing and arrive on your doorstep complete with gaskets, header bolts, and collector reducers. (Photo Courtesy Patriot/PerTronix)

Hedman offers terrific complete header packages with everything you need to get the job done. Shorty headers should be considered for tight applications. They also yield better low-end torque. If you have room, long-tube headers make more sense in terms of horsepower and torque. (Photo Courtesy Hedman)

proven before my eyes many times. Shorty headers yield better fit and don't take up as much room. However, they lose on the dyno compared with long tubes.

Shorties yield easy installation compared with long tubes. They're available in a variety of sizes for popular applications. You get improved ground clearance, especially in tight installations, and shorties offer a definite improvement over factory manifolds. What you lose in shorties is a slight loss of low- to mid-range torque in high power and high-RPM operation. Shorties suffer more restriction at the collector, which drives exhaust gas temperatures skyward.

Long-tube headers are clearly better for high-performance driving and power. They are designed specifically for racing and improved higher-RPM torque. Long tubes are best for high-RPM power. They come in a greater number of sizes and lengths, especially for 429/460 engines.

The downside to long tubes is that they're more challenging to install and offer less clearance, especially in Mustang, Cougar, Falcon, Comet, Fairlane and Torino. They're easily damaged due to ground clearance, which means extra caution going over speed bumps. Oftentimes, long tubes will not clear the factory Ford starter, which means you will need a compact high-torque starter.

Secondary Tubes and Collectors

Secondary tubes and collectors have a similar effect on torque peak. It comes down to secondary tube length coupled with diameter. Once you have established secondary tube length, you can then sort out size based on all of the elements mentioned earlier. This can get quite involved, but I am going to do my best to keep it simple.

Collectors and H-pipes/X-pipes mean something to torque production but not as much when it comes to horsepower. Drag racers, for example, don't sweat collector length much because it has little effect on horsepower, which is where drag racers live. However, if torque is important to you, collector size and length become very important.

Equal-Length, Step, and Tri-Y Headers

As if shorty- and long-tube and pipe sizing wasn't confusing enough, there's more to think about. Equal-length headers make fit a greater challenge, especially with a 385-series big-block. However, equal length does serve a purpose. Equal-length primary headers are more effective with an open exhaust system at high RPM yet make virtually no difference through mufflers on the street. Unless you intend to spin your big-block at high RPM through an open exhaust, equal-length headers make little sense.

Step headers, like their equal-length counterparts, are high RPM/open exhaust only if you are seeking significant results. The idea behind step headers is to create a broader, flatter torque curve. However, I personally have never seen any proof through actual testing that this is true. Considering the discussions I've had with experienced engine builders, racers, and header manufacturers, the step header doesn't make enough of a difference in performance to warrant its cost. In theory, the step header is an interesting concept. In practical function, there's little to be gained from using them.

Let's talk about what step headers actually do. A tuned-length primary exhaust header tube creates a negative low-pressure wave that comes back up the pipe after the exhaust pulse. With conventional headers, this negative low-pressure wave happens at the primary tube's collector union due to sudden gas expansion as this pulse enters the collector. The wave returns to the exhaust valve during valve overlap when both the intake and exhaust valves are off their seats, which would completely scavenge the chamber of residual hot gases.

Building step headers is a time-intensive approach to power and may not be worth the time and expense based on the gamble involved. It can be a lot of work for so little return on investment. This is something you have to get just right. Otherwise, you can even lose power.

Tri-Y headers are more common with small-block Fords and FE-series big-blocks than the 429/460. However, the Tri-Y header does exist for the 429/460 and here's why. The Tri-Y funnels hot exhaust pulses from four primary pipes into a two-into-one collector. This approach creates a broader torque curve primarily for racing where you need grunt coming out of a turn into the straights. In other words, Tri-Ys provide better low- to mid-range torque. This happens by pairing cylinders that fire farthest apart to create a pulsing momentum with improved scavenging. This momentum creates velocity and, depending upon cam profile, draws out hot gases while hauling in fresh air and fuel. The Tri-Y approach doesn't always work for all engines because its effectiveness is determined by firing order.

Exhaust System Selection

In addition, as much as we've complained about noise ordinances in certain areas around the country,

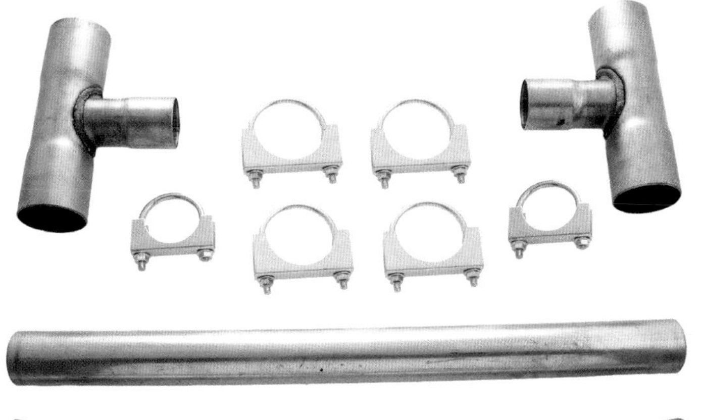

The market is rich in exhaust system kits and parts that enable you to do your own exhaust work. You can purchase all kinds of exhaust parts, J-bends, different degree bends, couplings, clamps, and more. This kit includes the crossover pipe, which should always be used to achieve balance. Without the crossover tube, your big-block will sound like a pop gun. (Photo Courtesy Summit Racing Equipment)

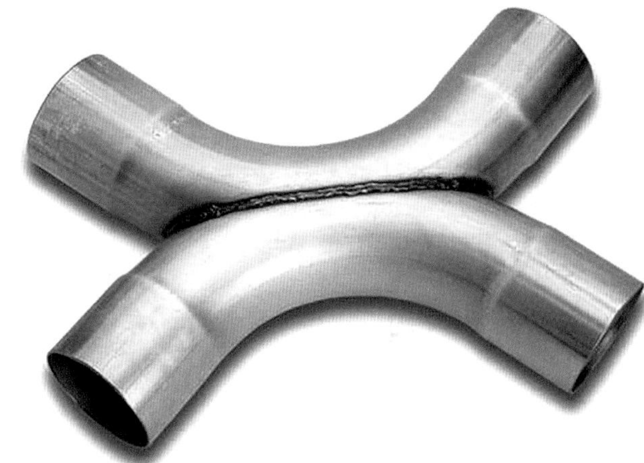

X-pipes and blend pipes are innovative in what they do for power. They will also give your 429/460 a snarly crackle at the tailpipes at high RPM. Simply put, the X-pipe organizes exhaust flow and smooths it out from both sides. (Photo Courtesy Summit Racing Equipment)

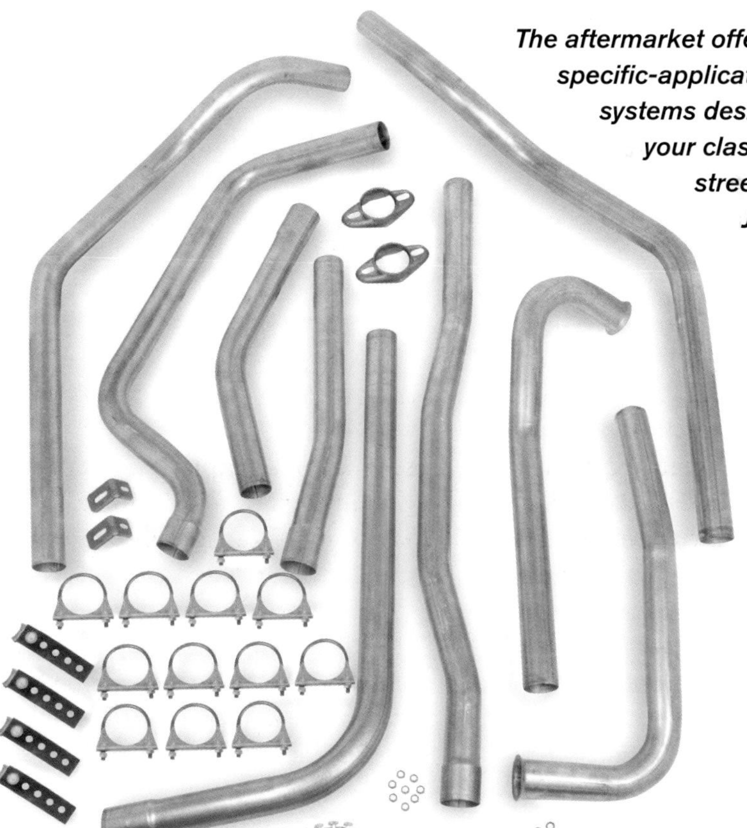

The aftermarket offers many specific-application exhaust systems designed to fit your classic muscle car, street rod, or truck. Just add mufflers. These systems offer custom fit, hangers, clamps, and hardware.

Flowmaster has long been the gold standard for sound and performance. This doesn't make Flowmaster your only choice. It is all in what you desire in both exhaust "throat" and power. Keep your hearing in mind when choosing a muffler. The Flowmaster Series 50 Delta Flow is a great street muffler. Resonance is non-existent and cabin noise is minimal. (Photo Courtesy Flowmaster)

I used to run Thrush Turbo mufflers decades ago and they sound terrific. They feature Tri-Flow Technology for better performance and sound. They are 100-percent aluminized coated shells for long life and are reversible (yes, really) for maximum flexibility to get the sound and fit you desire. (Photo Courtesy Summit Racing Equipment)

Dynomax's Super Turbo mufflers are the closest you can get to running an open pipe but a whole lot quieter. They're dyno proven. They have nice features that make them a good choice: less backpressure, durable construction, patented flow directors that channel exhaust gases in a very productive way along with fiberglass matting for a deep, throaty tone. It's a good muffler for the money. (Photo Courtesy Summit Racing Equipment)

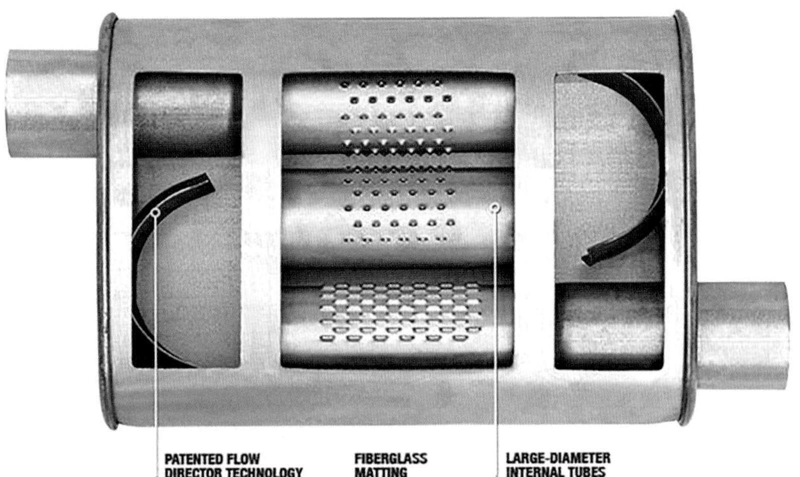

Here's a look inside the Dynomax Turbo Muffler. I like less restriction in a muffler along with a nice throaty tone at the tailpipes. What you want from a muffler is less cabin drone and resonance. Loud on the open road is uncool and damages hearing. (Photo Courtesy Summit Racing Equipment)

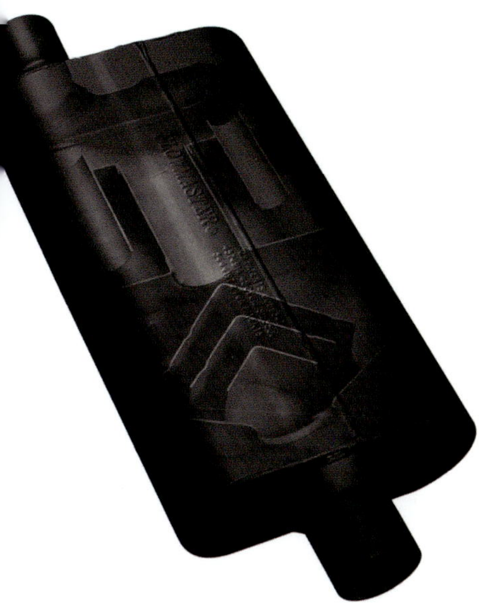

I tend to be partial to Flowmaster for its ability to engineer and tune what is undoubtedly the best-sounding muffler in the marketplace. It has that deep, rich "burble" at the tailpipes regardless of the type of engine you have. My best advice is to attend shows and cruises to decide what type of muffler is best for you.

If you're seeking all-out performance and the sound to go with it, Kooks race-series mufflers are optimum because they announce you have arrived. These race-series mufflers are made of 304-grade stainless steel and are polished to boot. These guys are reasonably priced too. (Photo Courtesy Summit Racing Equipment)

Exhaust Pipe Sizing				
Pipe Diameter (inches)	Pipe Area (inches squared)	Total Estimated CFM	Maximum Horsepower Per Pipe	Maximum Horsepower for Dual Exhaust
1.50	1.48	171	78	155
1.75	2.07	239	108	217
2.00	2.76	318	144	289
2.25	3.55	408	185	371
2.50	4.43	509	232	463
2.75	5.41	622	283	566
3.00	6.49	747	339	679
3.25	7.67	882	401	802
3.50	8.59	1029	468	935
Information Courtesy www.exhaustvideos.com				

we're finding noise just isn't what most people want anymore. Loud noise, no matter your age, causes deafness and makes conversation impossible. On the open road at speed, a loud exhaust system can take a toll on your hearing, which is a very real concern.

Racers are learning that there's torque hidden in those exhaust silencers. Companies such as Flowmaster, Magnaflow, Hooker, JBA, Doug's, Borla, and others are also discovering more horsepower and torque through advanced muffler design and pipe-sizing technology. For the street, I like the Flowmaster Delta Flow Series 50 for throatiness and cabin quiet. Gone is the resonance and ringing in your ears. Found is the torque you desire. These time-proven mufflers deliver real throat.

Summit Racing Equipment's website offers good information on how to design an exhaust system for your Ford muscle car. It suggests first knowing what size pipe to choose once you get past the header collectors. Fortunately, the automotive aftermarket offers a huge variety of complete exhaust systems for all kinds of vintage Ford muscle cars, which makes selection and installation easier. Not all off-the-shelf systems are a great fit. In fact, you will probably need the expertise of a good exhaust shop to install just about any system because nearly all require some kind of adjustment to achieve proper fit.

I suggest knowing the difference between a crush bend and mandrel bending, which affects exhaust flow, when you buy an exhaust system. Crush bending causes flow restriction along the way. Mandrel bending provides a smooth journey and it looks better. Always go with an H- or X-pipe dual-exhaust system (balance tube) for improved scavenging and better sound. Without a balance tube, performance suffers, and you will wind up with an exhaust system that sounds horrible.

National Parts Depot offers the most extensive line-up of exhaust systems for vintage Fords in the industry. You may combine these systems with a wide variety of aftermarket mufflers depending upon pipe size desired. Which muffler you choose for your 385-series engine project depends on desired performance and noise levels. The key is to get your pipe sizing correct and everything else will fall into place.

Header fitment has always been challenging depending upon the vehicle you're building. Choose headers first based on fitment, then primary and secondary tube sizing and configuration. If they won't fit in the first place, there's no point in going any further.

Here's a good chart to use, according to www.exhaustvideos.com.

Based on the chart, you should never need more than 3.000 inches of pipe diameter for a 600-hp 460. Remember that when you go too large, you lose torque, which is why you should keep pipe sizing conservative because larger isn't always better. The best path to pipe selection is common sense. You don't need 3.000-inch pipes with a 350-horse engine. You can get away with 2½-inch-diameter pipes with a 400- to 500-horse 460. Keep in mind how much space large-diameter pipes consume. It is very difficult to fit 2½- to 3-inch pipes underneath a Mustang or Torino.

The folks at www.exhaustvideos.com base their calculations on raw facts. They suggest your engine needs to flow 1.5 cfm through the intake per 1 engine horsepower. The exhaust system needs to flow 2.5 cfm per 1 engine horsepower because hot gases consume more space than cool incoming air. They suggest taking engine RPM x displacement, then dividing by two. This

These exhaust couplings make exhaust servicing a snap. You can weld these to mufflers, which would make muffler swaps straightforward. You may also use them in conjunction with header collectors where they can be disconnected for drag racing use. (Photo Courtesy Summit Racing Equipment)

ARP offers a wide variety of header bolt kits to facilitate your header installation. Each kit includes the specific number of parts required for your application, plus lock washers and either hex or 12-point heads. When you install headers, start all of the bolts, then tighten them crisscross style. Snug all of them, then apply torque to get them good and tight. (Photo Courtesy ARP)

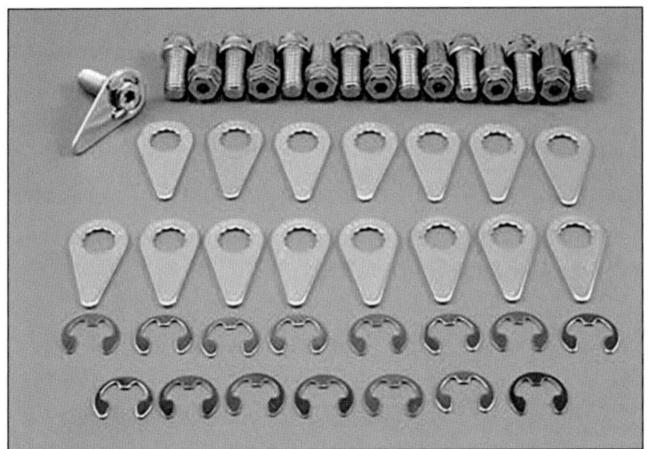

Stage-8 locking header fasteners use a patented system that consists of a grooved hex-head bolt or nut, a retainer, and a snap clip. They will not come loose, period. The retainer fits over the bolt head and locks the bolt against the header tube, and the snap clip holds the retainer in place. They cost more than conventional header bolts, but they are worth every penny in time saved. (Photo Courtesy Summit Racing Equipment)

is intake volume. When you take intake volume and figure in thermal expansion, this you get exhaust gas volume. Pipes typically handle 115 cfm per square inch according to www.exhaustvideos.com.

Stainless or Aluminized?

Another item we don't think about enough is material. Stainless or aluminized steel? Because exhaust systems are more a work of art these days as well as functional, additional thought must be given to material and aesthetics.

Aluminized exhaust systems are more affordable; however, they are more susceptible to rust as time passes, especially if you live where humidity is high. If appearance is important to you, you can ceramic-coat the headers and pipes. However, it is very expensive. The beauty of ceramic coating is color choice including a natural metal finish if you desire. Ceramic coatings such as Jet Hot can withstand temperatures up to 1,700°F. If you're going to dyno test your 429/460, remember that ceramic coating doesn't like the extreme heat of a dyno pull. It will fog badly. Dyno test with bare steel headers.

If your budget allows, stainless steel is the best choice for an exhaust system because it will last the life of a restoration. Although stainless is corrosion resistant, it is not corrosion proof. It can rust in pinpoint locations if not cared for.

Not much attention is paid to exhaust tips, but they will affect performance to some degree, not to mention sound. You want exhaust tips that are not restrictive, such as small quad-tips or those louvered first-generation Mustang trumpet tips. Both are quite restrictive though they're at the end of the system.

CHAPTER 10

BREAK-IN AND TUNING

When you fire an engine for the first time, all of your hard work either proves or disproves itself with the roar of combustion. It is a religious moment to fire an engine for the first time. Get your mind around proper break-in first. Don't get so caught up in the experience that you forget what you're supposed to be doing. Dyno-testing and break-in are crucial to how your engine is going to perform and endure.

All of your engine's moving parts must be soaking wet with lubrication before fire-up, which is why you should prime the oiling system to get bearings and cylinder walls soaking wet. There will be a lot of blue/

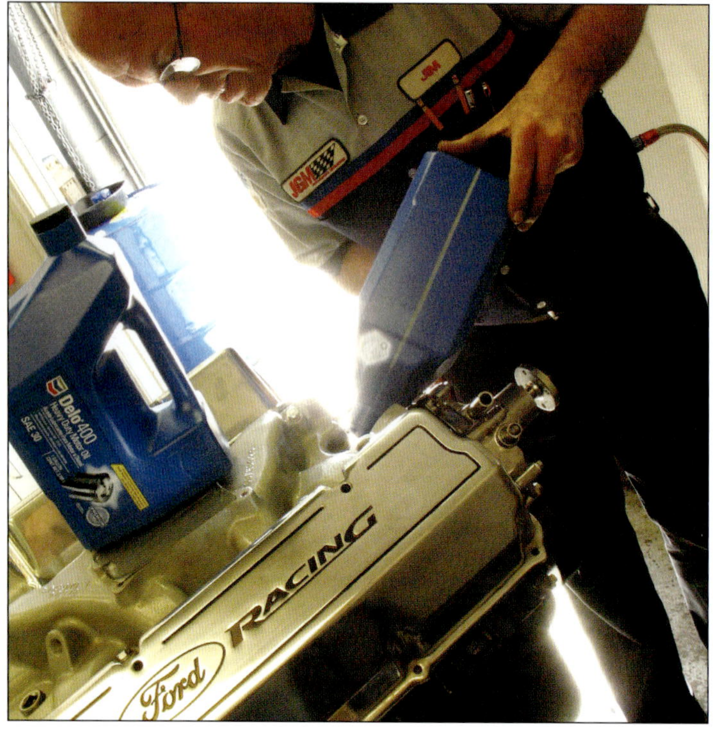

The first order of business is to put conventional 30-weight engine oil in the pan along with any break-in additives, such as ZDDP, which is good for any engine break-in. Whether you're running a flat-tappet or roller cam, an additive with zinc is good for a kinder, gentler break-in because it reduces wear issues.

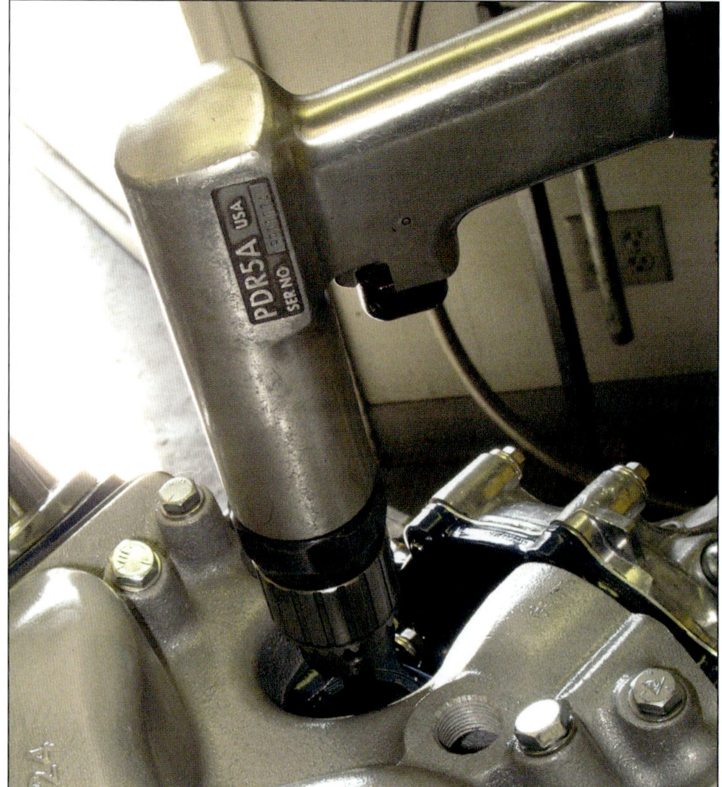

Priming the oil system with a 1/2-inch-drive electric or pneumatic drill gets moving parts slippery wet for a healthy start-up. Never fire an engine without first priming the oil system. Never use synthetic engine oil for break-in.

Use ethylene glycol coolant only after you've fired the engine and have confirmed it is free of leaks. Then, completely drain all coolant and begin with a dry block. Evans Non-Aqueous coolant is a nice alternative to conventional antifreeze. It is straight coolant without water, which means it is corrosion free and will last the life of your engine.

An anti-collapse spring should always be used in the lower radiator hose. Although there's controversy about this approach, it is the best approach because you don't want hose collapse at high RPM. If you are experiencing overheat on the open road but not in town, check the lower hose for collapse.

Fan shrouding means half of the fan should be out of the shroud for the best airflow and velocity. This fan is too deep into the shroud, which can cause air stagnation.

Coolant additives like Hy-Per Lube Super Coolant and Water Wetter improve coolant surface tension, which puts more coolant in contact with hot surfaces for better heat conductivity.

I suggest the use of a coolant filter in the upper radiator hose for the first 5,000 miles to capture any stray iron or aluminum casting particles that could plug up a radiator and heater core. Then, operate without the filter.

Comp Cams Break-In oil is conventional 30-weight engine oil with ZDDP additive to help work-harden cam lobes (flat tappet). You may also use a diesel-grade 30-weight engine oil, which automatically has zinc.

white smoke when the engine fires; however, all will be good with less risk of damage to dry bearings and seals. Fire the engine with straight SAE 30-weight conventional Castrol or Valvoline engine oil.

Make sure that your lubrication has the ZDDP (zinc) addictive, which is especially important if you're running a flat-tappet camshaft. Never use synthetic engine oil for break-in. Upon your first oil change, which should happen immediately following break-in, mix in a bottle of CamGuard. At the very least, you want a zinc additive or zinc-based engine oil to minimize wear, especially with a flat-tappet cam.

Break-In

The greatest favor you can do your engine (and your wallet) is to spend money on a good dyno pull, which accomplishes break-in and engine tuning to where it's ready to go in the vehicle without a hitch. Regardless of what type of cam you have, be it roller or flat-tappet, the rules of proper break-in apply to every type of engine because you want to seat rings and bearings with a proper run-in.

When the engine fires, confirm oil pressure and take it immediately to 2,500 rpm and let it run at this speed for at least 30 minutes. Under optimum conditions, you will fire your engine on a dyno with an experienced dyno technician and run it under a load after it has been running at 2,500 rpm for 30 minutes.

For good piston ring and bearing seating, you want a load at 2,500 to 3,000 rpm. Loading under throttle builds cylinder pressure, which allows rings to expand and seat into cylinder walls once oil is at operating temperature. You want a minimum 140°F coolant temperature before doing a power pull. If you have dyno access, you can break in an engine with proper tuning and operation to where all you have to do is install it in the car.

The first pull you should make is a jet check to establish air/fuel mixture. To perform a jet check, load the engine and go wide-open throttle for 15 seconds at 4,500 rpm and immediately shut down. Pull all eight spark plugs and inspect for proper color. All the basic rules of spark plug reading apply here: tan/beige, you're good; sooty black, rich; snow white, too lean. If you can see tiny dots of aluminum on the insulator, you are dangerously lean. When you are lean, go up several jet sizes toward

A spark plug firing tip is your best barometer of engine health. You want to see light tan to white. Snow white with dots of aluminum on the insulator means too lean and dangerous. Sooty black indicates too rich and/or high oil consumption. Jet sizing depends upon what you witness during the jet check.

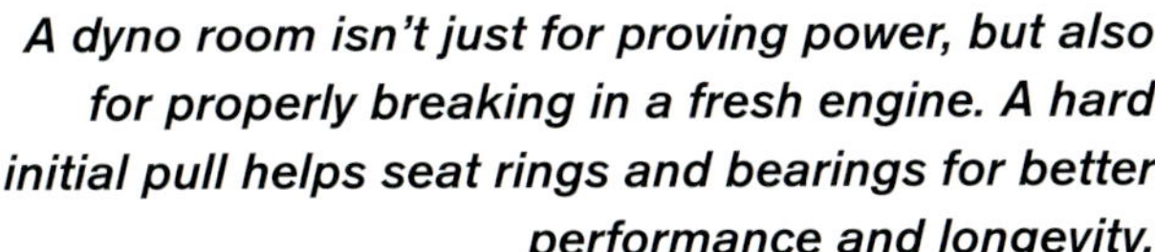

A dyno room isn't just for proving power, but also for properly breaking in a fresh engine. A hard initial pull helps seat rings and bearings for better performance and longevity.

rich, then come back to center in little steps and observe spark plug color. Spark plug insulator color is the best barometer of engine health and spirit.

Ignition timing should be somewhere around 6 to 12 degrees BTDC at idle and total timing at 34 to 36 degrees BTDC at 3,500 rpm. This minimizes the risk of detonation and engine damage. Some camshaft/cylinder head combinations lend themselves to more conservative ignition timing. You want air/fuel on the rich side to prevent detonation and a lean meltdown. It only takes a split second of detonation at 6,000 rpm under a load to blow an engine. You can always go leaner and more aggressive with time and testing. Oil pressure should be around 40 to 60 psi or 10 pounds per 1,000 rpm. At 5,000 rpm, you want a solid 50 pounds minimum.

Resist the desire to push ignition timing. Start out in the 32 to 36 BTDC total advance range at 3,500 rpm and watch your power curve. Testing under the controlled conditions of a dyno room is one thing. However, on the road in a hot engine compartment under varying conditions is another thing entirely. You can be fine in a dyno room at 38 to 40 degrees BTDC with 110-octane fuel. Out on the road with 92-octane fuel and a lot of underhood heat is another environment entirely. Keep ignition timing and fuel curves conservative.

After the Break-In

Once break-in is safely out of the way, what's next? I've learned from several reputable engine builders to observe the following. For the first 500 miles, keep your driving conservative. Continue those bursts of power periodically for ring and bearing seating. At 500 to 1,000 miles, change your oil using conventional SAE 10W30. At 1,000 to 2,000 miles, change oil going to a synthetic 10W30 or 10W40. Going synthetic is not mandatory. It is simply what I prefer. Wear data from synthetic engine oil is impressive. I've observed how well synthetic lubricants work. In engines driven 250,000 to 300,000 miles, there's virtually no wear. Synthetic is a good investment in your engine. Never opt for a cheap oil filter. I suggest using Mobil 1, Motorcraft, Wix, or Bosch oil filters.

At 1,500 miles, do a spark plug reading on all eight cylinders, examine coolant and thermostat function, inspect oil for color and content. Check underneath for leaks around the pan, timing cover, rear main seal, and freeze plugs.

When it comes to coolant, always opt for a 50/50 mix of antifreeze and distilled water. Never use tap water. Tap water can contain all kinds of minerals and contaminants that can damage your cooling system. Use distilled water only with antifreeze. Evans Non-Aqueous coolant is an excellent investment instead of conventional antifreeze because it virtually never has to be replaced and there's no corrosion. You run 100-percent Evans coolant and no water. Any water in the cooling system must be removed.

CHAPTER 11

Power Builds

I've had the good fortune of having worked with some of the best engine builders in the country and primarily on Ford engines. No matter how many engine builds I've covered for the magazines and in books, there has always been something new to learn from each build. Sometimes, the "tried and proven" doesn't always work. What works on a Chevy or Chrysler doesn't always work with a Ford.

What makes the 385-series big-block so terrific is its architecture and Ford-tested tough design and construction. You can hammer on this engine, and it always comes back for more. The factory 429/460 block can withstand up to 700 hp. If your budget allows for stock iron heads, there's a lot you can do with the factory castings, especially if you have access to good head porting talent. This is an engine born to make a lot of power at not much expense.

429 Super Cobra Jet

This is an excellent example of what the 429 Super Cobra Jet was from the factory and what makes it unique in the world of classic muscle cars. The 1970–1971 429 Super Cobra Jet was the last Ford muscle engine from the greatest muscle car era in vintage Detroit history. It was in great company with Chrysler's 426- and 440-ci wedges and the legendary Hemi, Chevy's 454, Buick/Olds/Pontiac's 455, and AMC's 401.

The 429 Cobra Jet had an aggressive hydraulic cam with Rochester Quadrajet carburetion. The Super Cobra Jet went beyond the Cobra Jet with a very aggressive mechanical tappet camshaft, Holley 780-cfm carburetion, and a "rumpity-rump-rump" idle. The darned thing was fast. The 429 Super Cobra Jet was badass whether it was in a Mustang or the intermediate Torino, Fairlane, or Cyclone. You have to love the clatter of mechanical lifters, throaty heads, and the abundant power this engine made.

It moved the earth . . .

JGM Performance Engineering in Valencia, California, took on this box-stock original 1970–1971 429 Super Cobra Jet and decided to enhance its power-making capabilities. On the dyno, they got 467 hp and 480 ft-lbs of torque. All of the power is in by 5,700 rpm.

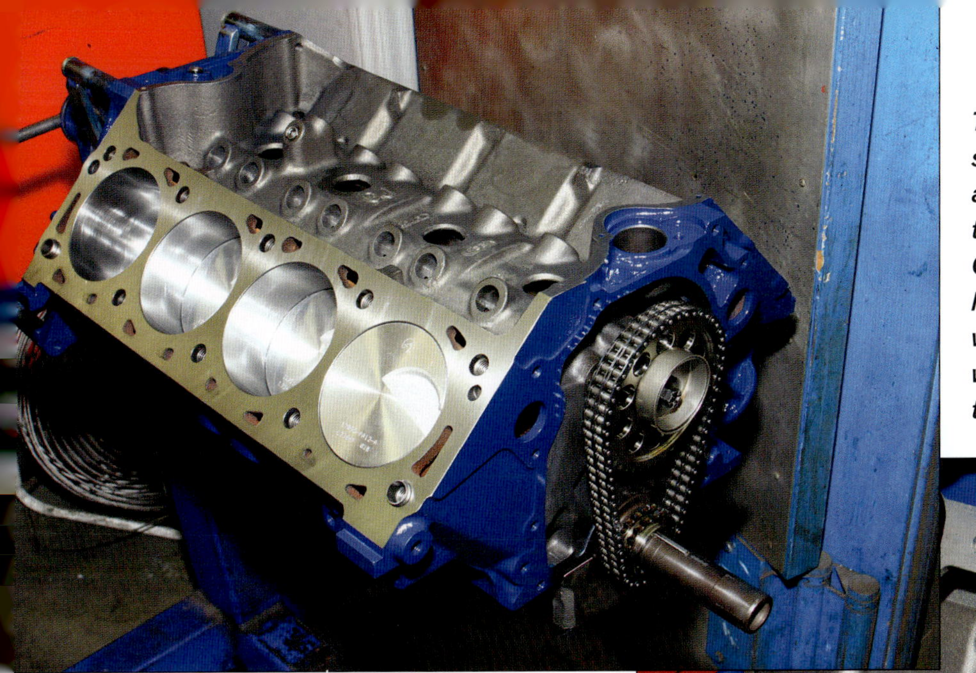

This is JGM's 429 Super Cobra Jet short-block with Speed Pro forged and coated 0.030-inch-oversize pistons, bearings, and ductile iron rings. Crane has provided a stock flat-tappet hydraulic cam. Comp Cams has provided special hydraulic lifters equipped with tiny 0.012-inch oil holes designed to keep lobes lubricated.

The 429 Cobra Jet block is a limited-production block casting (D0OE-B) with four-bolt mains, thicker main webs and cylinder walls, and a "CJ" cast in the lifter valley. There's also the 429 Police Interceptor block, which is basically the same casting with four-bolt mains.

JGM has opted for Speed Pro forged pistons and ARP Wave-Loc bolts. Stock rods have been reconditioned and strengthened.

This is how you build a 429 Super Cobra Jet. You can do this with any 385-series engine: four-bolt mains, heavy-duty rods, forged pistons, ARP main studs, and a Melling high-volume oil pump. There is also the 460 truck block option with a D7TE/D8TE/D9TE casting number also machined for four-bolt mains. You don't have to search high and low for a Cobra Jet or Police Interceptor block. You can turn any 429/460 block into a four-bolt main.

Rod bolts and main studs are given the once over with a torque wrench and marked as torqued with a felt-tip pen. This ensures all fasteners have been properly tightened.

The Super Cobra Jet 429 heads have 2.19/1.73-inch intake/exhaust valves, 72– to 74-cc chambers, and an adjustable studded valvetrain.

The Cobra Jet head sports huge drive-through ports engineered for high-RPM power. These heads have been cleaned up with a good port job.

JGM has upgraded the valvetrain with one-piece, 0.080-inch-thick-wall pushrods for durability.

A very important task with any 385-series build is confirming true TDC and degreeing the cam. If you don't check true TDC, nothing else about degreeing the cam will be right.

JGM has opted for reduced-friction components such as Crane roller rockers, two-piece fuel pump eccentric, and a Crane dual-roller timing set.

The 429 Super Cobra Jet was factory equipped with a flat-tappet mechanical cam, which calls for valve lash adjustment. Valve lash for the Super Cobra Jet is 0.024/0.026-inch intake/exhaust with valves closed. If lash seems excessive (noisy), tighten it up a bit to 0.020/0.022 inch. These numbers are based on builder feedback.

Crane Classic full-roller 1.70:1-ratio rocker arms offer precision and reduced friction performance. Valvetrain geometry has been checked.

Intake manifold studs in the corners ensure proper manifold alignment. Permatex The Right Stuff is applied only to the cooling passages.

Ford's 429-4V engine was fitted with two basic 4-barrel intake manifolds: D0OE-9425-D designed for the spread-bore carburetor (4-barrel and Cobra Jet) and D0OE-9425-C for the Holley 4150/4160 square-flange (Super Cobra Jet). Both are cast-iron and weigh a ton.

JGM opted for a 750-cfm Holley HP for this SCJ instead of the OEM-style 4150. The result was 467 hp and 480 ft-lbs of torque.

At 375 hp with 450 lb-ft of torque, the 385-series 429-ci big-block was the most powerful factory engine ever installed in a classic Mustang. It was a flash-bang grenade before the dead silence of the lame 1970s. For 1970–1971, the 429 got incredible wedge heads in two forms, Cobra Jet and Super Cobra Jet, which made it a whole lot better than the Lincoln's 460 luxury car mill.

The 429 was Ford's response to Chevrolet's 396-, 427-, and 454-ci big-blocks, and was developed to replace the FE-series 390-, 427-, and 428-ci big-blocks along with the heavy and outdated 462-ci MEL (Mercury-Edsel-Lincoln) big-block in 1968. The 429- and 460-ci big-blocks were a new generation of large-cube engines developed for both luxury and performance. The 429/460 engines were lighter than the big-cube engines they replaced.

The 429/460 employed a lightweight casting technique with similar architecture to Ford's more petite 90-degree Fairlane small-block, with skirtless block and poly-angle valve heads. In fact, the 429/460 heads borrow a lot of port and valve technology from the 351C engine and Chevrolet's 396/427/454-ci big-blocks.

The 1970–1971 429 Cobra Jet hit the option sheet with an aggressive flat-tappet hydraulic cam, fixed stamped bolt/fulcrum rockers, 715-cfm Rochester Quadrajet carburetion, dual-plane spread-bore iron manifold, four-bolt main block, and large-port cylinder heads with a factory rating of 370 hp with 450 ft-lbs of torque.

The mechanical tappet 429 Super Cobra Jet, a powerful upgrade, was a 1-2 punch response to Chevrolet's 450- and 465-horse 454-ci LS6 and LS7 big-blocks in the Chevelle. Ford gave it an aggressive mechanical cam, adjustable stud-mounted rockers, and 4150 Holley carburetion. Like the big 454-inch Chevy, Ford's 429 SCJ was grossly underrated at 375 hp. It made abundant horsepower and torque without breaking a sweat. JGM proved this out on the Super Flow dyno.

According to Ford insiders who were with the company at the time, the goal was to eventually take the 385-series engine to more than 500 ci had the battle for power not ended in 1970. Ford and other Detroit automakers backed off when priorities shifted from racing and performance to safety, emissions, and fuel economy. The Arab Oil Embargo in 1973–1974 ended any plan for high-performance muscle cars. Performance didn't return until the 1980s.

JGM Performance Engineering loves the 385-series 429/460-ci big-block engines and has built a lot of them. These engines make big torque for luxury cars and trucks. They can be dialed-in for drag racing horsepower. They also make robust street engines for freeway acceleration and the commute. JGM wanted to know how much power could be made from a 429 Super Cobra Jet with factory iron heads and intake along with a stock-grind Crane flat-tappet hydraulic camshaft.

Remember, this is the 429 Cobra Jet block with four-bolt mains, thick webs, 4.360-inch bores, and 10.310-inch deck height. On top are 429 Cobra Jet heads with 2.19/1.73-inch intake/exhaust valves, 72- to 74-cc chambers, and an adjustable valvetrain. Down below, a 4UA nodular iron crank with a 3.590-inch stroke along with a set of D0OE-A forged steel Cobra Jet rods. The rods were reconditioned and fitted with ARP bolts.

Speed Pro coated and forged the aluminum 0.030-inch-oversize pistons, Clevite 77 bearings, rings, and Fel-Pro gaskets, also from Summit. Crane provided a stock flat-tappet hydraulic cam, while Comp Cams set JGM up with hydraulic lifters equipped with tiny 0.012-inch oil holes designed to keep lobes lubricated.

JGM Performance Engineering opted for stainless steel Speed Pro 2.19/1.73-inch valves. With a little head port massaging, JGM Performance Engineering achieved 467 hp and 480 ft-lbs of torque. Not bad from a dead-stock 429 Super Cobra Jet. I am convinced that methodical engine building technique and the exceptional Holley HP made all the difference.

460 Street/Strip Build

Sometimes, all you need is displacement. Take what's basically a 460 truck block and 1973 460 heads to weave a high-revving personality into the build and you have an affordable ground-shaking street big-block. JGM Performance Engineering again shows how to make power with an all-iron 460 and both Summit Racing and COMP parts. They have taken standard 460 iron heads and massaged the ports for improved flow. JGM has also cleaned up the chambers to eliminate potential hot spots that could cause detonation.

JGM is easily one of the most knowledgeable 385-series build shops in the world. They understand how to spec, massage, cam, and head these engines to where they make power. When JGM approached me to build a 460, it was straightforward. They wanted it budget, boatloads of torque without the expense. Something the average enthusiast could build and enjoy.

The JGM 460 is all about brute street torque for the commute and weekend play. This is a civilized street mill with a smooth idle and tremendous torque. Give it a light throttle and it goes. I spent considerable time on the JGM dyno with different intake manifolds and Holley carburetion to see what I could get. In the end, Edelbrock won out in terms of power along with Holley 850-cfm carburetion.

More than 500 hp and more than 500 ft-lbs of torque with the Edelbrock Performer RPM 460 (7166) manifold and Holley 850-cfm Double Pumper. Not bad for iron heads and a Comp hydraulic roller cam.

JGM Street/Strip 460 Performance Numbers

RPM	Weiand/Holley Induction Corrected HP	Weiand/Holley Induction Corrected Torque ft-lbs	Edelbrock/Holley Induction Corrected HP	Edelbrock/Holley Induction Corrected Torque ft-lbs
3,500	345.8	521.3	383.9	576.5
4,000	402.7	531.9	439.4	580.0
4,500	441.1	518.2	483.0	567.5
5,000	471.8	498.9	504.2	533.6
5,500	491.4	471.6	505.5	485.5
5,600	487.3	458.7	498.1	469.2

Here's how you build an affordable powerhouse 460. This ported iron-head 460 sports a hot, yet streetable roller hydraulic cam, a Weiand Stealth intake, and Holley 850-cfm 4150 Double Pumper carburetion with an open 1-inch spacer. JGM ran 91-octane unleaded fuel with 1⅞-inch-long tube Hedman Hustler headers and 39 degrees of total ignition timing. We tested both Edelbrock and Weiand induction.

Speed Pro coated and forged pistons have been used with stock rods reconditioned and fitted with ARP bolts.

You can build a stout 460 (with a 0.060-inch overbore) for not much money with ARP main and rod bolts, two-bolt mains, forged pistons, a Melling oil pump, and a streetable roller cam and wind up with nearly 500 hp and more than 500 ft-lbs of torque.

Jim Grubbs has opted for an aggressive, yet quite streetable, roller hydraulic cam from Comp Cams.

Comp-linked hydraulic roller lifters complement the cam. I have learned that it is best to "kit" your cam selection, which includes the lifters and valve springs for solid compatibility.

Jim has a lot of bench time on these bread-and-butter iron castings. He performed port work and then went back to the flow bench.

Summit Racing offers a nice selection of affordable house-brand harmonic dampers. Jim Grubbs wanted this 500-horse 460 to be budget in the truest sense. Real affordable power for street and strip.

New stainless-steel valves are fitted to the factory iron heads for durability.

Head gasket thickness is figured into compression ratio along with volume above the piston ring package.

In the interest of durability, Jim has gone with ARP fasteners throughout.

I elected to try two dual-plane manifolds on the Grubbs Budget 460, the Weiand Stealth 460, and Edelbrock's Performer 460. With the Weiand, I made 491 hp and 532 ft-lbs of torque. I popped the Edelbrock on top and made 503 hp and 580 ft-lbs of torque.

Jim chose Trick Flow 1.73:1 roller rockers for reduced friction and durability. Adjustment with hydraulic roller tappets is zero lash valves closed, then 1/4 turn.

It is remarkable how much power is made from this iron-head 460. The best numbers came from the Edelbrock Performer 460 at 508.3 hp at 5,200 rpm and 580.1 at 4,200 rpm. This thing makes tremendous power and it's not even working hard. You can marry this formula to a Fairlane, Torino, Mustang, Cougar, or F-Series and scorch the pavement.

MCE 598-ci T-Rex Build

Marvin McAfee of Marvin Competition Engines (MCE) in Los Angeles knew how to make power in his day. His builds had a snarky aggressive bark when the throttles were pinned. Marvin assembled a good formula for big-cube power in his 598-ci T-Rex A460 Ford Performance build.

When Marvin penciled-out his 598-ci T-Rex vision a decade ago, his goal was between 800 and 900 hp and a comparable amount of torque in the 800 ft-lbs range with a single 4-barrel Holley carburetor. To stand any chance of getting there, he needed Ford Racing's new A460 race block with its thick wall construction, four-bolt mains, siamesed 4.600-inch bores, and steel main caps.

Marvin also needed a cylinder head, camshaft, and induction package that would deliver the kind of power he had planned. Seasoned engine builders are getting in excess of 1,000 hp from the A460 Ford block from a variety of new cylinder heads and induction systems that have come into the marketplace in recent years.

The Ford Racing C460 356-T6 aluminum cylinder head is a high-port job designed for professional racing. To repeat, this is not a street head. Valve angles are 7.5 degrees intake and 8.0 degrees exhaust void of side angles. Chamber size is 65 cc with suggested 2.450/1.900-inch valve sizing Manley Performance stainless and titanium steel valve sizing. Port and chamber sizing and shape are based on the successful Ford Racing Yates cylinder head.

Jon Kaase Racing Engines does a cool custom-ported Ford Racing C460 head that flows more than

500 cfm intake at 0.800-inch lift and more than 350 cfm at 0.800-inch-lift exhaust. The Kaase head ready to bolt on with Pro Stock port work, competition valve job, Manley Performance titanium steel valves, PSI valve springs, and titanium retainers is a good value for the money. This is how you make the C460 head even better than what you have right out of the box with Manley stainless steel valves and Comp Cams springs and retainers.

I am about to show you what can be done with these heads right out of the Ford Performance/Ford Racing box with little more than a port match and precision valvetrain components from Jesel, Comp Cams, and Manley Performance. Team MCE went to the dyno expecting 800 to 850 hp and a comparable amount of torque. Some may call this conservative, considering that engines of this caliber can make 1,000 hp and more than 900 ft-lbs of torque without breaking a sweat that power 8-second drag cars. Marvin always took a more conservative approach because he opted on the side of durability. He wanted an engine that would stay together while delivering planet-rocking power. Call it a balance of power and durability, which are challenging to achieve in a racing engine.

Defining Blueprint

There's blueprinting an engine, and then there's really blueprinting an engine. It isn't only about finite machine work and dynamic balance; it is getting all eight cylinders marching in unison with one another. You want them all doing the same thing. This is a tall order due to the imperfections of block castings, pistons, connecting rods, and crankshafts. None are perfect. However, you can get it close. You want identical compression ratio across the board, or as close as you can get it. You want bearing and piston/cylinder wall tolerances as uniform as you can get them.

The late Marvin McAfee of MCE Engines in Los Angeles was always a taskmaster for detail in blueprinting. He chased every bolt and bolt hole to get threads perfect and smooth because he wanted accurate torque readings. Once all the thread chasing and clean-up work was performed, Marvin lubricated bolt threads with SAE 30-weight engine oil or moly lube, stressing that you never fill the hole with oil. Excessive oil in bolt holes means you risk cracking the block because you cannot compress a liquid. Torque the bolt with no way for oil to escape and you "hydraulic" and crack the casting. Marvin stressed that when you install studs instead of bolts, never bottom-out the stud. Allow roughly 1/8 to 1/4 inch of gap at the bottom to allow room for oil to escape. What you want from a stud or a bolt when torque is applied is tension on the shank and threads. It is bolt or stud stretch and tension that provide clamping power on main and rod caps and other components.

Marvin's Ford Performance/MCE Engines big-inch big-block hasn't been the easiest engine project to undertake due to its limited production nature. You have a block and heads that enthusiasts don't encounter every day, which makes it tricky to find compatible components. Because the C460 isn't a mainstream off-the-shelf cylinder head, finding just the right headers exhausted most of Marvin's resources.

When Marvin contacted Custom Performance Racing in Gardena, California, they were glad to accommodate me and knew exactly what I needed to make the most of the T-Rex 598. Marvin wanted a custom equal-length step header with 2⅛-inch primary tubes segueing into 2¼-inch pipes down to 4½ inches. He had to go with a huge 4.000-inch collector because necessary raw materials (4½-inch pipe) weren't available at the time. The upside of 4-inch collectors is improved backpressure along with velocity for good scavenging depending upon valve overlap. Custom Performance Racing was able to fabricate a set of long-tube equal-length step headers just in time for the T-Rex 598 dyno session.

When you're about to test an engine like this, there's such anticipation. There were fitment issues with these headers because JGM Performance Engineering had an explosion-proof bell that was not compatible with these custom headers. Jeff Latimer of JGM Performance Engineering went above and beyond when he modified the bellhousing for use with these headers from Custom Performance Racing. This cost a lot of valuable time. What made the headers a tricky fit was Marvin's mandate for equal-length step plumbing to achieve and surpass my horsepower goal. This meant out-of-the-ordinary header tube routing to get the kind of power required.

Once on the dyno and running, there were problems that made continued pulls potentially destructive to the engine. Marvin had JGM perform three pulls. It was JGM's belief that the 598 had potentially blown a head gasket. Any additional pulls would have done engine damage and Marvin wasn't willing to risk that. He unloaded the engine and took it home. There was a plan to correct the 598's problems and get it back on the dyno. Age and health issues kept Marvin from returning to the dyno. In fact, two members of Team MCE, Benton Jackson and Fred Christian, both passed due to health issues. Marvin's health continued to decline to where he was never able to get back to the T-Rex project. The 1,000 hp was never realized in a dyno room.

However, what you have here is a great recipe for 1,000 hp and comparable torque from the 385-series family of strokers. Take these elements and tweak them to suit your performance agenda. Try a different cam profile and test it out. Opt for the sweet Kaase heads. Go with a full port job. The choice is yours.

MCE T-Rex 598 on the Dyno

Pull No. 1

Carburetor	Holley 1150-cfm Dominator #0-80673
Jetting	0.90/0.90
Ignition Timing	32 degrees BTDC at 3,500 rpm

Step pull in 500-rpm increments, beginning at 4,000 rpm.

RPM	Horsepower	Torque
4,000	567.1	744.6
4,500	672.7	785.1
5,000	764.1	802.6
5,500	821.4	784.4
6,000	859.7	752.5
6,500	895.4	723.5

In Pull 1, I learned the 598 was lean and in need of larger jetting. MCE began this dyno session with 0.90 jets in the primaries and secondaries. Based on air/fuel ratio and brake specific fuel consumption (BSFC) numbers, Marvin found we needed to step up to 0.92 jets in the primaries. Ignition timing was conservative at 32 degrees BTDC.

Pull No. 2

Carburetor	Holley 1150-cfm Dominator #0-80673
Jetting:	0.92/0.90
Ignition Timing	32 degrees BTDC at 3,500 rpm

Step pull in 500-rpm increments, beginning at 4,000 rpm.

RPM	Horsepower	Torque
4,000	503.9	661.6
4,500	690.4	805.8
5,000	784.1	823.6
5,500	838.3	800.5
6,000	878.9	769.3
6,500	909.8	735.1

Marvin learned with the second pull that he was still too lean. He increased jet size to 0.93. The 0.92 primary jets did add 14.4 hp and 21.0 ft-lbs of torque.

Pull No. 3

Carburetor	Holley 1150-cfm Dominator #0-80673
Jetting	0.92/0.93
Ignition Timing	32 degrees BTDC at 3500 rpm

Step Pull in 500-rpm increments, beginning at 4,000 rpm.

RPM	Horsepower	Torque
4,000	521.5	684.5
4,500	698.1	814.8
5,000	787.4	827.1
5,500	848.1	809.9
6,000	883.4	773.3
6,500	915.7	739.9

The MCE/Ford Performance T-Rex was designed from the start by the late Marvin McAfee of MCE Engines in Los Angeles. He expected anywhere from 800 to 1,000 hp and comparable torque from this engine. He ran into problems on the dyno with head gasket leakage and made 915.7 hp and 827.1 ft-lbs of torque.

This was admittedly a disappointing dyno session because I am convinced that given more dyno time and more adequate preparedness, this engine would have passed the 1,000-hp mark along with comparable torque. It did not reach its great potential. After three pulls, Marvin packed up the engine and went home. His health declined and this engine never returned to the dyno. It was JGM's belief the engine had detonated and blown a head gasket, which is another reason it never made 1,000 hp.

Valuable time was lost just setting up due to bellhousing/header issues, which were not anticipated ahead of time. This limited the session to three dyno pulls. It taught me the value of advanced planning and solid communication before going to the dyno. If you're going to the dyno, always communicate ahead of time with your dyno shop. Know what the dyno shop has and doesn't have, and be ready because dyno time is costly. If you want a specific header type, not to mention other parts critical to a dyno session, check this out with your dyno shop weeks in advance so you're not caught short on dyno day.

C460 Cylinder Head Flow Numbers Out of the Box

Lift	0.100	0.200	0.300	0.400	0.500	0.600	0.700	0.800
Flow/CFM	0	159/211	227/150	285/183	327/201	351/214	367/221	380/225

C460 Jon Kaase–Prepared Head Flow Numbers

Lift	0.100	0.200	0.300	0.400	0.500	0.600	0.700	0.800
Flow/CFM	0	160/130	245/170	323/194	400/280	450/315	478/340	500/355

Horsepower and torque numbers prove that Ford Racing has a terrific cylinder head in its C460 race head considering flow numbers shown above. Depending upon your budget, the professionally ported Jon Kaase C460 head can make a huge difference in horsepower and torque numbers.

The Ford Racing M-6010-A460 block is a cast-iron siamese-bore competition block you can use for street or strip. This is a race block with plenty of room for stroke. I'm talking 598 ci. It is a four-bolt main block with dowel-pin centered nodular iron main caps on mains 2, 3, and 4 for extraordinary strength. It is also a wet-sump design with 3.000-inch main journals tipping the scales at 290 pounds.

Marvin always ran Clevite H-series race bearings in his racing engines. Note how Marvin has staggered the two-piece rear main seal to get the ends away from the main cap seam.

Marvin ordered up a complete Eagle stroker kit with a steel crank, H-beam rods, and Mahle coated and forged pistons.

This 4340 forged steel crank from Eagle Specialty Products with its 3.000-inch mains and 2.200-inch polished rod journals with chamfered oil holes for improved lubrication is just the ticket for high-RPM 598-ci performance.

Moving parts need to remain lubricated should the engine be in storage for an extended period. Contact surfaces such as bearings, journals, cylinder walls, piston rings and skirts, and any other moving parts must be coated with engine assembly lube. This ring package is 1.5, 1.5, and 3.0 mm for reduced friction. A support rail keeps the oil ring package stable.

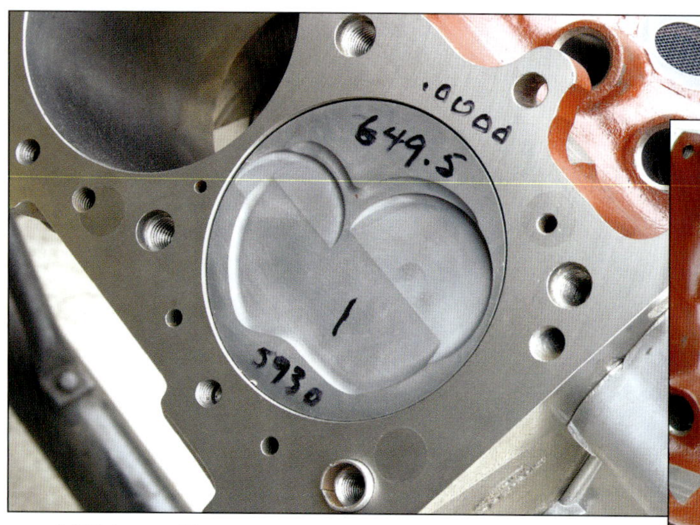

MCE specified forged Mahle pistons with a 15-cc dish are designed for the Eagle 598-ci stroker kit. The dish includes valve reliefs designed to clear the huge M-6049-C460 valves. This is basically a big-block Chevy piston. Mahle has relocated the wrist pin for the big-block Ford.

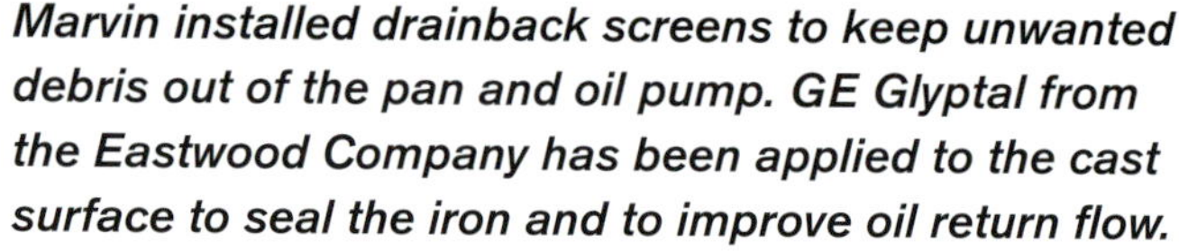

Marvin installed drainback screens to keep unwanted debris out of the pan and oil pump. GE Glyptal from the Eastwood Company has been applied to the cast surface to seal the iron and to improve oil return flow.

The 385-series big-block in box-stock factory form is bulletproof. This A460 block has been fitted with an Eagle stroker kit, which includes a forged steel crank, H-beam rods, and forged and coated Mahle pistons. Interference-fit four-bolt main caps with dowels keep things secure.

Marvin opted for the #34-850-9 mechanical roller camshaft from Comp Cams with an RPM range of 4,400 to 7,200, lobe centers of 112 degrees, lobe lift (intake/exhaust) of 0.421/0.421 inch, valve lift intake/exhaust of 0.727/0.727 inch, and duration at 0.050 inch of 275/281. He chose Comp #836-16 lifters.

The A460 block doesn't use a conventional 385-series cylinder head gasket. Instead, it calls for the Fel-Pro #1092 18-bolt steel core laminate head gasket with 4.700-inch bores. Gasket compression volume is 14.6 cc at a 0.051-inch crush. Marvin ran into one issue with these gaskets: the bolt hole size was too small. Marvin punched bolt holes out to the proper size of 9/16 inch.

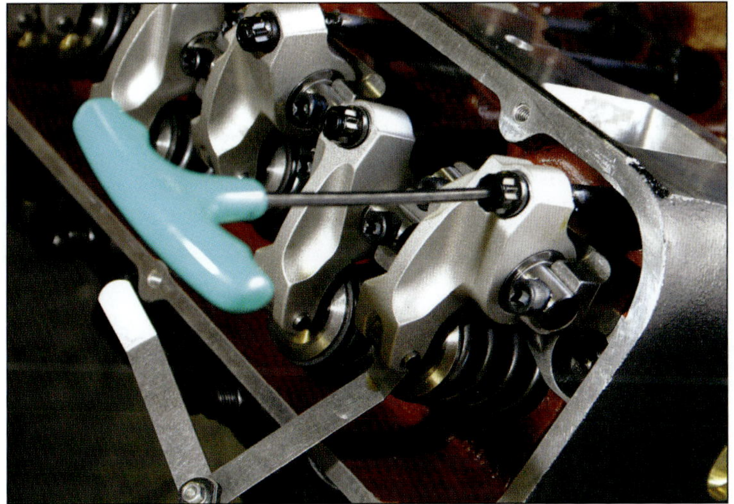

Jesel provided its best top-of-the-line Mohawk Beam Pro Series shaft assembly (#KPS-11057) for the 598-ci build. At 195 grams each, this is Jesel's stiffest, lightest rocker arm with the lowest moment of inertia while producing precise valve control with minimum frictional losses. These race-ready components stay adjusted once adjusted and locked down. Valve lash was 0.019/0.019-inch intake/ exhaust with more adjustments at the dyno.

Marvin slipped the C460 heads onto the studded block. There's great potential here for 1,000 hp and comparable torque. Marvin stressed the importance of proper torque and in proper sequence. All studs have been screwed into the block but not bottomed out.

Marvin went the only path he could: the Ford SVO Motorsport F3ZM-9424-C460 single-plane high-rise manifold with a Dominator flange to feed those Holland Tunnel-sized ports. Marvin chose to leave the manifold as was right out of the box except for port matching. His theory was that those rough-cast surfaces kept fuel droplets in suspension.

Marvin chose the Holley Dominator 1,150-cfm (#0-80673) carburetor right out of the box except for the installation of jet extenders. Jet extenders keep fuel around the jets in drag racing and hard acceleration. Marvin has also opted for a Holley mechanical fuel pump, #12-460-11 with 110 gallons per hour (gph).

Appendix

ENGINE MATH

When you're building an engine, it's nice to be armed with the facts necessary to do it successfully. Much of engine building is about math: machining dimensions, compression and rod ratios, bore sizes, stroke, journal diameters, carburetor and port sizes, dynamic balancing, and all the rest of it. Without math, you cannot successfully build an engine. What follows are quick facts that will help you in your Ford engine building.

Cubic-Inch Displacement

Cubic-inch displacement is calculated with this formula.

$$\text{Bore}^2 \times \text{Stroke} \times 0.7854 \times \text{Number of Cylinders}$$

Take the 302 for example:
4.000 x 4.000 x 3.00 x 0.7854 x 8 = 301.59 ci. Ford rounded off 301.59 to 302 ci or 4.9L.

Compression-Ratio Calculation

To calculate true compression, you must know piston/deck height, head gasket compressed thickness, combustion chamber volume, bore and stroke, piston dome volume (if there's a dome), or piston dish volume (if dished or with valve reliefs). These dimensions are measured in cubic centimeters (cc), not cubic inches (ci), so you simply divide the cc amount by 16.4. Measure piston/deck height with a dial indicator. Bring the piston to TDC and measure how far down the deck of the piston is from the deck of the block. This is normally somewhere between 0.008 and 0.025 inch. If the block deck has been machined, say 0.010 inch, then deck height will be smaller.

If you're checking a 302-ci engine, the process for the following example looks like this.

Bore	4.000 inches
Stroke	3.000 inches
Chamber Volume	60 cc
Head Gasket Thickness	0.038 inch
Deck Height	0.015 inch

First, convert chamber volume from cubic centimeters (cc) to cubic inches (ci) by dividing chamber volume by 16.4.

60 cc ÷16.4 = 3.6585365 ci

Next, convert head gasket thickness (gasket compressed) to volume in cubic inches by multiplying head gasket thickness times 0.7854 times bore^2.

0.038 x 0.7854 x 4.000 x 4.000 = 0.4775232 ci

Finally, convert piston/deck height into volume (ci) by multiplying deck height times 0.7854 times bore.

0.015 x 0.7854 x 4.000 = 0.047124 ci

Because you are dealing with a domed piston, in this case with a 30-cc dome, you reduce the number of cubic inches by displacing space with mass. If it's a domed piston, you're taking away cubic inches. If it's a dished piston or it has valve reliefs, you add cubic inches. Because you have a domed piston with 30 cc of dome, you need the formula for calculating dome volume.

Chamber volume (cc) ÷ 16.430 cc ÷ 16.4 = 1.8292682 ci

Calculating compression ratio is simple. Using a calculator, try this formula. Compression ratio is the total volume of the engine's cylinders (displacement) divided by the clearance volume of the engine. Imagine if you took one of the cylinders and measured its volume above the piston at BDC. Divide this amount by the amount of volume that is needed to fill the cylinder with the piston at TDC. The ratio of the two different volumes is the compression ratio.

For example, take volume above the piston at BDC compared to the volume at TDC.

The total volume of the cylinder includes the swept volume (bore x stroke) and the clearance volume (piston dish/dome, deck, head gasket, and chamber volume).

Compression ratio = (Swept volume + Clearance volume) ÷ Clearance volume

Bore: 4.030 inches
Stroke: 3.000 inches
Piston dome (or dish): 7 cc dome
Piston-to-deck clearance: 0.010 inch
Head gasket bore: 4.100 inches
Head gasket compressed thickness: 0.039 inch
Combustion chamber volume: 60 cc
Then, you can calculate cylinder swept volume.

Swept volume = (Cylinder diameter ÷ 2) squared x 3.14 x stroke

For example, with a 4.030-inch bore and a 3.000-inch stroke, the result is 38.2 ci (one cylinder of a 306-ci engine).

The conversion is:
1 ci = 16.387 cc
Example: 38.2 ci = 626.8 cc
Swept volume = 626.8 cc

Clearance Volume

Calculate the clearance volume, which includes the piston dish/dome, deck, head gasket, and combustion chamber volume.

Clearance volume = Piston volume + Deck volume + Gasket volume + Combustion chamber volume

It is true that most piston manufacturers list the volume of the dish or dome of their pistons. (If you don't know, you can use a cc'ing kit to measure.) Dish volume increases clearance volume and dome volume reduces clearance volume.

In our example, the piston has a 7-cc dome.

The block deck height, piston compression height, rod length, and stroke all affect how much a piston is down or out of the bore at TDC. This affects the clearance volume of the engine and must also be calculated.

Volume = (Cylinder diameter ÷ 2) squared x height

In our example, our piston is 0.010-inch below the deck at TDC. This equates to 0.13 ci, or 2.1 cc. Head gasket thickness also affects clearance volume. (The calculation for the gasket thickness is the same as the deck volume.)

The cylinder head gasket has a 4.100-inch diameter and is

0.039-inch thick. This gives us 0.51 ci, or 8.4 cc. Combustion chamber volume is also a major contributor of clearance volume. Check the head's specifications, specifically chamber volume. If you've installed new valves or modified the combustion chamber in any way, this will affect chamber volume. Chamber volume must be checked.

In our example, The cylinder head manufacturer lists 60 cc of combustion chamber volume. As a result, the total clearance volume is the sum of the piston volume (-7 cc), deck volume (2.1 cc), gasket volume (8.4 cc), and combustion chamber volume (60 cc).

Clearance volume = 63.5 cc

Adding our figures into the first equation:

Compression ratio = (Swept volume + Clearance volume) ÷ Clearance volume
Compression ratio = (626.8 cc + 63.5 cc) ÷ 63.5 cc
Compression ratio = 10.9:1
Check these numbers repeatedly to make sure they add up.

Or you take 22.119827 cubic inches divided by 1.8292682 cubic inches = 12.092205 or 12.1:1 compression ratio.

Carburetor Size

It seems a lot of folks specify a larger carburetor than they actually need. The following is an easy formula that will put you on target every time, as long as you're honest with yourself about where your engine's going to operate. You want to look at cubic inches and the best volumetric efficiency (VE). With street engines, volumetric efficiency is typically around 75 to 80 percent. Boost the performance and VE goes up to 80 to 95 percent. The best indicator of engine performance is an engine dynamometer. Here's how to pick your carburetor size.

Required Carburetor Size = VE Percent (Volumetric Efficiency) x Cubic Inches x Maximum RPMs ÷ 3,456

For example, if you've built a 460 that is performing strong on the dyno, the dyno figures tell you 85-percent VE. Then, 460 ci x 5,500 rpm ÷ 3,456 = 732.06018. Because you want 85 percent of 732.06018, that's 622.25 cfm. Opt for a 650-cfm carburetor.

Horsepower and Torque

"Horsepower" and "torque" are words you hear a lot in the automotive realm. Of the two words, which do you believe is more significant to power output? It may surprise you to learn that torque is the more significant number. Did you know horsepower and torque become the same at 5,252 rpm on any engine? Here's are two good formulas to remember:

Horsepower =
RPM x Torque ÷ 5,252 rpm
Torque =
5,252 rpm x horsepower ÷ RPM

Horsepower and torque can be determined with a simple quarter-mile pass at the drag strip. Begin by weighing your vehicle. Scales can be found at a farm coop or truck weigh scales along the interstate. Make several quarter-mile passes and calculate an average elapsed time and mph. Then use these formulas to make your calculations.

Horsepower =
Weight x 0.4 x 1/4-mile mph ÷ 282

For example:
3,000 lbs x 0.4 x 100 mph ÷ 282 =
425.53191 hp

Speed =
Horsepower ÷ Weight x 282 ÷ 0.4

For example:
425 hp ÷ 3,000 lbs x 282 ÷ 0.4 =
99.874952 or 100 mph

Torque =
5,252 x hp ÷ 6,000 rpm

For example,
5,252 x 425 ÷ 6,000 =
372 ft-lbs of torque

Save yourself the cost of a dyno and do the calculations yourself . These calculations are approximate, but close enough to determine your engine's output.

Torque Sequences and Specifications

429/460 ENGINE

Engine block

Bore diameter: 4.3600-4.3632
Taper limit: 0.001
Out of round limit: 0.001
Wear limit: 0.005

Crankshaft and connecting rods

Main journal diameter: 2.9994-3.0002
Taper limit: 0.0003 per inch
Out of round wear limit: 0.0004

Main bearing oil clearance:
Desired: 0.0005-0.0015.
Allowable: 0.0005-0.0025
Crankshaft end play: 0.0004-0.0008

Connecting rod journal diameter: 2.4992-2.5000
Taper limit: 0.0004 per inch
Out of round limit: 0.0004

Connecting rod oil clearance:
Desired: 0.0008-0.0015
Allowable: 0.0008-0.0026
Connecting rod side clearance: 0.010-0.020

Pistons and rings

Piston to bore clearance: 0.0014-0.0022
Piston ring side clearance:
First and second: 0.002-0.004
Oil ring: Snug
Piston ring end gap: 0.010-0.020

Cylinder heads and valve train

Warpage: 0.003 in any 6 inches, 0.007 overall
Valve stem to guide:
Intake and exhaust 0.0010-0.0027
(* Intake wear limit: 0.0045
* Exhaust wear limit: 0.0047)

Valve spring free length: 2.03
Valve spring installed height: 1 51/64-1 53/64

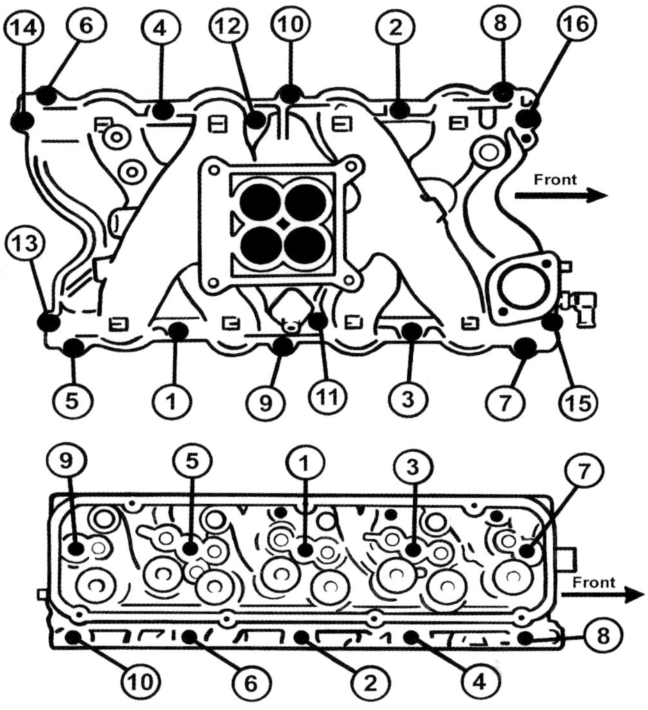

TORQUE LIMITS 429-460 V-8 ENGINES (Limits in ft-lbs)

Engine	Cylinder head bolts	Intake Manifold	Exhaust Manifolds
429-460	Step 1: 75 Step 2: 105 Step 3: 130-140	25-30	28-33
	Main Bearing cap bolts 95-105	Connecting Rod nuts 40-45	
	Flywheel to crankshaft 75-85	Damper to crankshaft 70-90	
	Oil Pump to block 20-25	Camshaft thrust plate 9-12	
	Camshaft sprocket to cam 40-45	Water Pump 12-15	

429 and 460 V-8 Torque Sequence

BOSS 429 BLUEPRINT SPECS

Main bearing clearance	0.0025 / 0.0030
Crankshaft end play	0.004 / 0.008
Connecting rod bearings	0.0025 / 0.0030
Connecting rod end play	0.018 / 0.028
Piston to bore	0.0055 / 0.0065
Piston to pin	0.0011 / 0.0009
Piston pin to connecting rod	0.0003 / 0.0005
Piston pin end play	0.005 / 0.010
Valve stem to guide (exhaust)	0.0020 / 0.0026
Valve stem to guide (intake)	0.0010 / 0.0016
Rocker arm to shaft	0.002 / 0.004
Rocker arm side clearance	0.001 / 0.016
Rocker arm shaft to support	0.001 / 0.004
Camshaft bearing	0.001 / 0.003
Camshaft end play	0.001 / 0.006
Damper to crankshaft	0.000 / 0.002 (interference)
Valve guide to cylinder head	0.001 / 0.003 (interference)
Centerline crank to top of block (NASCAR and street Boss)	10.300
Top of piston to top of block	0.030 minimum (NASCAR and street Boss)

Source Guide

Air Flow Research
661-257-8124
www.airflowresearch.com

Automotive Racing Products (ARP)
800-826-3045
805-339-2200
www.arp-bolts.com

BBK Performance
951-296-1771
www.bbkperformance.com

Comp Cams
800-999-0853
901/795-2400
www.compcams.com

Crane Cams
866-388-5120
386-310-4875
www.cranecams.com

Eagle Specialty Products, Inc.
662-796-7373
wwww.eaglerod.com

Edelbrock Corporation
800-416-8628
310-781-2222 (Tech Line Only)
www.edelbrock.com

Federal-Mogul
Speed Pro/Sealed Power/Fel-Pro
248-354-7700
www.federalmogul.com

Holley Performance Products
270-782-2900
270-781-9741
www.holley.com

Jesel
732-901-1800
www.jesel.com

JGM Performance Engineering
661-257-0101

Jon Kaase Racing Engines
770-307-0241
www.jonkaaseracingenginec.com

KB Pistons/Silv-O-Lite/Icon
Forged Racing Pistons
United Engine & Machine Company
800-648-7970
775-882-7790
www.kb-silvolite.com

Mahle/Clevite
www.mahle.com

Melling Engine Parts
517-787-8172
www.melling.com

Milodon
805-577-5970
www.milodon.com

MSD Ignition
915-857-5200
www.msdignition.com

Mustangs Etc.
818-787-7634
www.mustangsetc.com

Summit Racing Equipment
800-230-3030
330-630-3030
www.summitracing.com

Survival Motorsports
248-366-3309
248-931-0358 (After Hours Cell)
www.survivalmotorsports.com

Trick Flow Specialties
888-841-6556
330-630-1555
www.trickflow.com